NotebookLM: From Sources to Audio Overviews

NotebookLM — Master Google's AI Research Companion

Ken Tannenbaum

2026

Finnoybu Press

NotebookLM: From Sources to Audio Overviews

2026 Edition

NotebookLM — Master Google's AI Research Companion

Published by Finnoybu Press

For permissions and inquiries: press@finnoybu.org

First Edition: 2026

About the Author

Ken Tannenbaum is a technologist, entrepreneur, and AI governance researcher. He is the founder of Finnoybu Press and the founder/steward of the AEGIS Initiative, an open framework for AI safety and accountability. Learn more at aegis-initiative.com.

When he's not building governance standards for artificial intelligence, he's helping everyday people understand and use it.

Dedication

For everyone who has ever stared at a stack of PDFs, a folder of meeting notes, or a year's worth of reading and thought, *"There has to be a faster way to make sense of all this."*

There is. This book is about it.

The AI for Everyone Series

This book is part of the **AI for Everyone** series by Finnoybu Press, designed to help real people use AI tools effectively. Visit **press.finnoybu.org** for the latest titles and updates.

Collection One: Product Deep Dives

- *ChatGPT: The Definitive Guide (2026 Edition)*
- *ChatGPT: The Power User Guide (2026 Edition)*
- *Claude: The Definitive Guide (2026 Edition)*
- *Claude Code: The Power User Guide (2026 Edition)*
- *Gemini: The Complete Guide (2026 Edition)*
- *Gemini: The Advanced Guide (2026 Edition)*
- *Copilot: The Workplace AI Guide (2026 Edition)*
- *Copilot: The Advanced Workplace Guide (2026 Edition)*
- *Perplexity: The Research Playbook (2026 Edition)*
- *Perplexity: The Advanced Research Playbook (2026 Edition)*

Collection Two: Product Guides

- *NotebookLM: From Sources to Audio Overviews (2026 Edition)*
- *DeepSeek: Code, Math, and Reasoning (2026 Edition)*
- *Cursor: The AI Code Editor (2026 Edition)*
- *OpenClaw: Agentic AI for Everyday Work (2026 Edition)*

Collection Three: Cross-Platform Skills

- *AI Systems Playbook (2026 Edition)*
- *AI Prompt Engineering (2026 Edition)*
- *AI for Developers (2026 Edition)*
- *AI for Business (2026 Edition)*
- *AI for Students (2026 Edition)*
- *AI Governance for Practitioners (2026 Edition)*
- *Securing Agentic AI (2026 Edition)*

Table of Contents

Introduction

I wrote this book because most NotebookLM coverage falls into one of two categories: a 30-second viral demo of Audio Overviews ("OMG it made a podcast about my essay!"), or Google's own help documentation – accurate but written feature-by-feature, with no sense of how anyone actually uses the product.

Neither serves the person who has just uploaded their first PDF and is staring at the chat box wondering what to do next.

NotebookLM is, quietly, one of the most important AI tools to emerge from the post-ChatGPT era. It does something different from the chatbots most people have been using. It doesn't try to know everything. It tries to know *your things* – the documents you've collected, the research you've done, the meeting notes you've taken, the books you've read. It answers your questions using only those sources, with citations you can click and verify.

This is a different relationship with AI. Narrower, but more trustworthy. Once you know how to use it, it changes how you do research, how you study, how you brief executives, and how you turn a stack of source material into something a human being can understand.

Who This Book Is For

This book is for anyone who works with documents and wants a better way to make sense of them. That includes:

- **Students** preparing for exams from textbook chapters, lecture slides, and notes
- **Researchers and academics** synthesizing literature across dozens of papers
- **Knowledge workers** turning briefings, reports, and policy documents into actionable summaries
- **Analysts** comparing earnings reports, competitor filings, and market research
- **Content creators** producing podcasts, videos, and posts from their own research

- **Writers** drafting from a body of source material instead of from a blank page
- **Anyone curious** about what source-grounded AI can do that ChatGPT can't

You don't need any technical background. If you can drag a PDF onto a webpage, you have all the skills you need.

How to Read This Book

The book is organized in nine parts that progress from fundamentals to advanced use:

Part I: Getting Started (Chapters 1–5) takes you from zero to your first useful notebook. Even experienced users may discover sources, settings, and workflows they've overlooked.

Part II: Working with Sources (Chapters 6–9) covers the foundation of everything NotebookLM does — adding, organizing, and querying the documents your notebooks are built from.

Part III: The Studio (Chapters 10–15) is where NotebookLM stops being a smart search tool and starts being something new. Audio Overviews, Video Overviews, Mind Maps, Reports, Slide Decks, Flashcards, Quizzes, Infographics, Data Tables — every Studio output, explained and demonstrated.

Part IV: Going Deeper (Chapters 16–20) covers Deep Research, customization, Interactive Audio Overviews, very long documents, multilingual notebooks, and the mobile apps.

Part V: Getting Better Results (Chapters 21–23) teaches the source-curation strategy, prompting techniques, and verification habits that separate effective NotebookLM users from frustrated ones.

Part VI: NotebookLM for Your World (Chapters 24–27) provides targeted guidance for students, researchers, knowledge workers, and content creators.

Part VII: Sharing and Collaboration (Chapters 28–29) covers public sharing, team workflows, and the Plus-tier collaborative features.

Part VIII: Safety, Ethics, and Limitations (Chapters 30–32) covers what NotebookLM gets wrong, how to think about privacy and data, and the ethical questions every researcher should work through.

Part IX: Reference (Appendices A–F) gives you shortcuts, 60+ prompt templates, troubleshooting, a glossary, a 2026 changelog, and further resources.

You can read straight through or jump to the chapters that interest you most. Each chapter is designed to be useful on its own, though they build on each other when read in order.

A Note About Accuracy

NotebookLM changes frequently. Google ships updates monthly, sometimes weekly. New Studio outputs appear, the underlying Gemini model gets upgraded, the pricing tiers shift. This book is accurate as of early 2026, but specific details — menu locations, exact pricing, feature availability — may have changed by the time you read this.

The principles, techniques, and strategies have a longer shelf life than the interface details. How to curate a good set of sources, how to verify a citation, how to prompt for the output format you want — these skills transfer across versions and across other source-grounded AI tools.

When something looks different from what's described here, check Google's NotebookLM help center for the latest information.

Let's Get Started

NotebookLM is, in some ways, a quiet revolution in how people work with documents. It doesn't replace expertise. It doesn't replace reading. It doesn't replace the slow, careful thinking that good research requires. What it does — and does extraordinarily well — is collapse the time between *"I have these sources"* and *"I understand what they say."*

The only limit is knowing how to ask.

Turn the page. Let's fix that.

Part I: Getting Started

"To understand is to perceive patterns."

— Isaiah Berlin

Chapter 1: What Is NotebookLM?

In late 2024, a quiet feature inside an experimental Google product went unexpectedly viral. People were dragging research papers, business reports, even their own diaries into a tool called NotebookLM, clicking a single button, and getting back a fully produced podcast — two AI hosts, complete with banter, pauses, and the occasional "wow, that's fascinating" — discussing the contents of whatever they had uploaded. Spotify used the same technology to generate personalized year-in-review podcasts for every Wrapped user. Within months, a feature that almost nobody had heard of became a feature that almost everybody had tried.

If you're reading this book, you've probably encountered NotebookLM through one of those Audio Overviews. You may have generated one yourself and been delighted, confused, or both. You may have heard about the product but never figured out what it does. Or you may be picking it up for the first time.

Whatever brought you here, this chapter will give you a clear understanding of what NotebookLM is, how it differs from the AI tools you've already used, and what it can — and can't — do for you.

What NotebookLM Is

NotebookLM is a source-grounded AI research assistant built by Google. You upload documents — PDFs, web pages, YouTube videos, Google Docs, audio files, even photos of handwritten notes — and NotebookLM reads them. Then you ask questions, and it answers using only what's in those sources, with citations pointing back to the exact passage that supports each claim.

That's the simple version. Here's a slightly more complete one:

NotebookLM is powered by Gemini, Google's flagship large language model. But unlike Gemini's chat app — which tries to answer your question using everything it learned during training, plus the entire internet if web search is enabled — NotebookLM is deliberately constrained. It only knows what you've given it. If you ask a question and the answer isn't in your sources, it will tell you so, instead of making something up.

That constraint is the whole point. Most AI tools have a hallucination problem: they confidently state things that aren't true, especially about specific facts, dates, quotes, and citations. NotebookLM doesn't eliminate hallucination — no AI tool can — but it sharply reduces it by tying every answer back to a passage you can verify with a single click.

That's a fundamentally different relationship with an AI tool. ChatGPT is your knowledgeable friend who has read everything but sometimes misremembers. NotebookLM is your research assistant who has read only what you handed them and can show you exactly which page they got each fact from.

What NotebookLM Is Not

Understanding what NotebookLM *isn't* matters as much as understanding what it is. Clearing up these misconceptions early will save you frustration later.

NotebookLM is not a general-purpose chatbot. If you ask it a question that has nothing to do with your sources, you'll either get a polite refusal or an answer drawn from very limited general knowledge. It's not the right tool for "write me a poem" or "what's a good restaurant in Boston" or "explain quantum mechanics." Use ChatGPT, Claude, or Gemini for those.

NotebookLM is not a search engine for the web. It can pull web pages and YouTube videos in as sources, and Deep Research can fetch web information for you, but its primary mode is reading the documents you provide. If you want to search the open web first, then synthesize, reach for Perplexity.

NotebookLM is not a writing assistant. It can produce summaries, Briefing Docs, Study Guides, and even Blog Post drafts grounded in your sources. But it's not designed for the free-form generation that ChatGPT or Claude excels at. Use it to *understand* your sources, then take what you've learned somewhere else to write.

NotebookLM is not always right. This bears repeating because the source-grounding can lull you into trusting it too much. NotebookLM still makes mistakes. It can paraphrase a source in a way that subtly changes the meaning. It can cite a passage that doesn't actually support the claim it's making. The citations make verification easy — but only if you actually click them. We'll come back to this in Chapter 23.

A Brief History

NotebookLM didn't appear out of thin air. A short history helps you see what makes it different from other AI tools and where it's heading.

From Project Tailwind to NotebookLM

The product began life in May 2023 as **Project Tailwind**, an experimental tool out of Google Labs. The pitch was simple: an AI-powered notebook that learned from documents you uploaded. It was intentionally narrow — a research tool, not a chatbot — and it was developed by a small team that included author Steven Johnson, whose work on serendipity and the structure of innovation shaped the product's vision.

Tailwind was rebranded to **NotebookLM** in 2024 and graduated from experimental status to a stable product on **October 17, 2024**. By then, the team had added a feature that would change everything: Audio Overviews.

The Audio Overviews Moment

In **September 2024**, NotebookLM introduced the ability to generate podcast-style discussions from your sources — two AI hosts having a conversation about whatever you'd uploaded. The internet noticed. People generated Audio Overviews about their wedding photos, their tax returns, the lyrics of obscure '80s songs, the codebases of their startups. Spotify partnered with NotebookLM to produce **Spotify Wrapped 2024**, generating millions of personalized year-in-review podcasts on the same engine.

Audio Overviews did for NotebookLM what conversational chat did for GPT-3.5 in 2022 — it took something that had existed in technical form and turned it into something millions of people wanted to play with.

The Plus Tier and the Studio Explosion

In **December 2024**, Google launched **NotebookLM Plus** for enterprise customers, then extended it to individual users via Google AI subscriptions in **February 2025**. Throughout 2025 and into 2026, the product team kept adding new ways to transform sources into outputs:

- **Interactive Audio Overviews** (December 2024) — pause the podcast and ask the hosts a question
- **Video Overviews** (mid-2025) — the same idea as audio, but with visual slides, diagrams, and narration
- **Cinematic Video Mode** (July 29, 2025) — narrative-driven, more produced video output
- **Mind Maps** — visual hierarchy of concepts across sources
- **Slide Decks** (November 2025) — full presentation generation, with PPTX export and editable slides
- **Infographics** (November 2025) — visual summaries in ten distinct styles
- **Data Tables** (December 2025) — structured extraction across sources

By early 2026, NotebookLM had become less a chatbot and more a *Studio* — a workspace where the same set of sources could be transformed into a podcast, a video, a Study Guide, a Mind Map, a Slide Deck, a Quiz, an Infographic, or a structured Data Table, depending on what you needed.

Gemini 3 and the 2026 Restructure

In **March 2026**, Google upgraded the model under the hood to **Gemini 3**, sharply improving long-document reasoning, multilingual outputs, and the audio voice models that drive Audio Overviews. The pricing structure also evolved from a two-tier (Free/Plus) into a four-tier model — **Free, Plus, Pro, and Ultra** — bundled with broader Google AI subscriptions that include Gemini, expanded cloud storage, and other Google AI features. We'll cover the tradeoffs in Chapter 2.

How It Works (In Plain English)

You don't need to understand the technical details to use NotebookLM effectively, any more than you need to understand internal combustion to drive a car. But a basic mental model helps you get better results.

Retrieval-Augmented Generation

NotebookLM is built on a technique called **Retrieval-Augmented Generation**, or **RAG**. The name sounds intimidating; the idea is simple. When you ask NotebookLM a question, it doesn't try to answer from memory. It does three things:

1. **Retrieve** — search through your sources to find the passages most likely to be relevant to your question.
2. **Augment** — assemble those passages into context for the model to read.
3. **Generate** — produce an answer based on what those specific passages say, with pointers back to where each piece of the answer came from.

This is why NotebookLM's answers feel different from ChatGPT's. You're not asking a model what it learned during training. You're asking a model what *your sources* say. The model is the reader. You provide the books.

The Context Window

There is a limit, though. Each source can be up to about **one million tokens** — roughly 500,000 words, or a 1,500-page book. That's an enormous amount of text by historical standards, and enough for almost any single document you'd want to analyze. But it's a ceiling. Documents larger than that need to be split. We'll cover strategies for very long sources in Chapter 18.

The context window also limits how many sources you can effectively work across at once. NotebookLM is excellent at synthesis across five, ten, or fifty sources, but quality starts to degrade somewhere past a few hundred. The right way to think about it: one focused notebook per topic, not one giant notebook with everything you've ever read.

What NotebookLM Is Good At

NotebookLM excels in a specific range of tasks. Here are the areas where it consistently delivers strong results:

Synthesizing across multiple sources. This is where NotebookLM is genuinely better than every other AI tool. Upload ten papers on a topic, ask it to identify where they agree, where they disagree, and the gaps no paper has filled. It's an extraordinary literature-review tool.

Turning documents into multimedia. Audio Overviews, Video Overviews, Slide Decks, Infographics — NotebookLM can take a body of written content and reformat it into something easier to consume, share, or present. This is the workflow that has made it indispensable for content creators, teachers, and people who give a lot of presentations.

Answering specific questions with citations. Got a 200-page contract and a question about indemnification clauses? Upload it, ask, and get a sourced answer in seconds. The citations let you verify in one click.

Building study and learning aids. Flashcards, Quizzes, Study Guides, and Mind Maps generated from your own course materials are far more useful than generic study aids, because they're calibrated to exactly what you need to learn.

Briefing and summarization at length. Executive summaries, Briefing Docs, and Report digests grounded in real source material — not the vague AI-generated summary that could apply to anything, but a specific summary of what *this particular set of documents* actually says.

What NotebookLM Struggles With

Being honest about limitations makes you a better user:

Anything not in your sources. This sounds obvious but trips people up constantly. If you ask a question whose answer isn't in your uploaded documents, you'll get either a refusal or a weak general-knowledge answer. NotebookLM doesn't browse the web by default. It only knows what you've handed it.

Long, free-form generation. NotebookLM can produce a draft Blog Post or a Briefing Doc, but if you want a 3,000-word essay with original argumentation, ChatGPT or Claude is a better tool. NotebookLM is a synthesizer, not a writer.

Real-time data. NotebookLM doesn't know what happened yesterday. Even with Deep Research enabled, it's not the right tool for breaking news, live prices, or current events.

Code execution and computation. It can read code as a source and explain it. It can't run it, debug it, or execute analysis. Use ChatGPT's Code Interpreter or Claude's analysis tools for that.

Image and video generation. Studio outputs include some visual generation (Infographics, Slide Deck visuals), but it's not a tool for creating original artwork. Use DALL-E, Midjourney, Imagen, or Sora.

Subtle paraphrase errors. This is the big one. Because NotebookLM cites sources, people trust its answers more than they trust ChatGPT's. But the model can paraphrase a source in a way that subtly distorts the meaning, then cite the exact passage it just misrepresented. The citation looks like proof — but it only proves the source exists, not that it says what NotebookLM claims it says. **Always click through and verify.** We dedicate Chapter 23 to this habit.

Where NotebookLM Fits in the AI Landscape

NotebookLM is one of several major AI tools you might be using in 2026. Understanding how it fits in helps you make good choices about which tool to reach for:

- **ChatGPT** (by OpenAI) — General-purpose AI assistant. Knows about everything. Best for writing, brainstorming, creative work, coding, and conversation. Covered in *ChatGPT: The Definitive Guide*.
- **Claude** (by Anthropic) — Similar to ChatGPT in capability, with particular strength on long documents and careful, nuanced reasoning. Covered in *Claude: The Definitive Guide*.
- **Gemini** (by Google) — Google's general-purpose chatbot. Deeply integrated with Gmail, Docs, Drive, and the rest of the Google ecosystem. Shares the underlying model with NotebookLM, but with very different framing.
- **Perplexity** — A search-and-research engine. Best when you want to start with a question and let the AI find its own sources on the open web.
- **NotebookLM** — A source-grounded research assistant. Best when *you* control the sources, and you want answers tied to exactly what they say.

Many people use multiple AI tools. A typical workflow: use Perplexity to find good sources on a topic, save them, drop them into a NotebookLM notebook for synthesis, then use ChatGPT or Claude to draft something based on what you learned.

NotebookLM doesn't replace the others. It does something the others don't: it lets you work *with your own corpus* instead of an unbounded one. For research, study, analysis, and any work that depends on specific documents being treated as the source of truth, that's a fundamentally different — and more trustworthy — kind of AI.

What You'll Learn in This Book

This book is organized to take you from your first source upload to confident, productive daily use:

- **Part I (Chapters 1–5)** gets you set up: choosing a plan, creating your account, understanding sources as the foundation, and building your first useful notebook.
- **Part II (Chapters 6–9)** covers working with sources: adding, managing, asking questions, taking notes, and organizing across multiple notebooks.
- **Part III (Chapters 10–15)** explores the Studio — every output type, with concrete walkthroughs.
- **Part IV (Chapters 16–20)** goes deeper: Deep Research, customization, Interactive Audio Overviews, long-document strategies, and the mobile apps.
- **Part V (Chapters 21–23)** teaches the habits that separate effective NotebookLM users from frustrated ones: source curation, prompting, and citation verification.
- **Part VI (Chapters 24–27)** applies NotebookLM to your world: students, researchers, knowledge workers, and content creators.
- **Part VII (Chapters 28–29)** covers sharing and collaboration.
- **Part VIII (Chapters 30–32)** covers what you need to know about safety, limitations, ethics, and responsible use.
- **Part IX (Appendices A–F)** gives you reference material: shortcuts, 60+ prompt templates, troubleshooting, a glossary, a 2026 changelog, and resources for further learning.

Every chapter is designed to be read in order or dipped into as needed. If you're new, continue with Chapter 2. If you've been using NotebookLM for a while and want to level up, skip ahead to the features you haven't explored yet.

Let's get started. Chapter 2 will help you choose the right plan for your needs.

Chapter 2: Choosing the Right Plan

Most NotebookLM users never have to think about plans. The Free tier is genuinely useful — generous enough that a casual user could spend years on it without bumping into a wall. But the limits do exist, and if you start using NotebookLM seriously — for graduate research, for daily knowledge work, for content production — you'll hit them faster than you expect.

In early 2026, Google restructured NotebookLM's pricing into a four-tier model. NotebookLM is no longer sold as a standalone product; every paid tier comes bundled into a broader **Google AI** subscription that includes Gemini, expanded Google Drive storage, and other AI features across Google's product line.

This chapter walks through what each tier gives you, what it costs, and — most importantly — which tier fits the work you're doing.

The Four Tiers at a Glance

Here's the lay of the land in 2026:

- **Free** ($0) — 100 notebooks, 50 sources/notebook, 50 chats/day, 3 Audio/Video Overviews/day
- **Plus** ($7.99/mo) — 500 notebooks, 100 sources/notebook, 100 chats/day, ~6 overviews/day
- **Pro** ($19.99/mo, $9.99 student) — 500 chats/day; expanded quotas across the board
- **Ultra** ($249.99/mo) — 5,000 chats/day; maximum quotas; watermark-free outputs

The exact numbers shift as Google iterates on the product — these are the limits as of early 2026, and Google has been trending *upward* (raising Free-tier limits, adding features at the lower paid tiers). Check Google's current pricing page before committing to a plan.

The Free Tier: Better Than You'd Expect

The Free tier is not the toy version. It's a fully functional product:

- **100 notebooks.** That's enough to organize a year or two of serious work.
- **50 sources per notebook.** Enough for a literature review, a contract analysis, a multi-document research project.
- **50 chats per day.** The limit most users notice first. If you work in NotebookLM all day, asking question after question, you'll hit it. Casual users rarely do.
- **3 Audio Overviews per day.** Enough to experiment, generate one for the document you actually care about, and call it a productive afternoon.
- **All Studio outputs available.** Mind Maps, Reports, Flashcards, Quizzes, Slide Decks, Infographics, Data Tables — every output type is available on the Free tier, just at lower daily volume.
- **Mobile apps.** The Android and iOS apps work on Free.

If you're new to NotebookLM, **start here.** Don't pay until you actually hit a limit.

Google AI Plus: The First Upgrade Most People Need

Plus, at **$7.99/month**, is the smartest first upgrade for most regular users. The biggest unlocks compared to Free:

- **More of everything.** 500 notebooks, 100 sources per notebook, 100 chats per day, roughly 6 Audio/Video Overviews per day.
- **Access to Plus-tier collaborative features** (covered in Chapter 29).
- **Expanded Deep Research** quotas — the web-research feature becomes actually usable here.
- **Bundled Gemini access**, expanded Google Drive storage, and other Google AI features outside NotebookLM.

Two scenarios where Plus pays for itself almost immediately:

You hit the 50-chat daily limit on Free. The most common reason to upgrade. If you're working in NotebookLM for a few hours at a time — researching, asking follow-ups, refining queries — fifty chats goes faster than you think.

You want to share notebooks with collaborators. Free notebooks can be shared as read-only links. Plus unlocks real collaboration: multi-user editing, shared notes, the workflows that turn NotebookLM from a personal tool into a team tool.

If you're a casual user who pulls up NotebookLM once or twice a week, ignore Plus and stay on Free. If NotebookLM is part of your daily or weekly workflow, Plus pays for itself.

Google AI Pro: For Power Users and Heavy Producers

Pro, at **$19.99/month** (or **$9.99/month for verified students**), is for people who use NotebookLM intensively. The big jumps:

- **500 daily chats** — enough that you stop thinking about the limit entirely.
- **Expanded daily Studio output quota** — for people producing podcasts, videos, or Briefing Docs at volume.
- **Higher quotas across Deep Research and other paid-tier features.**
- **The full Google AI Pro subscription**, which bundles Gemini Pro, expanded storage, and tools that make Pro a reasonable upgrade even if NotebookLM is the only justification.

The student tier deserves special mention. At $9.99/month, Pro is cheap for what you get — and it lines up almost perfectly with the workflows of a serious graduate or undergraduate student doing research-heavy coursework. If you're a verified student, Pro is almost always the right tier; the half-price discount makes Plus look like a bad deal by comparison.

For non-students, the question is whether you actually use NotebookLM enough to need 500 chats a day. Most people don't. If you're producing daily briefings, generating multiple Audio Overviews per day for a podcast or content workflow, or running NotebookLM as the central tool of your research practice — yes, Pro is worth it. Otherwise, Plus is fine.

Google AI Ultra: For Teams and Power Producers

Ultra, at **$249.99/month**, is the maximum tier. It exists for two distinct audiences:

Teams that need maximum capacity. Small organizations running NotebookLM as a shared knowledge tool — research teams, consultancies, content studios — can hit even the Pro limits if they're producing at scale. Ultra removes the ceilings.

Producers who can't ship watermarks. Ultra removes the small NotebookLM watermark from generated Audio Overviews, Video Overviews, and other Studio outputs. For anyone publishing NotebookLM-generated content commercially — podcasters, video producers, course creators, agencies — this matters. If your business depends on outputs that look like *yours*, not *Google's*, Ultra is the only tier that makes that possible.

Ultra also typically gets first access to new Studio outputs and experimental features as Google rolls them out.

Which Plan Is Right for You?

Here's a decision flowchart that holds up for most users:

Have you ever used NotebookLM before? → No: Start on Free. Don't pay until you hit a limit.

Are you a verified student? → Yes, and you'll use NotebookLM regularly: Go straight to Pro at the student price ($9.99/mo). It's the best dollar-for-dollar deal in the lineup.

Do you use NotebookLM as part of weekly or daily work? → Yes, but not intensively: **Plus** ($7.99/mo). → Yes, intensively (multiple hours most days, hitting chat limits, generating multiple Studio outputs daily): **Pro** ($19.99/mo).

Are you producing NotebookLM content commercially, or running NotebookLM across a team? → Yes: **Ultra** ($249.99/mo). The watermark removal alone justifies it for commercial producers.

Are you a casual user who reaches for NotebookLM occasionally? → Stay on **Free**. The Free tier is generous enough that you'll likely never need to upgrade.

A Note on Bundling

One thing that surprises new users: NotebookLM cannot be purchased as a standalone subscription for individuals. Every paid NotebookLM tier comes bundled inside a Google AI subscription, which means you're also paying for — and getting:

- **Gemini Pro/Gemini Advanced** — Google's general-purpose AI assistant
- **Expanded Google Drive storage** — typically 2 TB at Plus, more at higher tiers
- **AI features in Gmail, Docs, Sheets, and other Google apps**
- **Other Google AI tools** that ship under the Google AI umbrella

For some people this is a feature — you were going to pay for Gemini anyway, and getting NotebookLM Plus included is a bonus. For others, especially people who don't otherwise use the Google ecosystem, it can feel like paying for things you don't need.

If you fall into the second camp, the math still tends to work out, because NotebookLM's Free tier is so capable that most non-Google-ecosystem users can stay on it indefinitely.

When to Upgrade — and When to Wait

The most common mistake new users make is upgrading too soon. NotebookLM's Free tier has been steadily improving, and Google has been generous with what they include at lower tiers. **The right moment to upgrade is when you've hit a specific limit that's actively blocking work you want to do** — not when you've heard that paid tiers exist.

Start free. Use it for two weeks. Notice which limit you bump into first. *That* tells you which tier you actually need.

Now that you've picked a plan — or wisely deferred the decision — let's get you set up. Chapter 3 walks through creating an account and configuring NotebookLM for the first time.

Chapter 3: Setting Up Your Account

NotebookLM is one of the easier pieces of software you'll ever set up. There's no installer, no license key, no configuration ritual. If you have a Google account — and roughly 1.8 billion people do — you can be inside NotebookLM and looking at an empty notebook in under a minute.

But the *easy* setup isn't always the *best* setup. A handful of decisions in the first ten minutes meaningfully affect your experience down the road: which Google account you sign in with, what your privacy and data settings look like, whether you install the mobile apps, and how you handle the inevitable moment when NotebookLM asks if it can train on your data.

This chapter walks you through all of it.

Creating Your Account

NotebookLM uses your Google account for authentication. There's no separate NotebookLM login.

To get started, go to **notebooklm.google.com** in any modern browser. You'll be prompted to sign in with a Google account if you aren't already.

You have three real options for which account to use:

A personal Gmail account. The simplest path, and what most individual users should pick. Your notebooks live under your personal Google account, accessible from anywhere you sign in.

A Google Workspace account (e.g., your work or school email running on Google Workspace). NotebookLM works here too, often with stronger data protections — your administrator may have configured the account so your data isn't used for model training, and may have additional retention or compliance controls. If your employer or school issues you a Workspace account, that's usually the right place to do work-related research.

A separate "NotebookLM-only" Google account. Some power users create a dedicated Google account for NotebookLM, especially if they're on the Free tier and want to keep their NotebookLM activity separated from the rest of their Google life. Overkill for most people, but worth knowing about.

The choice matters because **your notebooks are tied to the account you create them in.** If you start on a personal Gmail and later switch to Workspace, you can't easily migrate. Pick the right account at the start.

Where to Use NotebookLM

NotebookLM is available across three distinct surfaces:

The Web App

The web version at **notebooklm.google.com** is the primary product. New features appear here first. Almost every Studio output, every advanced setting, every workflow described in this book works on the web. If you're going to use NotebookLM seriously, the web app is home base.

It runs in any modern browser — Chrome, Edge, Safari, Firefox, Brave. There's no extension to install.

The Android App

The Android app (requires Android 10 or later) launched in 2025 and has been steadily catching up to the web version. As of early 2026, the app supports core source ingestion, chat, Audio Overview playback, and most Studio outputs. A handful of newer outputs lag the web by weeks to months as Google rolls them out.

The mobile app shines in two specific workflows: **listening to Audio Overviews on the go** (commute, walks, the gym) and **uploading sources from your phone** (photos of documents, screenshots, articles you're reading in mobile Safari). For deep work, the web is better.

The iOS App

The iOS app (requires iOS 17 or later, includes iPadOS) shipped at the same time as Android. Same pattern — core features work, newest features lag the web slightly. The iPad version is a pleasure for source review, since you can see chat and source side-by-side on a larger screen.

If you have any combination of these devices, install the apps. They share state across devices automatically — start a notebook on your laptop, listen to its Audio Overview on your phone during a commute.

Settings That Matter

Once you're signed in, click your profile icon in the top right and find the settings panel. Most defaults are reasonable, but a few are worth reviewing.

Language Preferences

NotebookLM auto-detects the language of your sources, but you can set a preferred language for chat responses and Studio outputs. This matters most for users working with sources in one language but wanting outputs in another — a common research workflow.

NotebookLM supports more than 80 languages for Audio and Video Overviews as of early 2026. Quality is best in major languages (English, Spanish, French, German, Mandarin, Japanese) and degrades gracefully in less common ones. We'll cover multilingual workflows in detail in Chapter 19.

Output Defaults

The settings panel lets you set defaults for some Studio outputs — preferred Audio Overview length, default Mind Map style, default Slide Deck format. These are conveniences; you can override them per generation.

If you're producing a lot of similar outputs — always generating "Brief" Audio Overviews for short research sessions, say — setting the default saves clicks.

Sharing Defaults

Decide whether new notebooks default to private or shared with your domain. For Workspace accounts, this can be set at the organization level and may be locked. For personal accounts, default to *private* unless you have a specific reason otherwise — it's far easier to share an existing notebook than to retroactively un-share one.

Privacy and Data

This is the most important section of this chapter. Read it carefully.

NotebookLM's data handling has two distinct dimensions: **what Google can do with your sources** and **what Google can do with your prompts and generated outputs.** They are governed by different rules, and the rules vary based on which account you're signed in with.

Personal (Gmail) Accounts

For personal Gmail accounts, the default is that **Google may use your interactions with NotebookLM to improve the product**, including reviewing some interactions for quality and training. Google has stated that source documents themselves are not used for training general-purpose Gemini models, but the boundaries here have shifted over time. Treat the live policy as the source of truth, not a screenshot or a blog post.

You can — and should — review the privacy settings in your Google account at **myaccount.google.com**, specifically the "Data & Privacy" section. There you can control whether your activity is used for personalization and product improvement.

If you're uploading anything sensitive — medical records, legal documents, internal company materials, personal financial information — **do not use a personal Gmail account.** Use a Workspace account instead, where data protections are stronger by default and configurable by an administrator.

Google Workspace and Education Accounts

For Workspace and Education accounts, **NotebookLM does not use your data to train models, and your administrator has additional controls** over retention, sharing, and external access.

That's a meaningful difference. If your organization has standardized on Workspace, you can use NotebookLM with internal documents under reasonable enterprise data controls. If you're a graduate student with a university Google account, your research notebooks have stronger protections than they would on a personal Gmail.

A Practical Rule

Use the right account for the right work. Personal Gmail for personal research, public sources, and experimentation. Workspace for anything you'd be uncomfortable seeing in the news. If you're not sure, default to the more protective option.

We'll go deeper on privacy, sensitive sources, and the 2026 voice-cloning lawsuit in Chapter 31.

Accessibility Features

NotebookLM ships with a growing set of accessibility features. Worth knowing about even if you don't personally need them — they often improve the experience for everyone:

- **Audio Overviews as accessibility tool.** For users with reading impairments or visual disabilities, the ability to convert any document into a podcast is transformative. Many blind and low-vision users have adopted NotebookLM as a primary research tool for exactly this reason.
- **Keyboard navigation.** The web app supports keyboard-only navigation through all primary interactions. We cover the specific shortcuts in Appendix A.
- **Screen reader support.** The web app implements ARIA correctly for the major screen readers (NVDA, JAWS, VoiceOver).
- **Mobile accessibility.** Both apps support iOS VoiceOver and Android TalkBack.
- **Caption support.** Video Overviews include captions; Audio Overviews can be paired with auto-generated transcripts.

Connecting to Google Drive

One setup decision pays dividends later: connect NotebookLM to Google Drive at first launch (or in settings).

This connection lets you add Google Docs, Sheets, and Slides as sources directly from your Drive instead of downloading them as PDFs and re-uploading. For anyone whose work already lives in Google Drive — most students, a lot of knowledge workers, anyone whose company runs on Workspace — this streamlines source upload dramatically.

The connection respects Drive permissions. NotebookLM can only see files you have access to. Files added as sources are *snapshotted* at upload time — if the underlying Drive doc changes later, your notebook still has the version you originally added, unless you re-add it.

Five Minutes of Setup, Years of Use

That's the entire first-time setup. You can do all of it in under five minutes:

1. Sign in at notebooklm.google.com with the right Google account
2. Review privacy settings at myaccount.google.com
3. Connect Google Drive
4. Install the mobile app on whichever phone you carry
5. (Optional) Set output defaults if you have strong preferences

Now you're ready to do the actual work. Chapter 4 covers sources — the foundation of everything NotebookLM does. Get sources right, and the rest of NotebookLM will feel like magic. Get sources wrong, and even the cleverest prompts won't save you.

Chapter 4: Sources — The Foundation of Everything

There's a phrase in computing that's been around since the punch-card era: *garbage in, garbage out.* It applies to databases, statistical models, machine learning, and — more than anywhere else — to source-grounded AI tools like NotebookLM.

NotebookLM is only as good as the sources you give it. Its model is excellent. Its retrieval is sophisticated. Its outputs are increasingly polished. None of that matters if you've fed it a folder full of low-quality, off-topic, or contradictory documents. The single most important skill for getting good results out of NotebookLM has nothing to do with prompts or features. It's choosing the right sources.

This chapter covers what counts as a source, what NotebookLM can read, what limits exist, and — most importantly — how to think about source selection before you upload anything.

What Counts as a Source

In NotebookLM, a *source* is anything you've added to a notebook for the AI to read. Think of a source as a book on a researcher's shelf: NotebookLM can refer to it, quote from it, summarize it, and cite specific passages, but it cannot infer beyond what's actually inside.

A notebook is a collection of sources, plus the chats, notes, and Studio outputs you've generated against them. The sources are the foundation; everything else is built on top.

What NotebookLM Can Read

In 2026, NotebookLM accepts a remarkable range of source types. The list keeps growing, but as of early 2026 it includes:

Documents

- **PDF** – the most common source type, and what NotebookLM is most thoroughly tested on. Almost any PDF works, including scanned PDFs (NotebookLM applies OCR automatically).
- **DOCX** – Microsoft Word documents, including formatting and embedded images.
- **TXT** – plain text files, useful for anything you've exported from another tool.
- **CSV** – structured tabular data. NotebookLM can read CSVs and answer questions across rows and columns, though for heavy data analysis a spreadsheet tool or ChatGPT's Code Interpreter is a better fit.

Images (with OCR)

- **PNG, JPG, GIF, WEBP** – NotebookLM applies OCR to extract text from images. Screenshots of articles, photos of book pages, phone-camera shots of handwritten notes, even diagrams with text labels can become sources. The OCR is good but not perfect, especially for handwriting and unusual layouts.

Audio

- **MP3, WAV** – NotebookLM transcribes audio sources automatically. Upload a recorded lecture, a podcast episode, an interview recording, or a voice memo, and it becomes searchable, summarizable, and citable just like a written document.

Video

- **MP4, AVI** – NotebookLM extracts both the audio (transcribed) and key visual content from video files.

Web and Embedded Sources

- **Websites** – paste a URL and NotebookLM fetches the page, extracts the readable content, and adds it as a source.
- **YouTube videos** – paste a YouTube URL and NotebookLM uses the video's transcript (auto-generated or creator-uploaded) as the source. Note: transcript-only – NotebookLM doesn't watch the video itself.

- **Google Docs, Sheets, and Slides** — directly from your connected Drive (covered in Chapter 3).

Generated Sources

- **Notes you've written** can be promoted into sources, so the AI can reference your own thinking alongside the documents you've uploaded.
- **Deep Research output** can be saved as a source, letting you build on top of NotebookLM's own web research (covered in Chapter 16).

The 1M-Token Ceiling

Each source can be up to about **one million tokens** — roughly 500,000 words, or a 1,500-page book. For almost any practical document, this is enormous. A typical research paper is 8,000–15,000 words. A long book is 100,000–150,000 words. A 200-page legal contract might be 80,000 words. NotebookLM handles all of these with room to spare.

The ceiling matters in two scenarios:

1. **Truly enormous documents.** Some technical manuals, historical archives, and long-form government reports exceed the limit. For these, split the document into multiple sources (covered in Chapter 18).

2. **Long-running audio and video sources.** A four-hour lecture, transcribed, can approach the limit. A multi-day conference recording will exceed it.

For 99% of users, you'll never bump into this ceiling on a single source. The tighter constraint is the per-notebook source count — 50 on Free, 100 on Plus, more on Pro and Ultra.

Source Limits Per Tier

Each tier sets a maximum number of sources per notebook:

Tier	Sources per notebook
Free	50
Plus	100
Pro	Expanded

Tier	Sources per notebook
Ultra	Maximum

Fifty sources per notebook is more than most users ever need for a single project. A typical literature review involves 15–30 papers; a contract analysis, 5–10 documents; a course notebook might pull in a dozen lectures, a textbook, and some supplementary readings.

The per-notebook limit becomes a problem only when people try to dump *everything* into a single notebook — every paper they've ever read, every meeting note from a year of work, every PDF they've collected. Don't do that. We'll cover the right way to organize across multiple notebooks in Chapter 9.

How NotebookLM Reads Your Sources

A broad-strokes view of what happens when you upload a source helps you make better decisions about what to upload.

When you add a source, NotebookLM:

1. **Ingests the file** — parsing the document format and extracting text. For PDFs, this includes layout analysis to handle multi-column documents, headers, footers, and tables. For images, OCR runs at this stage. For audio and video, transcription runs here.

2. **Generates a source summary** — a short overview of what the source contains, plus a list of key topics it covers. You'll see this when you click on the source in your notebook.

3. **Indexes the content for retrieval** — chunking the document into passages and creating embeddings (mathematical representations) that let NotebookLM quickly find relevant passages when you ask questions later.

4. **Makes the source available** for chat, Studio outputs, and notes.

This usually takes seconds for short documents and a minute or two for very long ones. While ingestion is happening, you can start exploring the document — but Studio output generation may need to wait until ingestion completes.

Source Summaries and Key Topics

Every source you add gets an automatically generated summary and a list of "key topics." These are useful in two distinct ways.

First, they let you **quickly verify what's actually in a source** before you start building on top of it. If you uploaded a PDF expecting a paper about machine learning interpretability, but the summary says "a survey of agricultural pesticide regulations," you've uploaded the wrong file. Better to catch that immediately than after generating an Audio Overview.

Second, the key topics serve as **inspiration for questions** you might want to ask. For a document you're not familiar with, scanning the topics list often surfaces angles you wouldn't have thought to query.

You can edit the source summary — sometimes the auto-generated one misses what *you* care about, and a custom summary will lead to better Studio output framing.

Source Curation: Quality Beats Quantity

Now we arrive at the most important idea in this chapter, and one of the most important ideas in the entire book.

A small set of high-quality, focused sources will outperform a large set of mixed-quality sources, every time.

This goes against the instinct most new users have: dump everything you have into a notebook on the theory that more = better. It's not. Here's why:

- **Retrieval gets noisier with more sources.** When you ask a question, NotebookLM searches across all your sources to find relevant passages. The more sources, the more chances for irrelevant passages to crowd out the relevant ones.

- **Contradictions create incoherent answers.** If you upload ten papers and three of them disagree with the others, NotebookLM may produce answers that paper over the disagreement or, worse, mix incompatible claims into a single "synthesis."

- **Off-topic sources dilute Studio outputs.** An Audio Overview from twenty focused sources sounds confident and clear. An Audio Overview from fifteen focused sources plus five off-topic ones sounds confused, because the AI is trying to make sense of a corpus that doesn't actually cohere.
- **Quality compounds.** Five great sources will give you better answers than fifty mediocre ones. The model is the same; the difference is what it's working with.

The discipline this requires is *curation*. Before you upload, ask: *Is this source actually relevant to the question I'll be asking? Is it credible? Is it current? Does it add something the other sources don't?*

If the answer to any of those is no, leave it out. You can always add it later if you find you needed it.

We'll come back to source curation as a deliberate practice in Chapter 21, where we cover strategy for assembling high-signal source sets.

What NotebookLM Cannot Do With Sources

A few things to set expectations:

It cannot edit your sources. NotebookLM is read-only. If you upload a PDF and then notice a typo, NotebookLM can't fix it. Fix the original and re-upload.

It cannot keep sources in sync with their originals. A Google Doc you added as a source is *snapshotted* at upload. If the underlying doc changes, your notebook still has the older version. That's a feature for stability and citability, but it can surprise people. Re-add the source if the original changes meaningfully.

It cannot run code embedded in sources. A Jupyter notebook uploaded as a PDF is a document NotebookLM can read. It is not an environment where the code can execute.

It cannot follow links inside sources. If a PDF references a URL or a citation, NotebookLM can see the text of the link but cannot click through and pull the linked content. (Deep Research, covered in Chapter 16, is how you bring external content into the notebook.)

It cannot see images inside PDFs as images. OCR extracts text, but charts, diagrams, and pure imagery in PDFs are largely invisible to NotebookLM unless their content is also described in the surrounding text. For source documents that depend heavily on visual content, that's a real limitation.

Sources Are Not Just Inputs — They're the Ground Truth

The most important shift in mindset for new NotebookLM users is recognizing that **sources are the ground truth.** In ChatGPT, you ask a question and the model answers from its training data. In NotebookLM, you ask a question and the model answers from your sources — and *only* your sources.

That means the quality of your work in NotebookLM isn't upstream of the model. It's downstream of your sources.

If you're getting bad answers, the first thing to check isn't your prompt or your settings. It's your sources. Are they relevant? Are they correct? Are there enough of them? Are there too many? Are some of them low-quality and dragging the rest down?

This is also why NotebookLM is so powerful *when you do it right*. Choose sources well, and you have an AI grounded in exactly the truth you care about — not the average of the internet, not the consensus of training data, not whatever the model happened to memorize. The truth you've assembled. The truth you've curated.

Now you're ready to actually build something. Chapter 5 walks through creating your first notebook — picking a source, asking your first questions, reading your first citations, and seeing what NotebookLM can do.

Chapter 5: Your First Notebook

Theory is good. Practice is better. This chapter walks you through your first real NotebookLM notebook from start to finish — picking a source, uploading it, asking your first questions, reading the citations, taking notes, and getting a feel for what the rest of the product can do.

We'll use a worked example throughout: turning a single research paper into a working knowledge base in about ten minutes. To follow along, pick a paper you've been meaning to read — anything in PDF form will do, ideally between 15 and 50 pages. If you don't have one handy, find a public-domain document that interests you (a government report, a Wikipedia-linked PDF, an academic paper from arXiv). Any source will work to demonstrate the workflow.

Creating the Notebook

Start at **notebooklm.google.com**. If this is your first visit, you'll see an empty workspace with a "Create new notebook" button. Click it.

You're now looking at NotebookLM's three-pane layout:

- **Sources** (left) — where you'll add the documents your notebook is built on
- **Chat** (center) — where you'll ask questions and read answers
- **Studio** (right) — where you'll generate Audio Overviews, Reports, Mind Maps, and other outputs

Right now all three panes are mostly empty. The only thing the notebook is asking you to do is add a source.

Adding Your First Source

Click "Add source." You'll see a dialog with several upload options:

- **Drag and drop** a file from your computer
- **Browse** for a file on your computer
- Enter a **URL** (web page or YouTube video)

- Connect from **Google Drive** (if you set this up in Chapter 3)
- Paste **text** directly

For this walkthrough, drag your PDF into the upload area. NotebookLM will spend a few seconds — or for longer documents, up to a minute or two — ingesting and indexing the source. A progress indicator runs while this happens.

When ingestion completes, the source appears in the left pane. Click on it. You'll see two things NotebookLM has already done for you:

1. **A source summary** — typically two or three paragraphs describing what the document is about
2. **A list of key topics** — concepts the document covers, displayed as tappable chips

Read the summary. This is your first sanity check: is this actually the document you meant to upload? Does the summary match what you think the document contains? If yes, great — you're ready to start asking questions. If the summary describes something completely different, you've uploaded the wrong file. This happens more often than you'd expect with similar filenames.

Your First Conversation

Click into the chat pane. NotebookLM has likely pre-populated a few suggested questions based on your source — things like "What is the main argument of this paper?" or "What evidence supports the conclusions?" Useful starting points, but for the first real question, type something specific that you actually want to know.

Some good first questions for almost any source:

- "What's the main claim or argument here?"
- "Summarize this in three paragraphs."
- "What are the three most important takeaways?"
- "What does the author seem most confident about, and what do they hedge?"
- "Who is this written for, and what does the author assume the reader already knows?"

Type your question and press enter. After a moment, NotebookLM produces an answer.

Read the answer. Then look immediately for the small numbered citations scattered through the response — they'll look like superscript numbers, like [1] or [2]. **Click one.**

Following Citations

When you click a citation, NotebookLM jumps you to the exact passage in the source that the answer is drawing on. The passage is highlighted, and you can read it in context.

This is the single most important habit to develop with NotebookLM, and we'll come back to it throughout the book. **Always click at least one citation per answer**, especially early in your work with a new source. You're checking two things:

1. **Does the cited passage actually exist in the source?** (Almost always yes — NotebookLM doesn't fabricate citations the way some AI tools do.)
2. **Does the cited passage actually support what NotebookLM said about it?** (Usually yes, but not always — and the cases where it doesn't are exactly the kind of subtle errors that will get you in trouble if you miss them.)

If the passage supports the claim, you can trust the answer. If the passage doesn't really say what NotebookLM claims, you've just learned something important about that particular answer — and possibly about the larger pattern of how NotebookLM is interpreting your source.

Asking Follow-Up Questions

NotebookLM remembers the context of your conversation. You can ask follow-ups like a normal conversation:

- "Can you say more about the second point?"
- "What evidence does the author give for that?"
- "How does this compare to what you said about [topic from earlier]?"

- “Quote the exact sentence where they say that.”

That last one is particularly useful. Asking NotebookLM to *quote* rather than *paraphrase* gives you the source’s actual language, with citations, and sharply reduces the chance of subtle paraphrase errors.

Try a few different kinds of questions:

- **A factual question.** “What year was this study conducted?”
- **An interpretive question.** “Does the author seem to be making a normative argument or a descriptive one?”
- **A comparative question.** “Does the conclusion in section 4 contradict the framing in the introduction?”
- **A summary question.** “Walk me through the methodology in plain language.”
- **A skeptic’s question.** “What’s the weakest part of this paper’s argument?”

NotebookLM is good at all of these. Pay attention to which kinds produce the most useful answers for your particular source — different documents reward different questions.

Taking Notes

While you’re working, you’ll come across answers worth keeping. Click the “Save to note” button under any response. The answer is saved as a note in your notebook, attached to a Notes section that lives alongside your sources and chats.

You can also write your own notes — observations, questions for later, your own paraphrases of what you’ve learned. Notes are working memory for the notebook. They’re how you build understanding over time, instead of just having a series of disposable conversations.

A useful pattern for any serious project: as you work, capture answers and observations as notes. By the end of a research session you have a structured, citation-grounded collection of insights you can come back to.

Notes can also be **promoted into sources** — turning an insight from one chat into something the AI can reference in future chats. That's how you build cumulative understanding across multiple working sessions.

Trying Your First Studio Output

You've asked questions. You've followed citations. You've taken notes. Now let's generate something.

In the right pane, you'll see Studio. Click "Generate" under **Audio Overview**.

This is the moment that made NotebookLM famous. Wait a couple of minutes (longer for very long sources) and you'll get back a full audio podcast — typically 8 to 15 minutes — featuring two AI hosts having a conversation about your document. They introduce the topic, discuss the main points, raise interesting tangents, and synthesize takeaways. The default style is conversational and accessible, like a well-produced explainer podcast.

Listen to a minute or two. Notice how the hosts:

- Explain the source in plain language without assuming background knowledge
- Pull out specific quotes or findings
- Pose questions to each other and answer them
- Sound, frankly, like real people having a discussion

This is also the moment most new users have a small revelation: this is genuinely useful, not a parlor trick. You can listen to a research paper while you're cooking dinner. You can turn a 60-page report into a 12-minute audio brief for your team. You can review course material while driving.

We'll go much deeper on Audio Overviews in Chapter 10 — how to customize them, when to use the different formats, how to steer them toward the topics you care about. For now, the goal is just to feel the shape of what NotebookLM can do.

Generating a Briefing Doc

Try one more output type before we wrap up. Back in Studio, find the **Reports** option. From the dropdown, pick "Briefing Doc."

NotebookLM generates a structured document with the key takeaways, organized by section, with citations throughout. It's the same source material you've been chatting about, but in a form designed to be skimmed by an executive or handed to a colleague who hasn't read the source.

This is the workflow that makes NotebookLM indispensable for knowledge workers: ten minutes reading and asking questions, one minute to generate the Briefing Doc, and now you have a polished, citation-grounded summary you can hand to someone else. What used to be an hour of work — read, take notes, write a summary — collapses into a tenth of the time.

What You've Just Learned

In about fifteen minutes you've done the entire core loop of NotebookLM:

1. **Created a notebook** and added a source
2. **Verified the source** by reading the summary
3. **Asked questions** and got citation-grounded answers
4. **Followed citations** to verify what NotebookLM said
5. **Took notes** to capture insights worth keeping
6. **Generated a Studio output** — an Audio Overview to consume passively
7. **Generated another Studio output** — a Briefing Doc to share

This is the entire shape of working with NotebookLM. Every workflow in the rest of the book is a refinement, expansion, or specialization of this loop. Multi-source synthesis (Part II) is the same loop with more sources. The Studio chapters (Part III) are the same loop with more output types. The audience-specific chapters (Part VI) are the same loop applied to particular kinds of work.

Once you have this loop in your hands, you can do real work. Even with the few skills you've picked up in this single chapter, you can:

- Read a paper in a quarter of the time
- Brief yourself on a new topic in twenty minutes instead of an afternoon
- Convert a stack of meeting notes into something coherent before a stakeholder asks
- Turn your own course readings into a working study system

A Few Closing Tips

A handful of things that are easy to learn now and hard to learn later:

Use one notebook per topic. The temptation to dump everything into a giant catch-all notebook is strong and almost always wrong. Ten focused notebooks beat one bloated one. We'll cover this in detail in Chapter 9.

Name your notebooks specifically. "Research" is not a useful name. "Indemnification clauses — Acme contract review — Q1 2026" is. Future-you will thank present-you.

Don't trust citations without clicking them. After a few good answers, it's tempting to start trusting NotebookLM's outputs without verification. Don't. Click citations. The discipline pays for itself many times over.

Save the good notes early. It's far easier to save an insight when you first encounter it than to find it again later in a long chat history.

Experiment with Studio. Each output type rewards different sources and different prompts. The only way to learn what each one is good for is to try.

That's Part I. You now know what NotebookLM is, which plan to use, how to set up your account, what counts as a source, and how to actually work in a notebook. The rest of the book goes deeper.

Part II picks up where Part I leaves off — the day-to-day craft of working with sources: adding and managing them, asking questions skillfully, organizing across notebooks, and getting fluent in the rhythm of source-grounded research.

Part II: Working with Sources

"The art of being wise is the art of knowing what to overlook."

— William James

Chapter 6: Adding and Managing Sources

Part I covered what sources *are* — what counts as one, what NotebookLM can read, and the principle that source quality determines output quality. This chapter is about the mechanics of working with sources day to day: adding them efficiently, organizing them inside a notebook, and handling the situations that come up once you have more than three or four to manage.

Most of this is small craft. None of it is hard. But the difference between a source pane that's a chaotic dump of unlabeled PDFs and one that's a deliberate, navigable collection is the difference between fighting NotebookLM and having it work for you.

Adding Sources Efficiently

The basic upload mechanics from Chapter 5 — drag-and-drop, browse, paste a URL, pull from Google Drive — work fine for one or two sources at a time. Once you're working on a real research project, you'll want the faster paths.

Bulk Uploads

NotebookLM accepts multiple files in a single upload. Drag a folder or a multi-selection of files into the upload area, and they'll ingest in parallel. If you've already collected ten or twenty PDFs in a folder on your computer, this is the fastest path: select all, drag in, walk away for a minute, come back to a fully populated notebook.

Bulk uploads count against your per-notebook source limit just like single uploads. Try to add 60 sources to a Free notebook (limit: 50) and you'll get an error — drop the count or split into multiple notebooks.

URL Lists

For web sources, you can paste multiple URLs at once (typically one per line) and NotebookLM will fetch and ingest each as a separate source. Useful when you've collected articles or papers as links rather than downloaded files.

Fetching isn't always reliable — sites with paywalls, JavaScript-heavy rendering, or aggressive bot detection may not extract well. If a fetched source's auto-generated summary looks wrong ("page not found," "subscribe to read"), the fetch failed and you'll need to download the article as a PDF and upload it directly.

YouTube Playlists and Channels

You can add YouTube videos one at a time by URL. There's no native "import a playlist" function, but the common workflow is to copy the video URLs out of a playlist (most playlists let you do this from a context menu or via a third-party tool) and paste them as a list.

Remember that YouTube sources are *transcript-only* — NotebookLM uses the auto-generated or creator-uploaded transcript, not the video frames. For lectures, interviews, and talks, this is fine and often perfect. For visual content (cooking demos, art tutorials, anything where you need to *see* what's happening), the transcript captures a fraction of what's there.

Naming and Renaming Sources

Every source gets an auto-generated name based on its filename or page title. These default names are often terrible — `Untitled1.pdf`, `12345_Final_v3_REVISED.docx`, `bing.com - Search Results`.

Rename your sources. Click the source in the left pane, then click the title to edit it. Give each one a name that tells you, six months from now, what it actually is.

Good source naming patterns:

- **For papers:** `Author (Year) - Short title` — e.g., `Smith (2023) - Causal inference in observational studies`
- **For reports:** `Org - Report title - Year` — e.g., `McKinsey - State of AI 2025`
- **For internal docs:** `Type - Project - Date` — e.g., `Postmortem - Migration outage - 2026-03-12`
- **For long-form content:** `Author - Title (Source)` — e.g., `Karpathy - Software 3.0 (talk)`

This sounds like a small detail. It isn't. When NotebookLM cites a source, the source name is what shows up in the citation. Clear names mean readable citations. Garbled names mean citations that look like noise.

Reordering and Grouping

Within a notebook, sources can be reordered by drag-and-drop in the left pane. NotebookLM doesn't currently support folders or hierarchical groups inside a notebook, but two practical patterns work well:

Order by importance. Put your most central sources at the top, supplementary sources below. This is purely visual — NotebookLM doesn't weight retrieval by source order — but it helps *you* navigate.

Order by category. Group related sources together (all the papers on one sub-topic, then the next, then primary sources, then commentary). This doesn't change how NotebookLM searches, but it makes the source pane scannable.

For real categorization, use multiple notebooks (covered in Chapter 9). NotebookLM is built around the notebook as the primary organizational unit — if you find yourself wanting subfolders inside one, that's usually a sign you should split into two.

Selecting Sources for a Query

Here's a feature most new users miss for weeks: you can **select a subset of your sources** for any chat or Studio output, and NotebookLM will only consider the selected sources when answering.

Look for the checkboxes next to each source in the left pane. By default, all are selected. Uncheck the ones you don't want NotebookLM to consider, and your next chat will be answered using only the rest.

This is genuinely powerful and worth using deliberately:

- **Comparing sources.** Select just two sources and ask "what do these two disagree about?" — far cleaner than asking the same question against a notebook of fifteen.

- **Avoiding contamination.** If you've added a source you're not sure about (incorrect, outdated, biased), uncheck it for queries where it might mislead.
- **Focused Studio outputs.** Generate an Audio Overview for three sources rather than all ten — you'll get a tighter, more coherent podcast.
- **Working through a notebook progressively.** Read source-by-source by selecting one at a time, asking questions of it specifically, then expanding to the others.

The selection persists per session but resets when you reload — it's a working tool, not a permanent setting.

Removing Sources

You'll occasionally want to remove a source — you uploaded the wrong file, found a better version, or the source turned out to be lower quality than you thought. Click it, then look for the delete option in its menu (typically a trash icon or a "Remove" button).

Two things happen when you remove a source:

1. **The source is gone from the notebook.** Your source count drops by one, freeing space for another upload.
2. **Existing chats and Studio outputs that referenced it still exist** — but their citations are now broken. The citation links won't go anywhere, and any insights that depended on the removed source are unanchored.

If you've already done significant work in a notebook and you're considering removing a source, think carefully. It's often better to *deselect* it (uncheck the box) than to remove it — the source stays available for citation but doesn't influence new queries.

If you're sure you want it gone (it's wrong, sensitive, or you're cleaning up an experimental notebook), the removal is final. There's no undo.

Updating Sources

NotebookLM doesn't update sources automatically. A source you added is *snapshotted* at upload time, even if the underlying file or web page changes later.

This is by design — it gives you stable, reproducible answers and citations that mean something. But it surprises people in two scenarios:

A Google Doc you added gets edited. The notebook still has the version that existed when you uploaded. To pull in changes, remove the old source and re-add it (or add the updated version alongside as a new source).

A web page you fetched gets updated. Same situation — you have the snapshot. Re-add the URL to grab the current version.

For research projects where the sources are stable (papers, books, recorded talks), this is rarely an issue. For workflows that depend on living documents (an evolving spec, an ongoing report), build a habit of refreshing sources at the start of each session.

Source Summaries and Custom Summaries

In Chapter 4 we covered source summaries — the auto-generated overview that appears when you click on any source. The defaults are reasonable but generic.

You can edit a source summary by clicking into it. The custom summary you write is what NotebookLM uses to *frame* the source in Studio outputs. If the auto-generated summary says "a research paper on language model evaluation" but you care specifically about the methodology section, edit the summary to emphasize that — and your Audio Overviews and Reports will weight the methodology more.

Worth doing for sources you'll be working with intensively. Not worth doing for casual sources you're dropping in for a one-off question.

Source-Level Notes

Some Studio outputs let you attach notes or context to specific sources. When you generate a Video Overview, for example, you can add a per-source note like "focus on the regulatory implications" — and that source will be read through that lens.

This is most useful when you have a heterogeneous source set (a paper, a news article, a podcast transcript, a press release) and you want NotebookLM to use each one differently. Without per-source notes, it treats them all as equivalent inputs. With them, you can shape how each contributes.

When You Have Too Many Sources

Eventually you'll hit one of two ceilings:

The hard limit. Free is capped at 50 sources per notebook, Plus at 100, with higher caps on Pro and Ultra. When you bump into the cap, NotebookLM stops accepting new uploads.

The soft limit. Long before the hard cap, you'll notice quality degrading. Answers get hedgier, Studio outputs get muddier, retrieval starts pulling passages from off-topic sources. There's no precise threshold, but for most users the soft ceiling sits somewhere between 20 and 40 well-chosen sources. Beyond that, more sources hurt more than they help.

When you hit either limit, the answer is almost always the same: **split into multiple notebooks.** One per topic, one per project, one per sub-question of a larger investigation. Chapter 9 covers organizing across notebooks in detail; for now, treat the per-notebook ceiling as a nudge toward better organization rather than a limitation to fight.

The Source Pane as Working Memory

There's a useful way to think about the source pane that makes the rest of NotebookLM feel more natural: **the source pane is your working memory for this notebook.**

It's not an archive. It's not a bibliography. It's the set of documents that, right now, you want NotebookLM actively reasoning about. A good sourcc panc is:

- **Curated.** Every source is there for a reason.
- **Named clearly.** You can tell what each source is at a glance.
- **Up to date.** Outdated or superseded sources have been removed or replaced.
- **The right size.** Big enough to support the synthesis you need; small enough that retrieval stays sharp.

Treating the source pane as a deliberate working set rather than a passive accumulation changes how you use NotebookLM. Before each session you start asking: *Are these still the right sources? Is anything missing? Is anything dragging the rest down?*

That habit pays off everywhere. Better questions get asked of better sources, and the quality of everything downstream improves.

With the source pane in good shape, the next chapter covers the other half of the equation: how to ask questions skillfully.

Chapter 7: Asking Questions

If sources are NotebookLM's foundation, questions are its primary interface. You'll spend more time typing into the chat box than doing anything else. Getting good at questions — knowing what to ask, how to phrase it, when to push back, when to start over — is the single highest-leverage skill in source-grounded AI.

The good news: it's not a complicated skill. The bad news: most people who've spent serious time with ChatGPT bring habits that work *worse* in NotebookLM than in a general-purpose chatbot. This chapter is about adjusting those habits and developing new ones tuned to how source-grounded AI actually works.

What Makes NotebookLM Different

In ChatGPT or Claude, the model is the source of truth. You ask a question, and the model answers from everything it learned during training. Prompting those tools is largely about *eliciting* the right knowledge from a model that knows an enormous amount about almost everything.

In NotebookLM, the model is the *reader*, not the source. You ask a question, the model searches your sources for relevant passages, and it composes an answer from what it finds. Prompting NotebookLM is more like asking a research assistant a good question: clear scope, specific framing, explicit about what you want and why.

Three practical consequences:

1. Vague questions get vague answers. A general-purpose chatbot can fill in around a vague question with general knowledge. NotebookLM can't — it's bounded by your sources. "Tell me about this paper" produces a generic summary. "What evidence does this paper offer for its main causal claim, and which piece is the strongest?" produces a useful one.

2. Out-of-scope questions return weak answers. If you ask something whose answer isn't in your sources, NotebookLM will either tell you so (good) or attempt a weak general-knowledge answer with no citations (less good — and a sign you should reframe the question or add a relevant source).

3. The same question phrased differently can yield very different results. True of all AI tools, but especially true of retrieval-based ones. A question that pulls back the wrong passages produces an answer composed from the wrong foundation. Often the fix isn't a better question but a *differently scoped* one.

The Anatomy of a Good NotebookLM Question

The best NotebookLM questions tend to share four features:

Scope. What part of your sources you want NotebookLM to focus on. "Across all the papers" is one scope. "The methodology section of the third paper" is another. The more specific, the more focused the answer.

Specificity. The actual ask. "Summarize" is vague. "Identify the three main findings and the evidence each rests on" is specific.

Framing. What lens or perspective you want NotebookLM to use. "Explain this for a non-expert" is one. "Analyze this from a regulatory compliance perspective" is another. "Find the weaknesses in this argument" is a third. Framing changes which passages NotebookLM treats as most relevant.

Format. What you want the answer to look like. A short paragraph, a bulleted list, a comparison table, a quoted passage. NotebookLM is responsive to format requests, and asking for the right one saves a follow-up turn.

You don't need all four in every question. But a question that has none of them — "What's this about?" — will produce a much weaker answer than one with even two or three.

Question Patterns That Work

Here are question patterns that come up constantly. They're not magic — they're just specific enough to give NotebookLM clear traction.

The Targeted Summary

> "Summarize section 3 of [source] in three paragraphs, focusing on the methodology and what makes it different from the prior literature."

This combines scope (section 3 of a specific source), specificity (methodology focus), framing (in contrast to prior literature), and format (three paragraphs). The answer will be substantially more useful than "summarize this paper."

The Cross-Source Comparison

> "Compare what [Source A] and [Source B] say about [specific topic]. Where do they agree, where do they disagree, and how do they frame the question differently?"

This is where NotebookLM genuinely outperforms reading the sources yourself. Especially powerful for literature reviews, contract reviews, and any work that hinges on identifying agreement and disagreement across documents.

The Quote Hunt

> "Find the exact passage where [Source] discusses [specific concept]. Quote it directly with the surrounding context."

When you need an actual quote — for a paper you're writing, a contract you're analyzing, a brief you're preparing — ask NotebookLM to *quote* rather than paraphrase. This dramatically reduces the risk of subtle paraphrase errors (covered in detail in Chapter 23).

The Inventory

> "List every distinct [thing] mentioned across all sources. For each one, briefly note what's said about it and which source(s) discuss it."

Useful for building a structured view of what's in your corpus. "Every regulatory body mentioned." "Every named technique." "Every author cited as influential." NotebookLM is good at exhaustive inventory work — better than scrolling through PDFs, in most cases.

The Skeptic's Question

> "What's the weakest part of [Source's] argument? Where is the evidence thinnest, and what would a critic likely target first?"

NotebookLM leans toward agreement and synthesis if you let it. Explicitly asking it to look for weaknesses, contradictions, and gaps produces more useful critical analysis than asking "is this argument sound?"

The Re-Frame

> "Re-explain [concept from source] for a [specific audience], without using technical jargon and using a concrete analogy."

Excellent for learning workflows. NotebookLM is genuinely good at adjusting register — explaining the same thing for a five-year-old, a non-expert adult, a working professional, a domain expert. Specifying the audience pulls a far better answer than asking generically for a "simpler explanation."

The Steel-Man

> "Make the strongest possible case for [position] using only what's in the sources. Then make the strongest possible case against."

Valuable for contested topics, policy questions, and any work where you need to understand multiple perspectives. The two-pass structure forces NotebookLM to give each side its due.

Single-Source vs. Cross-Source Queries

Recall from Chapter 6 that you can select a subset of your sources for any query. This is the difference between a single-source question and a cross-source one, and the right mode depends on what you're trying to do.

Use a single source when: - You're trying to deeply understand one specific document - You're checking what one source says, independent of the others - You're doing close-reading work (quotes, exact passages, careful interpretation) - You want to verify or fact-check a specific claim

Use multiple sources when: - You're synthesizing across the corpus - You're looking for patterns, agreements, disagreements - You're building Studio outputs (Audio Overviews, Reports, Mind Maps) meant to cover the whole notebook - You're answering a question that no single source fully addresses

A common mistake is leaving all sources selected for every query, even when you're really only thinking about one. That's not wrong, but it's noisier. If you're working through a single source, select just that one. The answers get sharper.

Refining and Following Up

NotebookLM remembers the context of your conversation, which makes follow-ups natural and productive:

- **"Say more about that."**
- **"What's the evidence for the second point?"**
- **"How does that compare to what was said in the previous answer?"**
- **"Quote the exact passage."**
- **"Now do the same analysis but for [different sub-topic]."**

A useful pattern: ask a broad question first to map the territory, then drill in with follow-ups on the most interesting parts. Don't try to write the perfect single-shot question. NotebookLM works better as a conversation than as a one-shot oracle.

When NotebookLM Says "I Don't Know"

This is a feature, not a bug. NotebookLM will sometimes refuse to answer, or will answer with explicit caveats like "I don't see this addressed in the sources" or "the sources don't directly answer this question."

When this happens, it usually means one of three things:

1. The answer genuinely isn't in your sources. You're asking about something the documents don't cover. Either reframe the question to one your sources can answer, or add new sources that cover the gap.

2. The answer is in your sources but phrased differently than your question. Retrieval failed to surface the relevant passages. Try rephrasing using terms more likely to appear in the source text. If the source talks about "endpoint protection" and you asked about "antivirus," try the source's preferred term.

3. The answer is in your sources but spread across passages that don't obviously connect. NotebookLM is better at retrieving single relevant passages than at stitching scattered fragments. Try a more decomposed question, or build up the answer through multiple related queries.

The instinct, when NotebookLM says "I don't know," is to assume it's wrong and push harder. Sometimes it is wrong, and rephrasing helps. But often the refusal is honest, and the right move is to update your model of what's actually in the sources — not to bully the AI into making something up.

When to Push Back

Sometimes NotebookLM gives you an answer that seems wrong. You read a citation and the cited passage doesn't say what NotebookLM claims. Or the answer contradicts something you know to be true in the source.

Push back. Be direct.

> "I don't think that's quite right. Source X actually says [your understanding]. Can you re-read the relevant passages and reconsider?"

NotebookLM is good at correcting itself when given specific feedback. It's poor at correcting itself in response to vague pushback — "are you sure?" produces sycophantic backpedaling without actually improving the answer.

The discipline this requires is your own attention. You have to read enough of the sources, click enough citations, to know when to push back. NotebookLM won't catch its own subtle errors — but it will fix them when you do.

When to Start a New Chat

A single chat in a NotebookLM notebook can run a long time, but conversations have a kind of accumulating drift. After many turns, NotebookLM can lose track of what was established earlier, or get stuck in a pattern that's not serving you.

Signs it's time to start a new chat:

- Answers are circular — you're hearing the same points repeated
- The conversation drifted off the topic you actually care about and you're trying to drag it back
- You're moving to a fundamentally different question or a different sub-section of your sources
- A previous answer was wrong and you're worried it's biasing the ones that follow

Starting a new chat is cheap. NotebookLM keeps your full chat history available in the sidebar — you can always come back to a previous conversation. There's no penalty for working in many shorter conversations rather than one sprawling one.

A Note on Conversational Style

NotebookLM doesn't reward chatty preambles or politeness rituals. "Could you please be so kind as to summarize this for me?" is a wasted prompt. So is "I'm sorry to bother you, but..."

Be direct. Specific. Imperative. Not because NotebookLM has feelings to spare, but because the parts of your prompt that aren't carrying signal are competing with the parts that are.

Compare:

- ❌ *"Hi! I was hoping you could help me with something. I have this paper and I'd love to know what it's about. Could you summarize it for me when you have a chance?"*
- ✅ *"Summarize the paper in three paragraphs. Focus on the methodology and the main empirical claim."*

Both will get you a summary. The second one will get you a better summary in one turn.

The Question Behind the Question

Here's a final habit worth developing: before you type a question, ask yourself what you're actually trying to find out. The question you type is often a proxy for a deeper one.

You typed: *"What does this report say about Q4 revenue?"*

What you actually wanted to know: *"Is this report's revenue framing consistent with what they said in the previous quarter, and if not, what changed?"*

The first is easy and produces a one-line answer. The second is harder and produces real insight. The skill of NotebookLM use, ultimately, is the skill of articulating the question behind the question — and asking *that* one instead.

We'll come back to the craft of prompting in Chapter 22 with templates organized by use case. But the fundamentals in this chapter — scope, specificity, framing, format, and the discipline of asking the question behind the question — will carry you through most real work.

Next chapter: notes, the workspace, and how to capture what you're learning so it doesn't dissolve back into the chat history the moment you close the tab.

Chapter 8: Notes and the Workspace

There's a moment in every NotebookLM session that separates casual users from people who are building something. NotebookLM gives you an answer. It's good — better than you expected, exactly the framing you needed, with citations you've verified. You read it, nod, and... move on to the next question.

A week later, you remember the answer existed but can't find it. You scroll through chat history. You re-ask a similar question and get a slightly different response. The insight you wanted is gone.

Notes are the fix. They're how you turn NotebookLM from a chat interface into a working knowledge base. This chapter covers what notes are, how to use them well, and how to think about the workspace as a whole — sources on the left, chat in the middle, Studio on the right, and notes weaving across all three.

What Notes Are

In NotebookLM, a *note* is a small text artifact that lives in your notebook alongside the sources. You'll find them in their own section, typically below or alongside the sources in the left or center pane (Google iterates on layout — look for a "Notes" tab or panel).

A note can contain:

- **An answer NotebookLM gave you** that you wanted to keep
- **Your own writing** — observations, paraphrases, working hypotheses, questions for later
- **A combination** — an AI-generated answer with your annotation on top

Notes are tied to the notebook they live in. They're available across all your chats in that notebook, can be promoted into sources (more on this below), and persist when you close and reopen.

Saving Answers as Notes

Every chat response has a "Save to note" button — typically a small icon below the answer, sometimes labeled "Pin" or shown as a bookmark icon depending on the interface version.

Click it. The answer is saved as a note, with a link back to the chat it came from and the citations it included.

This sounds trivial. It's not. The discipline of saving good answers in the moment changes how productive your sessions are. Without it, your work in NotebookLM is ephemeral — every chat is its own bubble, and the moment you ask a follow-up you risk losing the answer you wanted. With it, a session naturally produces a structured collection of insights you can come back to.

A useful rhythm:

1. Ask a question
2. Read the answer
3. Click at least one citation to verify
4. If the answer is worth keeping — *save the note immediately*
5. Move on to the next question

The "save immediately" step is what most people skip. It costs one click. It saves you hours of re-asking and re-reading later.

Writing Your Own Notes

Notes aren't just for storing AI output. You can write your own — and you should.

Use cases for handwritten notes:

- **Hypotheses you want to test.** "Authors seem to be conflating two distinct definitions of [concept]. Verify by re-reading section 4."
- **Questions to come back to.** "What does this paper's framing imply for the regulatory question we discussed last week?"
- **Synthesis across answers.** A note that pulls together insights from three different chats into a coherent picture.

- **Working drafts.** A paragraph you're trying to write, refined across multiple NotebookLM-assisted iterations.
- **Observations the AI didn't make.** Things you noticed that NotebookLM missed.

Handwritten notes serve a function the AI's notes don't: they capture *your* thinking, in your voice, with whatever idiosyncratic framing makes sense to you. In a long-running notebook, the handwritten notes become the actual product of your work — the AI is the assistant, your notes are the document being built.

Promoting Notes to Sources

Here's a feature that takes most users a while to discover but transforms how you can use NotebookLM: **you can promote a note into a source.**

When you do, the note moves from the Notes section into the Sources section. From that point on, NotebookLM treats it like any other source — it can be cited, included in Studio outputs, used in synthesis across the corpus.

This unlocks a powerful pattern: **building cumulative understanding within a single notebook.**

Here's how it works in practice:

1. You ask NotebookLM a series of questions across your sources, generating answers
2. You save the most useful answers as notes
3. You write a synthesis note in your own words that pulls together what you've learned so far
4. You promote that synthesis note to a source
5. Future queries can now reference your synthesis directly, alongside the original sources

Now NotebookLM isn't just searching your raw sources — it's searching them *plus your accumulated thinking about them*. Your insights compound.

This is powerful for long-running research projects. After a few weeks, your notebook contains not just the original PDFs but a layered structure of synthesis notes, each building on prior ones. NotebookLM can reason across the whole stack.

A few cautions:

- **Promote sparingly.** A notebook full of promoted notes becomes hard to manage. Promote synthesis notes that are genuinely useful as future reference, not every casual observation.
- **Mark your own work clearly.** Give promoted notes names that distinguish them from the originals — e.g., `MY SYNTHESIS – How the three frameworks compare` rather than just `synthesis`.
- **Watch the citation trail.** When NotebookLM cites a promoted-note source, the citation points to your own synthesis, not the underlying papers. For published or shareable work, you'll need to dig deeper to cite the originals.

Organizing Notes

NotebookLM doesn't currently support folders, tags, or hierarchical organization for notes within a notebook. Notes are a flat list. So: name them clearly.

Patterns that work:

- **Date-prefixed for chronological notebooks.** `2026-04-15 – Methodology summary` makes it easy to scan a long notebook for the work from a specific session.
- **Topic-prefixed for thematic notebooks.** `[Regulation] FDA position on adversarial models` lets you quickly find all notes on a sub-topic.
- **Verb-led for action-oriented notes.** `TODO: Verify the third citation in §2.3` tells you at a glance that this needs follow-up.

If you need more structure than naming can provide, that's usually a signal to split into multiple notebooks — one per major topic or sub-investigation.

The Workspace as a Whole

Step back from any individual feature and the NotebookLM workspace has a coherent shape:

- **Sources** are what you're working *with* — the documents, transcripts, web pages, images that anchor everything.

- **Chat** is how you *interact* with the sources — questions, refinements, synthesis on demand.
- **Notes** are what you *retain* — the insights, hypotheses, and synthesis you want to keep.
- **Studio** is what you *produce* — Audio Overviews, Reports, Mind Maps, Slide Decks, the artifacts you'll consume later or share with others.

Each pane has a different temporal character. Sources are stable (mostly snapshotted at upload). Chat is ephemeral (lots of it, only some kept). Notes are accumulated (deliberately curated over time). Studio outputs are episodic (generated when you need them, often shared and then archived).

Effective NotebookLM use means moving fluidly across all four. You're not stuck in chat. You're not just consuming Studio outputs. You're working — adding sources when you need them, asking questions when you have them, capturing notes when answers are worth keeping, generating Studio outputs when you need to share or consume.

A Working Session, End to End

To make this concrete, here's what a productive 90-minute NotebookLM session might look like:

0–10 minutes: Setup. Open the notebook. Skim the existing sources and any synthesis notes from your last session. Review what you were planning to do.

10–15 minutes: Add sources. Drop in any new documents you've collected since last time. Rename them, verify the auto-generated summaries match your understanding.

15–55 minutes: Working chat. Ask questions, follow citations, refine, follow up. Save useful answers as notes as you go. When a chat drifts, start a new one. Use source selection to scope queries appropriately.

55–70 minutes: Synthesis. Write a handwritten note capturing what you learned this session. Maybe pull together insights across multiple chats. If the synthesis is significant enough, promote it to a source so future sessions can build on it.

70–85 minutes: Studio output. Generate a Briefing Doc or Audio Overview that captures where the work stands. Useful for sharing with collaborators, or for letting yourself listen back over the session while you make dinner.

85–90 minutes: Cleanup. Rename anything ambiguously named. Mark any TODO notes that need follow-up. Note what you want to do next session.

Not every session needs all of these phases. Quick exploratory sessions are mostly chat. Deep work sessions are mostly synthesis. The structure is a default, not a requirement.

Why This Matters

The biggest difference between people who get a lot out of NotebookLM and people who don't is whether they treat it as a chat interface or as a workspace.

If you treat it as a chat interface — open it, ask questions, get answers, close it — you'll get what a chat interface gives you: useful answers in the moment, mostly forgotten by the time you need them again.

If you treat it as a workspace — sources curated, notes accumulated, synthesis built up over time, Studio outputs generated when you need to consume or share — NotebookLM becomes the central place where a body of knowledge actually lives. Months into a project, your notebook is the most valuable artifact of the work — not because the AI is doing the thinking, but because the workspace is structured to let *your* thinking compound.

This is why naming, saving, and synthesis matter more than they sound. They're the small habits that turn a fancy chat tool into a research environment.

With a good model of how a single notebook works, the next chapter zooms out: how to organize across multiple notebooks, when to split, when to merge, and how to think about NotebookLM at the scale of a year of work rather than a single session.

Chapter 9: Organizing Multiple Notebooks

Most NotebookLM users start with a single notebook. They upload a few sources, ask some questions, generate an Audio Overview, and call it a day. For casual use, this is fine — one notebook, lightly used, can serve indefinitely.

The trouble starts when NotebookLM becomes part of how you actually work. Once you're using it for multiple projects, multiple research threads, multiple recurring topics, how to organize *across* notebooks matters more than how to organize within any single one. Get this right and your library becomes a personal knowledge system that grows in value over years. Get it wrong and you end up with a sprawling mess of overlapping notebooks, none of which contains quite the sources you need.

This chapter is about the organizational craft. There aren't many features to learn — NotebookLM keeps the structure flat on purpose. The skill is in your discipline.

One Topic, One Notebook

The single most important rule, and the one most new users get wrong: **one topic per notebook.**

The temptation, especially when sources are tier-limited, is to dump everything you might want to reference into a single mega-notebook. "AI research." "Work stuff." "Reading list." This always ends badly. Here's why:

- **Retrieval gets noisier.** With unrelated sources in the same notebook, NotebookLM's search has more chances to surface off-topic passages. Answers get hedgier.
- **Studio outputs become incoherent.** An Audio Overview generated from a notebook full of unrelated topics sounds confused, because there's no coherent topic to discuss.
- **Synthesis breaks down.** NotebookLM is good at finding patterns across related sources. It's bad at finding patterns across sources that have nothing to do with each other.

- **You hit source limits faster.** Even at Plus's 100-source ceiling, an "everything I'm reading this year" notebook fills up in months. A focused notebook rarely does.

The right granularity varies by how you work, but useful patterns include:

- **One notebook per active research project.** A literature review. A contract analysis. A market study. Each gets its own.
- **One notebook per recurring topic you reference.** "Quarterly earnings — Acme Corp." "Internal architecture documents." "Course readings — Spring 2026."
- **One notebook per client or project, for consultants and freelancers.** Easy to share, easy to wind down when the engagement ends.
- **One notebook per book or major source you're studying intensively.** A notebook dedicated to a single dense book, with your notes and supplementary readings, becomes a working companion to that book over weeks.

If you're not sure whether two collections of sources belong in the same notebook, default to *separate*. It's much easier to consolidate later than to disentangle.

The Notebook Gallery

The home screen of NotebookLM (where you land after signing in) is your notebook gallery — a grid of all the notebooks you've created, with thumbnails, titles, and last-modified dates.

A few quality-of-life features to know:

Search. A search bar at the top searches notebook titles. It does not (currently) search inside notebook content — for that, you have to open the notebook and search there. This makes notebook *titles* much more important than they'd otherwise be.

Sort. Notebooks can typically be sorted by recently modified, recently created, or alphabetical. Recently modified is the default and usually what you want.

Pinning. Some interface versions let you pin a notebook to the top of the gallery. Use this for the two or three you're working in most actively.

The gallery is your library. Treating it intentionally — naming notebooks well, archiving inactive ones, keeping the active set small — is what makes a NotebookLM library useful at scale.

Naming Notebooks

A notebook name is the only thing visible in the gallery. Treat it like a label on a file folder: specific enough that future-you can find what you need without opening it.

Bad names: "Research." "Project." "Stuff." "Untitled notebook."

Good names follow a pattern. Pick one and stick with it. Some that work:

Date + topic. `2026-Q1 – Pricing strategy research`. Useful when you have many notebooks across many time periods.

Project + scope. `Acme contract review – indemnification clauses`. Useful when you have multiple notebooks within the same project.

Type + topic. `LITREV – Causal inference methods (2020-2025)`. Useful for academic work where the type of investigation matters.

Audience + topic. `Client briefing – Apex M&A – diligence materials`. Useful for client-facing work you'll later share.

The specific pattern matters less than the consistency. Pick one, use it everywhere, and your gallery becomes navigable at a glance.

When to Split a Notebook

Sometimes a notebook starts as one project and naturally bifurcates. You started with "European energy regulation," and three months in you have so many sources on grid storage specifically that "grid storage" wants to be its own notebook.

Signs it's time to split:

- **The source list has clear sub-clusters.** Two or three groups of sources that don't cross-reference each other.

- **Your queries naturally divide.** You're never asking questions that span the full source set — you're always asking about one sub-area at a time.
- **Studio outputs are getting muddier.** Audio Overviews and Briefing Docs are losing focus because the underlying source set is too heterogeneous.
- **You're hitting source limits.** A notebook that's full and growing wants to be split.

Splitting is straightforward: create a new notebook, move (or re-add) the relevant sources, and let the old one keep what's left. You may need to re-create some chats and notes in the new notebook — there's no native "move this note to another notebook" function — so do the split before you've accumulated huge amounts of work in the original.

When to Merge Notebooks

Less commonly, you'll find two notebooks should really be one. You were investigating two questions that turn out to be the same question. Or two related projects converged into a single deliverable.

Merging is harder than splitting because NotebookLM has no native merge. Practically, you:

1. Pick which of the two notebooks will absorb the other
2. In the second, identify the sources worth bringing over
3. Add those sources to the first (re-uploading from local copies, or using shared Drive links)
4. Re-create any critical notes by copy-pasting them into the merged notebook

Notes and chats from the second notebook *don't* automatically come along. You'll lose chat history that wasn't captured as notes. Plan accordingly.

In practice: try not to merge. Splitting is cheap; merging is expensive. Create a new notebook only when you're confident the topic is distinct.

Templates and Starter Notebooks

If you do similar investigations repeatedly — quarterly briefings, monthly literature reviews, client onboarding research — you'll find yourself setting up notebooks the same way each time: same source naming conventions, same starter questions, same Studio outputs at the end.

NotebookLM has no built-in template feature, but you can fake one:

1. Create a notebook called `TEMPLATE – Quarterly briefing` (or whatever pattern you use)
2. Set it up with the default sources, custom summaries, naming conventions, and starter notes you'd want every instance to begin with
3. When you start a new instance, *duplicate* the template (or create a new notebook and copy in the relevant pieces)
4. Rename to the actual project name and proceed

More friction than a real template feature, but worth doing for any workflow you repeat more than three or four times. The starter notes alone — "first questions to ask," "things to check before generating outputs" — pay for the setup cost.

Shared and Team Notebooks

If you're on Plus or higher, notebooks can be shared with other Google accounts (covered in detail in Chapter 29). In a team setting, the organizational rules shift slightly:

- **Be even more explicit about naming.** A teammate opening a shared notebook for the first time should be able to tell what it is from the title alone.
- **Establish team conventions.** If your team adopts NotebookLM, agree on a naming pattern and notebook structure (e.g., one notebook per active investigation, named `[Team] – [Project] – [Phase]`).
- **Be careful with promoted-note sources.** A note you promoted as "synthesis of my thinking" may not be what a teammate expects when they see it in the source list. Mark personal synthesis clearly.

- **Designate notebook owners.** For shared notebooks with multiple editors, decide who's responsible for the source list, who keeps the gallery tidy, and who's allowed to delete.

Shared notebooks are powerful for team research and collaborative knowledge work, but they require more deliberate stewardship than personal notebooks. Disorganization that's annoying in a personal library is actively expensive when it's shared across a team.

Pruning the Library

Over time your gallery accumulates notebooks. Some are active. Some served a purpose months ago and are no longer useful. Some were experimental and never amounted to anything. Some were one-off investigations you don't plan to return to.

A periodic pruning ritual — once a quarter is reasonable — keeps the library navigable:

- **Archive or delete completed projects.** A notebook for a project that finished six months ago can be deleted, exported (more on this below), or renamed to indicate it's archived (`[ARCHIVED] Q3 strategic review`) so it doesn't clutter the active gallery.
- **Delete experimental notebooks.** If you tried something and it didn't pan out, the notebook isn't doing anything for you. Delete.
- **Consolidate stragglers.** A notebook with three sources and four chats from eight months ago, on a topic you haven't touched since — almost certainly deletable.
- **Promote synthesis notes from archived notebooks.** Before deleting an old notebook, skim the notes for anything worth keeping. Promote it to a source in a current notebook, or save it externally.

The goal isn't ruthlessness — some notebooks are worth keeping forever, even if you only check them once a year. The goal is to make the gallery *legible*, so you can find what you need without scrolling through a graveyard of stale work.

Exporting and Backup

NotebookLM, like most cloud-only tools, has limited native export. You can typically:

- Export individual Studio outputs (Briefing Docs as DOCX or PDF, Slide Decks as PPTX, Audio Overviews as MP3)
- Copy chat responses and notes manually
- Take screenshots

You cannot, as of early 2026, export an entire notebook as a single bundle, or back up your whole library. So: if a notebook contains work you can't afford to lose, *export the critical artifacts* (Briefing Docs, key Audio Overviews, handwritten notes) to durable storage outside NotebookLM.

This matters more than it sounds. NotebookLM's data isn't going to disappear in any normal scenario, but products change, accounts get locked, features get deprecated. Critical work should always exist somewhere outside the single tool that produced it.

A Library That Grows in Value

The right way to think about a NotebookLM library, after a year or two of serious use, is as personal knowledge infrastructure. Not a set of one-off conversations. A *library* — curated, navigable, layered with synthesis, available when you need it.

That kind of library doesn't happen by accident. It happens because you:

- Created notebooks intentionally (one topic per notebook)
- Named them clearly
- Pruned the inactive ones periodically
- Captured synthesis notes in the active ones
- Knew when to split, when to merge, and when to start fresh

None of this is hard. All of it requires a small amount of attention sustained over time. But the payoff — being able, six months from now, to pull up a notebook on a topic and immediately have the sources, the prior thinking, and the structure you need to keep working — is one of the things that separates NotebookLM-as-toy from NotebookLM-as-tool.

That closes Part II. You now have everything you need to use NotebookLM as a working environment: sources curated, questions asked skillfully, notes captured deliberately, and a library organized to grow.

Part III is where things get interesting. The Studio is what makes NotebookLM uniquely powerful — Audio Overviews, Video Overviews, Mind Maps, Reports, Slide Decks, Flashcards, Quizzes, Infographics, Data Tables. We'll cover every output type, with worked examples, in the chapters that follow.

Part III: The Studio

"The medium is the message."

— Marshall McLuhan

Chapter 10: Audio Overviews

This is the feature that made NotebookLM famous. In September 2024, Google added a button labeled "Generate Audio Overview" to what had been a quiet research utility known mostly to early adopters and Google Labs followers. Within weeks, the feature was everywhere — research papers turned into podcasts, wedding photos turned into podcasts, the lyrics of obscure songs turned into podcasts, the entire codebase of someone's startup turned into a podcast. Spotify used the same engine to generate personalized year-in-review podcasts for hundreds of millions of Wrapped users.

The reason it caught fire is simple: it produces something that doesn't feel like AI. Two AI-generated hosts, sounding remarkably like real people, having a real-feeling conversation about whatever you handed them. The first time you generate one for a document you wrote yourself, the experience is uncanny.

This chapter is about how to use Audio Overviews well — not as a parlor trick but as a working tool. We'll cover the formats, the customization options, when to use which, and the workflows that have emerged in the year and a half since launch.

What an Audio Overview Actually Is

An Audio Overview is a generated audio track in which two AI hosts discuss the contents of your selected sources. Default length runs between 8 and 15 minutes; the format is conversational and explanatory, with the hosts trading turns asking questions, offering observations, and synthesizing the source material.

A few things to understand about how it works:

The hosts are AI-generated. Their voices, their names (sometimes assigned, sometimes left implicit), and their personas are all model-generated. They don't correspond to real people. Google has been deliberately vague about which voice models power them — they've been upgraded multiple times since launch, most recently with the move to Gemini 3 in March 2026.

The script is generated, not improvised. Behind the scenes, NotebookLM produces a full text script first, then renders it as audio. This is why the conversational rhythm feels natural — it's a written conversation, polished for delivery.

Citations exist but aren't surfaced in audio. The generation is grounded in your sources, but you don't hear citations spoken aloud. If you need traceable claims, the chat interface and Reports are better tools.

The podcast is "about" your sources, not "from" them. The hosts talk *about* your documents. They don't read them aloud. They summarize, paraphrase, contextualize, and synthesize. This is usually what you want, but worth being clear about.

Generating Your First Audio Overview

The basic flow:

1. In your notebook, select the sources you want the Audio Overview to cover (use the source checkboxes from Chapter 6).
2. In the Studio panel, find Audio Overview and click "Generate."
3. Wait. Generation takes a few minutes for short source sets, longer (5–10 minutes) for larger ones.
4. When ready, click play.

The result also downloads — most interface versions let you export the MP3 directly, useful for offline listening or sharing.

The most common first-time mistake: generating an Audio Overview against *all* sources in a notebook by default. If your notebook has a focused topic and only a few related sources, that's fine. If it has a heterogeneous source set, the resulting podcast will feel scattered. Select sources deliberately.

The Default Format and Its Limits

Out of the box, NotebookLM generates a "Deep Dive" Audio Overview — the conversational, explanatory format that became the viral hit. This format is excellent for:

- Introducing yourself to a new topic
- Reviewing a single substantial source (a paper, a book chapter, a long report)

- Producing something a non-expert can listen to and understand

It's less ideal for:

- Specific factual reference (you can't easily skim audio for one fact)
- Highly technical material with many precise details
- Anything where the *exact* claims matter (paraphrase is the medium)

Knowing what the default format is good for — and what it isn't — is what separates power users from people who generate one Audio Overview, find it impressive, and never think to use the customization features.

The Other Formats

Beyond Deep Dive, NotebookLM offers several format variants. The exact list shifts as Google iterates, but as of early 2026 the major options include:

Brief. A shorter, more concentrated Audio Overview — typically 3–5 minutes. Same conversational format, less depth. Useful when you want a quick overview rather than a thorough discussion.

Critique. The hosts adopt a skeptical stance, focusing on the limitations, weaknesses, and unanswered questions in the source material. Excellent when you want a critical lens — for evaluating an argument, reviewing a paper before citing it, or pressure-testing a claim.

Debate. The hosts take opposing positions and argue with each other. Useful for genuinely contested topics where the value is in hearing both sides articulated. Less useful for settled topics — the format manufactures conflict that may not exist.

Custom. Provide your own framing and the format follows your direction. This is the most powerful option once you know how to use it (covered in Chapter 17).

Each format has its place. The discipline is matching the format to the goal:

- Want to learn? Deep Dive.
- Want to brief a colleague in five minutes? Brief.
- Want to evaluate? Critique.
- Want to understand multiple perspectives? Debate.

- Want something specific the defaults don't give you? Custom.

Source Selection for Audio Overviews

The sources you select for an Audio Overview shape what kind of podcast you get more than any other variable. Some practical guidance:

One to three focused sources usually beats five or more mixed sources. The hosts can go deeper on each source when there are fewer of them. With many sources, the conversation becomes high-level synthesis at the cost of specifics.

Closely related sources cohere; loosely related ones don't. Three papers on the same topic produce a tight discussion. Three papers on tangentially related topics produce a podcast that feels like the hosts are jumping around.

Single very-long sources work surprisingly well. A 200-page report distilled into a 15-minute podcast is one of the things NotebookLM does best. Don't be afraid to generate against just one substantial source — the result is often more useful than synthesis across many shorter ones.

Mixed-medium sources can be powerful. A research paper plus a press release plus a podcast transcript on the same topic produces a podcast that brings in multiple perspectives and registers. Worth experimenting with.

Length and Pacing

NotebookLM gives you some control over Audio Overview length. The exact controls vary, but typically you can request "shorter," "longer," or specify a target length range when generating.

A few practical notes:

- **Shorter Audio Overviews are not always better.** A 5-minute Audio Overview on a 200-page report will necessarily skim. A 12-minute one has room to dig in.
- **Very long Audio Overviews lose listeners.** Past about 20 minutes, attention drops. If you have so much material that a single Audio Overview can't cover it, generate multiple Audio Overviews on different sub-topics.

- **The hosts pace themselves naturally.** You usually don't need to specify pace. The model handles the rhythm.

Topic Focus Prompts

The single most underused feature of Audio Overviews is the **topic focus prompt** — a short text instruction you can provide when generating, telling the hosts what to emphasize.

Without a focus prompt, the hosts decide for themselves what to highlight, based on what they identify as central in the sources. That's fine for general overviews. For specific use cases, a focus prompt sharpens the result dramatically.

Examples:

- *"Focus on the methodology and what makes it different from prior approaches. Spend less time on the literature review and conclusions."*
- *"Discuss this from the perspective of a regulatory compliance officer. What in this paper would be relevant to compliance teams, and what should they be skeptical of?"*
- *"This is for a general audience with no background. Use analogies, avoid jargon, and explain technical terms when they come up."*
- *"The audience is a board of directors. Keep the discussion strategic, focus on business implications, and don't get into technical details."*
- *"Focus specifically on the limitations and open questions, not the main findings. Treat this as a critical review."*

Topic focus prompts work best when they specify three things: **what to emphasize, what to de-emphasize, and who the audience is.** Generic instructions ("make it good") don't help. Specific direction ("for a non-expert, focused on the regulatory implications, skipping the technical sections") shapes the entire output.

Languages

As of early 2026, NotebookLM supports Audio Overviews in more than 80 languages. The mechanics are straightforward: in the generation settings, select the target language, and the hosts will speak in it.

Quality is best in the major languages — English, Spanish, French, German, Mandarin, Japanese, Portuguese, Italian. It degrades gracefully in less common languages but is usually still good.

A few cross-language workflows worth knowing:

Sources in one language, output in another. Upload English sources, generate the Audio Overview in Spanish. NotebookLM handles the cross-language synthesis — useful for international research and multilingual teams.

Multiple languages in the same notebook. A notebook can mix sources in different languages. Audio Overviews will draw across all of them and produce output in whichever language you select.

Bilingual hosts. A few experimental options let the hosts code-switch or alternate languages, useful for language-learning workflows. Availability and quality vary.

We cover multilingual workflows in detail in Chapter 19.

When to Use Audio Overviews

Audio Overviews are not universally the right output format. They shine in specific scenarios:

Passive consumption. When you want to learn about something while doing something else — driving, exercising, cooking, walking. A 12-minute Audio Overview is a productive use of a commute.

Quick orientation to a new topic. Before diving into a stack of papers, listen to a Brief Audio Overview to get the lay of the land.

Sharing with collaborators. A teammate is faster to listen to a 10-minute Audio Overview than to read a 50-page report. Generate, share the link or the MP3, save them an hour.

Reviewing your own work. Hearing your own writing summarized by a third party (even an AI third party) is a surprisingly useful way to evaluate it. Generate an Audio Overview of your own draft to hear what comes across and what doesn't.

Producing content. For podcasters, content creators, and educators, Audio Overviews can be raw material — generated, edited, supplemented with their own commentary, then published. (Note: commercial publication of unmodified Audio Overviews comes with watermarks unless you're on Ultra; see Chapter 32 for the ethics discussion.)

When Not to Use Audio Overviews

Equally important to know:

You need precise information. Audio is a poor medium for facts you'll need to look up later. Use Reports or chat instead.

The source material is detail-dense. A heavy mathematical paper, a complex legal contract, a detailed technical specification — all of these flatten into something less useful in audio form. The chat interface and Reports preserve the precision.

You're trying to verify a specific claim. Audio doesn't surface citations. To verify, use chat with explicit citation-following.

The source material is short or simple. A two-page memo doesn't need a 10-minute podcast about it.

A Practical Walkthrough

Let's run through a concrete example. Suppose you've added a single 40-page research paper to your notebook and want to use it as a learning tool.

First pass — quick orientation. Generate a Brief Audio Overview with no focus prompt. Listen on your commute. Get the rough shape: what's the paper about, what's the main claim, what kind of evidence does it offer?

Second pass — depth on the part that matters. Now you know the paper's structure. Generate a Deep Dive Audio Overview with a focus prompt: *"Focus specifically on the methodology section. Walk through the experimental design and explain the choices the authors made."* Listen while reading the methodology section in parallel.

Third pass — critical review. Generate a Critique with a focus prompt: *"What are the weakest parts of this paper's argument? What would a peer reviewer raise as concerns?"* Use this to inform your own evaluation of the work.

You've now spent roughly 30 minutes of audio time and arrived at a much deeper understanding of the paper than reading alone would have produced — not because the audio is doing the thinking for you, but because each Audio Overview is a different lens on the same source, and the combination of lenses produces understanding the source alone wouldn't.

One More Thing: Watermarks

Audio Overviews generated on Free, Plus, and Pro tiers include a small NotebookLM watermark — a brief identifier at the start, end, or both. It doesn't affect the listening experience but marks the audio as AI-generated.

For most use cases this is fine and arguably good (transparency about AI generation). For commercial podcast producers and content creators who need watermark-free audio, the only path is the Ultra tier ($249.99/month). We covered this in the plan-selection chapter.

Audio Overviews are the showcase feature, but they're one of many in the Studio. The next chapter goes deeper on a more recent twist on the format: Interactive Audio Overviews, where you can pause the conversation and ask the hosts a question of your own.

Chapter 11: Interactive Audio Overviews

In December 2024, three months after Audio Overviews launched, NotebookLM added what looked like a small twist on the existing format: a "Join" button that lets you interrupt the AI hosts and ask them a question of your own. They pause. They consider. They answer. Then they pick the conversation back up.

In practice, the twist changes the medium. A regular Audio Overview is a podcast — a thing you listen to. An Interactive Audio Overview is a conversation — a thing you participate in. The shift from passive consumption to active dialogue, while you're commuting or on a walk or working out, opens use cases the original format couldn't.

This chapter covers what Interactive Audio Overviews are, when they earn their keep, what they're bad at, and the best ways to use them.

How Interactive Mode Works

Generate an Audio Overview the normal way (Chapter 10). When playback starts, look for a control labeled "Join" or "Talk" — typically a microphone icon or a button below the playback controls.

Tap it. The hosts pause mid-sentence. The interface shows it's listening. You ask your question — out loud, in the same voice you'd use with a real person.

The hosts respond. Sometimes one takes the question, sometimes both engage. They draw on the same source material that produced the original Audio Overview, so their answers are grounded in your sources. Once they've answered, the original conversation resumes — sometimes circling back to incorporate what was just discussed, sometimes picking up where they left off.

You can interrupt as often as you want. Each interruption is logged — depending on the interface version, you may see a transcript of your questions and the hosts' answers in a sidebar.

What Kinds of Questions Work

Interactive Audio Overviews handle some kinds of questions much better than others.

Questions That Work Well

Clarifications about something just said. "Wait — when you mentioned the second methodology, can you say more about that?" The hosts have just established the context, so they can drill into a specific point cleanly.

Asking for an example. "Can you give a specific example of that?" The hosts pull from the source material to ground an abstract claim in a concrete instance.

Pushing for more depth. "That was interesting — go deeper on the implications you just mentioned." Often produces a few more minutes of focused discussion on the topic you cared about.

Asking how something connects. "How does this relate to what you said earlier about [topic]?" The hosts maintain context within the conversation and can reason about connections.

Re-framing for a different audience. "Can you re-explain that as if I'm a beginner?" or "Explain it from the perspective of [different audience]." Useful when the discussion is pitched at the wrong level for your purpose.

Questions That Work Less Well

Highly specific factual questions. "What was the exact effect size in study 3?" The hosts may give you a number, but you're better off pausing and checking the chat or the source itself for precise facts.

Questions about things outside the source material. "How does this compare to last week's news?" The hosts won't know — they only know your sources. They'll either say so or improvise badly.

Long compound questions. "Can you explain X, then walk through Y, then connect both to Z?" The format is conversational. Long compound questions get truncated answers. Break them up.

Questions that need citations. Audio doesn't surface citations. If you need traceable claims, use the chat interface or a Report.

When Interactive Mode Earns Its Keep

A few use cases where Interactive Audio Overviews are genuinely the right tool:

Active learning while doing something else. You're walking the dog and listening to an Audio Overview about a paper you'll need to discuss tomorrow. A point comes up that you don't fully understand. Instead of waiting until you're back at your desk, you ask right then. Understanding compounds across the listening session instead of building a mental queue of follow-ups for later.

Studying for an exam. Generate an Audio Overview of your course materials and listen interactively. When the hosts cover a topic you don't have down, ask them to drill in or quiz you on it. The combination of audio review and on-demand clarification is more efficient than either alone.

Briefing in transit. You're in a car on the way to a meeting. The Audio Overview is covering the report you'll be discussing. A question occurs to you about a specific detail — ask it, get the answer, arrive at the meeting having actually addressed it instead of carrying a mental note to look it up.

Exploring a long source. A 200-page report has more in it than a 12-minute Audio Overview can cover. As the hosts skim past topics that interest you, ask them to come back and go deeper — effectively building your own customized overview as you listen.

Generative confusion. Sometimes you don't know what question to ask until you hear the wrong answer. Listening interactively to an Audio Overview about a topic you're trying to understand surfaces questions you wouldn't have thought to ask sitting in front of a chat box.

When to Use Standard Mode Instead

Interactive mode isn't always better than standard.

When you want a finished product. If you're generating an Audio Overview to share with a colleague or publish as content, you want the standard version —

a complete, polished podcast. Interactive interruptions break the produced quality.

When you're truly multitasking. If you're listening while doing focused work, interactive mode pulls you out of the work. Standard mode is better for true background listening.

When you don't have questions. If the source is straightforward and the Audio Overview is hitting the right notes, there's nothing to interrupt for. Don't force it.

When voice input is awkward. Walking around outside is fine. Sitting in a coffee shop and asking AI hosts a question out loud is awkward. Read the room.

Voice Input Quality and Tips

Interactive mode depends on speech recognition. A few practical tips for getting consistent recognition:

Speak naturally but clearly. You don't need to enunciate like a newsreader, but mumbling into headphones in the wind doesn't work well.

Use full questions. "Wait – what about the second case study?" works better than "Second case study?" The recognizer and the model both have more to work with when the question is a complete utterance.

Don't expect perfect recall of names or numbers. Speech recognition has gotten dramatically better, but it still struggles with proper nouns, technical jargon, and precise numbers, especially in noisy environments. If you need to reference a specific named entity, you may need to spell it or repeat it.

Pause before tapping Join. Some interface versions need a beat to stop playback before the recognizer is ready. A half-second pause prevents your first words from being clipped.

What the Hosts Do Well

After enough sessions with Interactive Audio Overviews, you start to notice the hosts have personalities – not full personalities, but tendencies. They're encouraging when you ask basic questions, more analytical when you push on specifics, and sometimes pleasantly self-aware about the limits of what they can answer ("That's outside what we've been discussing — I'd want to look at the source directly to be sure").

This is by design. The conversational format is part of what makes the medium work. People are more willing to ask questions of an apparent conversational partner than of a text box. Interactive mode leans into that.

It also has limits. The hosts are generated by a language model and share that model's failure modes — a tendency toward agreement, occasional fabrication when pushed past their actual knowledge, and a smoothness of delivery that can hide uncertainty. The same skepticism you'd apply to chat answers applies here. Maybe more so, because audio doesn't show citations.

Use Cases by Audience

Different audiences get different value from interactive mode:

Students. Generate Audio Overviews of course materials, listen interactively, ask the hosts to quiz you, ask them to drill in on weak spots. The combination of audio and interactivity makes for an effective study companion.

Professionals on the move. Briefing in transit, with the ability to clarify in real time. Particularly valuable for client-facing roles where you need to internalize material you couldn't fully prep before.

Researchers exploring a corpus. When you have a notebook full of papers and want to explore — not target a specific question, but wander through what's there — interactive mode rewards the wandering. You stumble onto something interesting, ask about it, and the conversation shifts.

Accessibility users. For users with reading impairments or visual disabilities, the combination of audio output and voice input means the entire research workflow can happen without touching a keyboard.

Creators and educators developing content. Listening interactively to your own source material is one way to identify what your audience will find unclear — the questions you find yourself asking the hosts are often the questions your audience would ask you.

A Practical Walkthrough

Suppose you've added a quarterly earnings report to a notebook the morning of an earnings call. You don't have time to read all 60 pages.

Generate a Brief Audio Overview with the focus prompt: *"Focus on year-over-year growth, margin pressure, and any new strategic initiatives. Skip standard boilerplate."* Listen on the way to the office in interactive mode.

The hosts cover the core financials. As they mention a new product initiative, you ask: "What's the spend commitment on that?" They look it up in the source and answer. As they discuss margin pressure, you ask: "Did they say anything about pricing changes to address it?" They find the relevant passage and discuss it.

By the time you arrive, you haven't just listened to a 5-minute summary — you've had a 12-minute conversation that addressed your specific questions. You walk in prepared in a way passive listening alone wouldn't have made possible.

This is the use case interactive mode is built for: the moment between *I have material I need to understand* and *I need to act on that understanding*, when you don't have the time or context for focused desk work.

What Comes Next

Interactive Audio Overviews don't fully land until you've used them in real circumstances. The first time you tap Join during a podcast about a paper you're trying to understand and get a clarifying answer back, the value clicks immediately.

The next chapter moves to the visual side of the Studio: Video Overviews and Cinematic Mode, which take the same source-grounded approach and translate it into something you can watch instead of listen to.

Chapter 12: Video Overviews and Cinematic Mode

Audio Overviews proved that NotebookLM could turn documents into media. Video Overviews proved it could turn them into media you could *watch*.

Launched in 2025 and significantly expanded with the Cinematic Video Mode in July of that year, Video Overviews are the visual sibling of Audio Overviews. Same source-grounded approach. Same hosts (when applicable). Different medium, different use cases, different things to know.

This chapter covers what Video Overviews are, the difference between the explainer-style default and Cinematic Mode, the visual style options, and the workflows where video genuinely beats audio.

What a Video Overview Is

A Video Overview combines AI-generated narration with visual elements — slides, diagrams, illustrations, occasional animations — drawn from your source material. The narrator (or sometimes narrators) speaks while the visuals advance, walking the viewer through the content in a format closer to an educational explainer video than a podcast.

Default length depends on source size and selected format, but typical Video Overviews land between 3 and 10 minutes. Output is MP4, suitable for sharing or embedding.

A few important things to understand:

The visuals are generated, not extracted. Video Overviews don't pull screenshots from your source PDFs. They generate new visuals — diagrams, infographics, illustrative images — designed to support the narration. The look and feel can be substantially different from the source material.

It's narration, not a conversation. Default Video Overviews use a single narrator rather than the two-host conversational format of Audio Overviews.

(Some format variants use two voices; the conventions shift as Google iterates.) The result feels more like a produced explainer video than a podcast.

The pacing is slower than audio. Video moves more slowly than audio because visuals need time to register. A Video Overview covering the same material as an Audio Overview will typically be longer.

Visual Style Options

NotebookLM offers several visual style variants for Video Overviews. The exact list shifts, but as of early 2026 the main options include:

Whiteboard. Hand-drawn-looking diagrams, sketches, and annotations in a whiteboard-style interface. Friendly, accessible, slightly informal. Excellent for educational and explanatory content where you want visuals that feel drawn for you rather than presented to you.

Watercolor. Softer, more illustrated visuals with a watercolor-painted aesthetic. Lower information density, higher emotional warmth. Good for narrative-driven content, personal subjects, or anything where you want a less corporate feel.

Kawaii. Cute, cartoon-style illustrations. Surprisingly effective for making dry technical material feel approachable. Used to good effect for educational content aimed at younger audiences and for taking the edge off intimidating subjects.

Classic. A traditional, polished presentation aesthetic. Cleaner typography, more structured layouts, fewer flourishes. The right choice when the content is professional or formal — financial reports, regulatory documents, business communications.

Style changes the feel of the output substantially. The same source can become a friendly whiteboard explainer or a polished classic presentation depending on the choice. If you're producing video for a specific audience, the style choice is non-trivial.

When Video Beats Audio

Audio Overviews and Video Overviews cover overlapping ground, but each shines in different scenarios.

Visual content is part of the source. If your source includes diagrams, charts, screenshots, or visual layouts that matter, video can show them (or generate analogues). Audio cannot. For a paper whose argument depends on its figures, video is the right format.

Sharing for asynchronous viewing. A 5-minute video sent to a colleague is something they can watch on their schedule, including in noisy environments where audio doesn't work. Audio is harder to share casually.

Demonstration and walkthrough content. Step-by-step explanations work better with visuals tracking each step. A walkthrough of a process, a technical concept, or a multi-stage analysis is easier to follow with visual support.

Public-facing or marketing content. Video carries a higher production-value perception. For content shared externally — to clients, to a website, to social media — video reads as more polished than audio.

Audiences that don't have time for podcasts. A 5-minute video gets watched. A 12-minute podcast gets queued and forgotten. For colleagues who won't carve out audio listening time, video is more accessible.

When Audio Beats Video

The reverse cases:

Passive consumption while doing something else. You can listen to audio while driving, exercising, or cooking. You can't easily watch video.

Conversational format matters. The two-host dialogue of Audio Overviews has an explanatory power that single-narrator video doesn't quite match. For complex topics, the conversational structure helps the listener stay engaged.

Long-form material. A 15-minute audio podcast is comfortable. A 15-minute video is long. For longer treatments, audio is more forgiving.

Speed and lower production cost. Audio Overviews generate faster and cost fewer Studio quota credits than Video Overviews. For rapid iteration, audio is friction-free.

Cinematic Video Mode

Released July 29, 2025, Cinematic Video Mode is the more produced sibling of standard Video Overviews. The difference is meaningful.

Standard Video Overviews are educational explainers — narration over visuals, pleasant and clear. Cinematic Mode aims higher, with:

- More fluid animation and motion design
- Narrative structure (a beginning, middle, and end as a story rather than a topic walkthrough)
- Higher visual production values (richer color, more sophisticated compositions)
- A more emotionally resonant aesthetic — the difference between a documentary and a lecture

Cinematic Mode is overkill for most everyday research workflows. But for specific use cases it's transformative:

Pitch and presentation content. A Cinematic Video Overview of a strategic plan, market opportunity, or product vision lands differently than a standard explainer. It has the production polish you'd otherwise need a video team for.

Narrative source material. A historical account, a personal story, a case study with dramatic structure — all of these benefit from cinematic framing. Standard video flattens them; Cinematic Mode honors them.

External-facing marketing. For content where the production value is part of the message — a brand-aligned explainer, a recruitment video, a public communication — Cinematic Mode produces output that holds up to public scrutiny.

Special-purpose content. Year-end retrospectives, milestone announcements, public-facing reports. The kind of communications where you want the medium to do part of the talking.

The tradeoffs: Cinematic Mode generates more slowly, costs more Studio quota, and isn't always the right vibe. For a quick brief on a research paper, it's the wrong tool. For a customer-facing product story, it's often exactly right.

Customizing Video Overviews

Like Audio Overviews, Video Overviews accept customization parameters when generating. The key controls:

Format. Explainer (default) or brief (shorter, more concentrated).

Visual style. Whiteboard, watercolor, kawaii, classic, or whatever new options Google has shipped since this was written.

Language. 80+ language support, same as audio.

Topic focus prompt. The same kind of focus prompt that works for Audio Overviews works here. Specify what to emphasize, what to skip, what audience you're producing for.

Length controls. Some interface versions let you specify a target length. Others derive length from format choice and source size.

The most underused customization, again, is the topic focus prompt. A Video Overview with no focus prompt is a generic walkthrough of your source material. One with a clear focus — *"Explain this for a non-technical executive audience, emphasizing business implications and skipping technical details"* — is substantially more useful for that audience.

Editability (or the Lack of It)

A practical limitation worth knowing: as of early 2026, **most Video Overviews can't be edited after generation.** What you generate is what you get. If a section doesn't work, you regenerate the whole video.

A few partial workarounds:

- **Generate multiple variants and pick the best one.** Studio quota permitting, generate two or three versions with slightly different focus prompts. Use the best.
- **Use the source-selection trick.** Different selected sources produce different videos. Try a more focused source set if a broader one isn't working.

- **Edit externally.** The output is an MP4. Take it into a video editor, cut sections, add your own annotations. This breaks any "no human in the loop" pretense, but lets you ship a final product that actually works.

The lack of native editing is one of the bigger product gaps in Studio outputs as of this writing. Watch for changes — Google has been steadily adding post-generation editing to other Studio outputs (notably Slide Decks), and Video Overview editing is a likely roadmap item.

Sharing and Embedding

Generated Video Overviews can be:

- **Played in NotebookLM directly** (no download required)
- **Downloaded as MP4** for offline use, sharing, or further editing
- **Shared via direct link** (with appropriate permissions on your notebook)
- **Embedded** in some contexts (the embed support has been growing; check current capabilities)

For workflows where the video will be the primary deliverable — a briefing for a stakeholder, a piece of educational content — download as MP4 and host wherever your audience consumes content (your website, an LMS, internal video platform, etc.).

A Practical Walkthrough

A concrete scenario: you've been asked to give a 10-minute internal presentation summarizing a competitive analysis your team produced. The analysis is a 30-page document with charts.

You could spend three hours building slides. Or:

1. Add the analysis as the source in a focused notebook.
2. Generate a standard Video Overview, classic style, with the focus prompt: *"Produce a 7-minute summary suitable for an internal team presentation. Focus on the three main competitive insights and their strategic implications. Skip methodology details."*
3. Watch the result. If a section needs more depth, regenerate with refined framing and try again.

4. When you have a version that works, download the MP4 and present it directly, or use it as the spine of slides you'll narrate yourself.

You've gone from 30-page document to presentable summary in under an hour, with a video that captures what the analysis actually says — not a generic AI summary, but a specific summary of *this* analysis, grounded in the actual document.

For the same scenario with an external audience — a customer briefing or a public-facing version — switch to Cinematic Mode and accept the longer generation time for the higher production value.

Watermarks, Again

Same as Audio Overviews: Video Overviews on Free, Plus, and Pro tiers carry a small NotebookLM watermark. For commercial or public-facing content where you need watermark-free output, Ultra is the only path.

For internal use, briefings, learning, and most day-to-day workflows, the watermark is a non-issue.

Where Video Fits

The instinct, when a new output format appears, is to use it for everything. Don't. Video Overviews aren't better than Audio Overviews — they're different. Use video when the source content benefits from visuals, when your audience will watch but won't listen, when production polish matters, or when you need to share asynchronously.

Use audio everywhere else. The two formats are complementary tools, not competitors.

The next chapter shifts away from generative media into the more text-centric Studio outputs: Reports — Briefing Docs, Study Guides, Blog Posts — the formats that turn your sources into readable, shareable, structured documents.

Chapter 13: Reports — Briefing Docs, Study Guides, Blog Posts

Audio Overviews and Video Overviews get the headlines. But for serious knowledge work, the most-used Studio output is probably the most boring-sounding one: **Reports.**

Reports take your sources and produce structured written documents – Briefing Docs, Study Guides, Blog Post drafts, custom-formatted summaries. They're what you reach for when you need something readable and shareable rather than something you'll listen to or watch. For knowledge workers who spend their days writing memos, briefing executives, preparing client materials, or producing study aids, Reports are the workhorse output.

This chapter covers each of the standard Report formats, when to use which, and how to get more out of the generation options than the defaults give you.

What Reports Are

In NotebookLM's Studio panel, Reports is a category that contains several distinct output types. The exact list shifts as Google adds formats, but as of early 2026 the standard menu includes:

- **Briefing Doc** – executive-style summary with structured sections
- **Study Guide** – learning aid with key concepts, questions, and study aids
- **Blog Post** – narrative draft suitable for publication or further editing
- **FAQ** – question-and-answer format covering the source material
- **Timeline** – chronological organization of events and developments
- **Custom Report** – provide your own framing and the report follows your direction

Each Report type pulls from the same source material but organizes it for a different purpose. The Briefing Doc is for someone who needs the takeaways. The Study Guide is for someone who needs to learn the material. The Blog Post is for someone who needs to publish it. Choosing the right format matters.

Reports come out as readable documents — typically with headings, bullet points, sub-sections, and inline citations back to the source material. They're substantial: a Briefing Doc on a 30-page report might run 3–5 pages; a Study Guide for a textbook chapter might run longer. Most Report formats export as DOCX or PDF.

Briefing Docs

The Briefing Doc is the format you'll use most often. It's the closest analogue to what executives, project leads, and decision-makers actually want when handed a stack of source material: *tell me what's in here, what matters, and what I should do with it.*

A typical Briefing Doc is structured as:

- **Executive summary** — three or four sentences capturing the essence
- **Key findings** — the most important conclusions, structured as discrete points
- **Background and context** — what's needed to understand the findings
- **Detailed analysis** — sub-sections covering the main themes or topics in depth
- **Implications and recommendations** — what the findings mean and what to do
- **Open questions** — what remains unclear or unaddressed

The structure shifts based on source material. A Briefing Doc for a research paper looks different from one for a strategic plan or a contract. NotebookLM does a reasonable job of adapting structure to content.

Where Briefing Docs shine:

Briefing executives or stakeholders. A 30-page report becomes a 3-page brief that captures what they need. Take the brief, top it with your own framing, and you have a polished deliverable.

Self-orientation to a new domain. When you're getting up to speed on a topic, a Briefing Doc on a foundational source is faster to read than the full source and more structured than a chat summary.

Meeting prep. Generate a Briefing Doc on materials you'll discuss in a meeting. Read it on your way in. Go in actually prepared.

Newsletter and digest writing. A Briefing Doc on a recent paper or report makes a strong starting point for a newsletter section, Blog Post intro, or social media thread.

The biggest customization lever is the topic focus prompt. A generic Briefing Doc gives you a generic structure. A Briefing Doc generated with *"For a CFO. Focus on financial implications, cost projections, and risks. Skip methodology and academic framing"* gives you something tailored to a specific audience.

Study Guides

The Study Guide format reorganizes source material as a learning aid. Where a Briefing Doc is structured for someone who wants takeaways, a Study Guide is structured for someone who needs to internalize the material.

A typical Study Guide includes:

- **Key concepts and terms** — definitions and explanations of the important vocabulary
- **Main themes and arguments** — structured discussion of the central content
- **Discussion questions** — questions designed to test understanding
- **Practice questions or exercises** — when applicable to the source material
- **Connections to other topics** — how the material relates to broader subjects
- **Summary and review** — recap of the most important points

Study Guides are a natural fit for:

Students preparing for exams. Generate a Study Guide from your textbook chapter, lecture notes, and supplementary readings. Use it for review.

Onboarding new team members. A Study Guide on internal documentation gives a new hire structured, citation-grounded learning material.

Self-study of a new domain. Reading a difficult book? Generate a Study Guide chapter by chapter. Use it to test your understanding before moving on.

Teaching prep. Educators can use Study Guides as structured starting points for lesson planning — identify the key concepts NotebookLM extracts, then build curriculum around them.

The customization that matters most is difficulty level. Specify in the topic focus prompt whether the Study Guide is for a beginner, an intermediate learner, or an advanced student. *"This is for a first-year undergraduate. Use accessible language and explain technical terms when they appear"* produces something quite different from *"This is for a graduate student preparing qualifying exams. Assume strong background and emphasize nuances and contested points."*

Blog Posts

The Blog Post format produces narrative-style drafts suitable for publication, after editing. Typically 1,500–3,000 words, structured with introduction, body sections, and conclusion, in a style that reads as a piece of writing rather than as a structured document.

A few important caveats up front:

These are drafts. AI-generated Blog Posts are starting points, not finished work. They need editing — for voice, for structure, for the specific framing you want, for accuracy. NotebookLM produces serviceable drafts; turning them into something you'd publish under your own name is your job.

Voice will be generic by default. The default Blog Post voice is competent but characterless. To get something that sounds like *you*, either heavily edit the draft or guide the generation with detailed voice instructions in the topic focus prompt.

Disclosure matters. If you're publishing AI-assisted content, the ethical defaults around disclosure apply. We cover this in Chapter 32.

When Blog Posts are useful:

As a starting point for your own writing. Generate a Blog Post draft, then rewrite it section by section in your own voice with your own framing. Faster than starting from a blank page.

For internal-only publishing. Newsletters, internal Blog Posts, communications where the audience knows AI was involved and the bar is information transfer rather than literary craft.

As a structural exercise. Even if you don't use the generated text, the structure NotebookLM imposes can suggest organizational patterns you hadn't considered.

For producing first drafts at volume. Content marketers, communications teams, and others who produce a lot of similar content can use Blog Posts as scaffolding to be filled in.

The risk: publishing AI-generated drafts without sufficient editing produces the kind of generic, characterless content that has flooded the open web in the AI era. Don't add to it.

FAQ

The FAQ format restructures source material as questions and answers. NotebookLM identifies the questions someone might have about the material, then answers each one from the sources.

Useful for:

Documentation. A FAQ generated from internal docs is often immediately publishable as a help-center article.

Training material. New employees, customers, or stakeholders tend to have predictable questions. A NotebookLM-generated FAQ surfaces them and provides citation-grounded answers.

Self-check. A FAQ on material you're trying to learn surfaces questions you didn't know you should be asking. Useful as a thinking tool even if you don't publish the result.

The default FAQ tends toward obvious questions. To get more useful results, guide it: *"Generate a FAQ for technical practitioners, focusing on edge cases, integration questions, and common misconceptions"* produces a much more useful FAQ than the unguided default.

Timelines

The Timeline format extracts and organizes events from your sources into a chronological structure. For source material with a temporal dimension — historical accounts, project records, evolving regulatory frameworks, biographical material — Timelines turn what's scattered across sources into a coherent narrative arc.

Best uses:

Historical research. A Timeline pulled from multiple historical sources gives you a structured chronology that would have taken hours to assemble manually.

Project retrospectives. A Timeline of a project from meeting notes, decision documents, and communications produces an organizing structure for a postmortem.

Tracking the evolution of an idea. A Timeline of how a concept has been treated across sources over time can reveal trajectories that aren't obvious from any single source.

Onboarding to a long-running situation. Joining a team or topic mid-stream? A Timeline gives you the prior context as a structured narrative.

Custom Reports

The Custom Report option is the most powerful and most underused. Instead of selecting a pre-defined format, you describe what you want.

Examples of useful custom report specifications:

> "Produce a comparison table of how each source addresses [specific question]. For each source, list its position, its evidence, and its limitations."
>
> "Generate a one-page memo for [specific audience] covering [specific topic], in the format of [reference document]."
>
> "Produce a literature review section suitable for the introduction of an academic paper, following standard conventions for the field."

"Generate a competitive analysis structured as a strengths/weaknesses/opportunities/threats matrix, with each cell populated from the source material."

"Produce a checklist of every recommendation across the sources, organized by priority and tagged with which source(s) made each recommendation."

Custom Reports get you exactly what you want, when no pre-defined format quite fits. The catch: you have to know what you want. The defaults are useful precisely because they tell NotebookLM what good output looks like for common cases. Custom Reports require you to articulate that yourself.

Citations and Verification

All Report formats produce text with inline citations back to the source material. The citations work the same way they do in chat: clickable links that take you to the exact passage being referenced.

The same discipline applies: **don't trust an AI-generated report without verifying its citations.** Reports feel more authoritative than chat answers — they're polished, structured, and look like documents written by humans. That polish doesn't make them more reliable. The same paraphrase errors and subtle misrepresentations that can occur in chat can occur in Reports, and the polish makes them harder to catch.

Before sharing or publishing a Report, work through it citation by citation, especially for any claim load-bearing for the conclusions. This is tedious. It's also non-negotiable for any work where accuracy matters.

Editing and Iteration

Most Report formats can be edited after generation. The exact mechanism varies — some interface versions let you edit in place, others let you regenerate specific sections, and you can always export to DOCX or PDF and edit externally.

A useful pattern:

1. Generate a Report with a focus prompt
2. Read it critically

3. Identify sections that don't quite work
4. Either regenerate those sections with refined framing, or edit them by hand
5. Export the final version

Trying to nail the perfect Report in one generation usually fails. Two or three rounds of generate → review → refine produces much better results than fighting to get it right in a single shot.

When Not to Use a Report

Reports are powerful, but they're not always the right tool:

For passive consumption. If you're going to listen rather than read, generate an Audio Overview instead.

For visual content. If the content benefits from diagrams and visuals, a Video Overview or Mind Map is a better fit.

For one-time questions. If you just need to answer a specific question, ask in chat. A Report is overkill for "what does the source say about X?"

When you don't have a clear use case. A Report generated "just in case" rarely gets used. Generate Reports when you know what you'll do with them — share with a stakeholder, study from, publish, or file for reference.

A Practical Walkthrough

Suppose you're a consultant prepping for a client meeting. The client has handed you a stack of internal documents — strategic plans, financial reports, customer research, market analysis — totaling about 200 pages.

You can read for two days. Or:

1. Add all the documents as sources in a focused notebook.
2. Generate a **Briefing Doc** with the focus prompt: *"For a strategic consulting engagement. Focus on the client's stated priorities, the competitive position, and the most acute organizational challenges. Identify implicit tensions or inconsistencies across documents."*

3. Read the Briefing Doc — about 4–5 pages — to get the lay of the land. Click citations on anything load-bearing to verify.
4. Generate a **FAQ** with the focus prompt: *"Generate the questions a consultant would need to ask the client to clarify gaps and tensions in these materials."* Use this to prep your client interview agenda.
5. Generate a **Timeline** with the focus prompt: *"Map the strategic decisions and changes documented in these materials over the past three years."* Use this to understand the trajectory.
6. After the client meeting, when you have new information from the conversation, return to the notebook, add notes capturing what you learned, and generate a fresh **Briefing Doc** integrating the new context.

In about 90 minutes you've covered the equivalent of two days of reading, with structured outputs you can use directly in your engagement. The work is faster, but not worse — it's *more thorough*, because you've now read across the entire source set rather than just the documents you would have prioritized.

That's the workhorse use of Reports: not one impressive output, but multiple complementary Reports as scaffolding for actual knowledge work.

The next chapter covers two more visual outputs — Mind Maps and Slide Decks — that often pair naturally with the Report formats covered here.

Chapter 14: Mind Maps and Slide Decks

Reports give you structured prose. Audio and Video Overviews give you generated media. Sometimes what you need is something in between — a visual structure that exposes how concepts relate, or a presentation you can stand in front of and walk through.

That's where Mind Maps and Slide Decks come in. They're the visual cousins of the Report formats covered in the last chapter, and they fit some scenarios — particularly synthesis and presentation work — better than anything else in the Studio.

This chapter covers both formats: what they're good for, when they fall short, and the practical considerations for using them in real work.

Mind Maps

A NotebookLM Mind Map is a visual hierarchical diagram of the concepts in your sources. The central topic sits in the middle. Major branches radiate outward representing the main themes or sub-topics. Each branch has its own sub-branches, building up a tree that captures how the source material decomposes.

The output is interactive — you can click on any node to see citations back to the source passages it draws from, and many interface versions let you expand or collapse branches to focus on specific parts of the map.

When Mind Maps Beat Other Formats

Mind Maps shine in a specific cognitive niche: **understanding how concepts relate and where the territory's boundaries are.**

A Briefing Doc tells you what's in the sources. An Audio Overview discusses it. Neither makes the *structure* of the material visible. A Mind Map does.

Some scenarios where this matters:

Onboarding to a new domain. When you don't know what you don't know, a Mind Map shows you the shape of the field. You can see at a glance which areas are central, which are peripheral, and where the connections are.

Identifying gaps. A Mind Map of your sources reveals what's *not* there. If a major sub-topic has only one or two thin branches, you've probably under-sourced that area.

Teaching and explanation. A Mind Map is an excellent visual aid when explaining a complex topic to someone else. It externalizes the structure in a way that's easier to follow than prose.

Brainstorming and ideation. A Mind Map of an existing source set can suggest connections you hadn't seen — often the basis for new questions, new directions, or new sources to add.

Pre-writing. Before drafting a long piece, a Mind Map can help you see the topic's shape and decide what to include and exclude.

Limits of Mind Maps

Mind Maps don't currently accept much customization beyond source selection. You generate one against a set of sources and get whatever the model produces. You can't easily tell it to focus on a specific sub-topic or organize the map a particular way.

This is a meaningful limitation for power users. Sometimes you have a strong opinion about how the material *should* be organized, and the auto-generated structure doesn't match. Workarounds:

- **Generate against a smaller, more focused source selection.** A Mind Map of three sources has a tighter structure than one of fifteen.
- **Generate multiple Mind Maps with different source subsets.** Each one captures a different facet.
- **Use the Mind Map as a starting point, then redraw your own.** External mind-mapping tools (Miro, Whimsical, paper) let you take the structure NotebookLM proposes and refine it with your own judgment.

Mind Maps Are Not Outlines

A common confusion: people generate a Mind Map expecting an outline of an argument or a sequence of points. It isn't. Mind Maps are *topological*, not *sequential*. They show how concepts relate, not in what order to discuss them.

If what you need is structure for an argument or a presentation, you want a Briefing Doc, an Outline Report (custom format), or a Slide Deck — not a Mind Map.

Exporting Mind Maps

Mind Maps can be exported as images (PNG) for inclusion in slides, documents, or shared files. Some interface versions support more sophisticated export to mind-mapping tools, but these capabilities are evolving.

For most uses — sharing with a colleague, including in a brief, using as a slide in a presentation — PNG export is sufficient.

Slide Decks

NotebookLM's Slide Deck output, launched in November 2025, generates full presentations from your source material. The output is a structured deck with title slides, content slides, and conclusions, formatted for either detailed reading or live presentation.

This is one of the more transformative Studio outputs for knowledge workers. Building a presentation from scratch — outlining content, structuring slides, drafting bullet points, finding visuals — is among the most time-consuming things many professionals do. NotebookLM compresses the work dramatically.

Format Variants

NotebookLM offers (at least) two Slide Deck formats:

Detailed. Information-dense slides designed to be read. Each slide carries substantive text — full sentences, multiple bullet points, detailed explanations. Good for slides shared as a document for asynchronous reading.

Presenter-focused. Sparser slides designed for live presentation. Less text per slide, more visual focus, structured to support a speaker rather than to be read independently. Good for slides you'll actually stand in front of and speak to.

Pick the format that matches the use case. Detailed for documents that go in inboxes; presenter-focused for live talks. A common mistake is generating a detailed deck and then wondering why it doesn't work for presentation — the answer is to regenerate as presenter-focused, not to fight with the result.

PPTX Export

The most consequential capability of Slide Decks is **PPTX export.** What you generate isn't trapped inside NotebookLM — you can download a standard PowerPoint file, open it in PowerPoint, Keynote, or Google Slides, and edit freely.

This matters because:

- **Slide Decks are starting points, not finished products.** You'll always want to edit — adjust voice, customize for the audience, add your own visuals, tweak the structure. PPTX export makes this trivial.
- **Brand consistency.** Most organizations have visual standards their slides need to match. NotebookLM's default styling won't match your brand. Export, then re-skin in your standard template.
- **Version control.** Once a deck is in PowerPoint or Google Slides, it lives in your normal workflow — comments, versions, sharing, the whole apparatus.

Customizing Slide Decks

The same topic focus prompts that work for other Studio outputs work here. Specify the audience, the angle, the emphasis. Examples:

> *"Generate a 12-slide investor pitch deck. Focus on market opportunity, traction to date, and the ask. Use presenter-focused format."*
>
> *"Produce a 30-slide deep-dive deck for an internal engineering review. Include technical detail. Use detailed format."*
>
> *"Generate a 6-slide executive summary deck. Each slide should have a single chart or callout, minimal text, suitable for a 10-minute board update."*

The clearer the framing, the more useful the result.

A useful pattern: specify the slide count. Without a target, NotebookLM picks one that may not match your needs. With a target — *"15 slides"* or *"around 10 slides"* — you get closer to the deck you'll actually use.

Editable in Place

Some interface versions let you edit slides directly inside NotebookLM — change titles, edit bullet points, rearrange slides — before exporting. This is faster than full PPTX export-and-edit for small adjustments, and worth using when you only need light cleanup before sharing.

When Slide Decks Are the Right Output

Slide Decks earn their keep in a few common scenarios:

Internal presentations from research. You did a research project. You need to present it. Generate a Slide Deck from the source materials and your synthesis notes. Edit, present.

Status updates and briefings. Recurring presentations — quarterly updates, project status — can be partially automated. Add new sources, regenerate the deck, edit.

Teaching material. Generate Slide Decks from course readings, edit for your teaching style and emphasis, use directly.

Client deliverables. Consultants and agencies often deliver Slide Decks as the primary artifact. NotebookLM can produce a strong first draft from the underlying source material in minutes rather than hours.

Pre-meeting prep. Sometimes you don't need to *give* a presentation but you need to think in slide form to organize your thinking. A Slide Deck is a useful artifact for that.

When Slide Decks Are the Wrong Output

A few scenarios where Slide Decks are overkill or off-target:

For yourself only. If you're the only audience, a Briefing Doc is faster to consume than a deck.

For very short content. If the source material is short or the takeaway is simple, a deck is overkill. A short report or chat answer is better.

For content that doesn't decompose into slides. Some material — narrative arguments, complex case studies, single-thread analyses — doesn't fit slide form. Forcing it produces a deck that fights its own format.

When the visuals are the point. If you need slides with custom diagrams, branded visuals, or specific photography, NotebookLM's default visual approach won't satisfy. Do the visual work elsewhere.

Combining Mind Maps and Slide Decks

A useful pattern that combines both formats:

1. **Mind Map first** to understand the structure of your source material and decide what to cover
2. **Slide Deck second**, with a focus prompt that reflects the structure you decided on after looking at the Mind Map

The Mind Map exposes the territory. The Slide Deck commits to a specific path through it. Doing them in this order produces better decks than going straight to the deck.

You can also use a Mind Map *as a slide* in a Slide Deck — export it as PNG, drop it into the deck during editing. For internal communications and educational decks, a Mind Map slide is often more informative than the equivalent text or chart.

Citations and Trust, Again

Slide Decks include citations back to source material, just like other Studio outputs. The same discipline applies: **don't ship a deck without verifying its citations**, especially for any load-bearing claim.

The polish of a generated Slide Deck creates a trust gradient that doesn't match its actual reliability. A bullet point in a clean professional template feels more authoritative than the same content in a chat answer. It isn't. The model that generated both is the same model. Verify before you present.

A Practical Walkthrough

You've spent two weeks researching a competitive landscape for an internal strategy meeting. You have 15 sources in your notebook — competitor reports, market research, customer interviews, internal docs. You need a 20-slide deck for the meeting on Friday.

The traditional path: spend most of Thursday in PowerPoint, building the deck slide by slide.

A better path:

1. **Generate a Mind Map** of all 15 sources to confirm the structural picture and identify the main themes you want to cover.
2. **Generate a Briefing Doc** with a focus prompt for the strategy team's perspective. Read it. Note the framings that work and the ones that don't.
3. **Generate a Slide Deck** with the focus prompt: *"20-slide internal strategy deck for our leadership team. Cover the four main competitive positions, our relative strengths and weaknesses on each, and the three strategic options we should consider. Presenter-focused format."*
4. **Export to PPTX**, open in your normal slide tool, and spend 90 minutes editing — adjusting voice, replacing default visuals with your team's standard charts, refining the strategic framing based on your own judgment.
5. **Present** Friday with a deck that captures the breadth of the research, structured around your team's actual decision points, produced in a fraction of the usual time.

The deck is yours, not NotebookLM's. But the scaffolding NotebookLM gave you collapsed what would have been a day of structural work into about two hours.

That's the highest-leverage way to use both Mind Maps and Slide Decks: not as final products, but as scaffolding for work you would have done by hand — in a fraction of the time, with better source-grounding than you could have managed alone.

The next chapter rounds out the Studio — covering Flashcards, Quizzes, Infographics, and Data Tables. These are the smaller, more specialized outputs that often pair with the larger ones we've covered so far.

Chapter 15: Flashcards, Quizzes, Infographics, and Data Tables

Audio Overviews, Video Overviews, Reports, Mind Maps, and Slide Decks are the Studio's headline outputs. Several smaller, more specialized outputs round out the menu, each optimized for a specific use case.

This chapter covers the four most useful of them as of early 2026: Flashcards and Quizzes (for learning), Infographics (for visual summary and sharing), and Data Tables (for structured extraction from messy source material). None of these is something you'll generate every day, but for the right task each one is the right tool.

Flashcards

Flashcards turn your source material into question-and-answer cards designed for active recall — the well-validated learning technique where you test yourself on concepts rather than rereading material.

NotebookLM's Flashcards output generates a stack of cards from your selected sources, with:

- **Question or prompt on the front** — a concept, term, or idea from the source
- **Answer or explanation on the back** — the sourced response with a citation
- **Difficulty levels** — most interface versions let you specify whether you want easier (recall-focused) or harder (synthesis-focused) cards
- **Topic focus** — you can direct generation toward specific sub-areas of the source material
- **Quantity** — typical generation produces 20–50 cards per session, with some control over the count

Flashcards work best when:

You're studying for an exam. The obvious case. Generate Flashcards from your textbook chapter, lecture slides, and notes. Use them for spaced repetition.

You're learning a new domain. New vocabulary, new concepts, new mental models — Flashcards force the active engagement that reading doesn't.

You're onboarding to a body of knowledge. A new job, a new technology, a new field. Flashcards from the foundational sources accelerate absorption.

You're preparing for an interview or presentation. Generate Flashcards on the material you need to be conversant in. Self-test until the answers come quickly.

A practical limitation: NotebookLM's Flashcards output is currently meant for review *inside NotebookLM*, not for export to dedicated spaced-repetition tools like Anki or Quizlet. Some users copy the cards manually into their preferred system. The lack of native export to standard flashcard formats is a real gap — worth checking whether Google has shipped it by the time you read this.

Quizzes

Quizzes are Flashcards' close cousin, optimized for assessment rather than review. Where flashcards are typically open-ended (read the question, recall the answer), quizzes can include:

- **Multiple choice** with several plausible distractors
- **True/false** statements
- **Short answer** questions
- **Fill-in-the-blank** items

NotebookLM generates Quizzes from selected sources with adjustable parameters: question count, difficulty, topic focus, and question type mix.

Where Quizzes earn their keep:

Self-assessment after study. You've read the material. You think you understand it. Generate a quiz to find out where you actually do.

Teaching assessment. Educators can generate Quizzes from course materials for student practice or as starting points for assessments. (Generated Quizzes need editorial review before being used as actual graded assessments — for the same reasons all AI-generated material does.)

Onboarding checks. New hires can take Quizzes on training material to confirm comprehension before moving on.

Pre-meeting prep. Take a quiz on the materials you'll discuss in a meeting. Identify which concepts you can't articulate cleanly. Review those before the meeting.

The same limitation as Flashcards applies: quiz output is primarily designed for use within NotebookLM, with limited export support. For published assessments, you'll likely need to copy questions into your own system.

A note for educators: AI-generated quiz questions can be subtly off — distractors that aren't quite plausible, correct answers that depend on a particular reading of the source, ambiguities human judgment would catch. Always review before using in any setting where the assessment matters.

Infographics

Launched in November 2025, the Infographics output is one of NotebookLM's most visually impressive features. Powered by Google's Nano Banana Pro image generation pipeline, it produces visual summaries of your source material in a range of distinct styles.

As of early 2026, the available styles include:

- **Sketch Note** — hand-drawn-feeling illustration with handwritten-style text and informal layouts
- **Kawaii** — cute, cartoon-style with friendly characters and soft colors
- **Professional** — polished business aesthetic, suitable for corporate or formal contexts
- **Scientific** — diagrammatic and analytical, with technical visual conventions
- **Anime** — Japanese illustration style with characteristic visual tropes
- **Clay** — 3D-rendered claymation aesthetic
- **Editorial** — magazine-style layouts with strong typography and visual hierarchy

- **Instructional** — step-by-step educational layout suitable for tutorials
- **Bento Grid** — compartmentalized layout (like a bento box) with discrete information cells
- **Bricks** — modular, blocky composition

Each style produces a meaningfully different output. The same source material rendered as Sketch Note vs. Scientific vs. Bento Grid produces three quite different Infographics, each suited for different audiences and uses.

Practical considerations:

Style choice matters more than topic focus. The biggest variable in Infographic output is style. Scientific produces dense, information-rich Infographics. Kawaii produces friendly, approachable ones. Pick the style that matches your audience.

Orientation and detail level are typically configurable. You can usually choose portrait vs. landscape and a target detail level (sparse, medium, dense). For social sharing, sparse is often better. For internal documentation, denser layouts pack more information per image.

Language affects layout. Different languages produce different text lengths, which affects layout. NotebookLM handles this reasonably, but expect style variation across languages.

When Infographics are the right output:

Social media and shareable content. A well-designed Infographic spreads where a Briefing Doc doesn't.

Visual summaries for non-readers. Some audiences won't read a 5-page brief but will look at an Infographic.

Reference posters. A Bento Grid or Scientific Infographic can serve as a visual reference document — pin to a wall, reference at a glance.

Educational handouts. For student or training audiences, an Infographic captures key concepts in a memorable visual form.

When Infographics are the wrong output:

For dense factual content. An Infographic can communicate maybe a dozen discrete facts cleanly. Beyond that, the format breaks down.

For evolving content. Infographics are static. If the underlying information will change, you'll have to regenerate — which (as with most Studio outputs) doesn't always produce a consistent visual identity across versions.

When you need editability. Like Video Overviews, Infographics aren't easily edited after generation. What you generate is what you get.

Data Tables

Released December 2025, Data Tables are one of NotebookLM's most useful outputs for analytical work. The format extracts structured tabular data from your source material — pulling values, categories, and relationships out of unstructured text and presenting them as actual tables.

You provide a prompt describing the structure you want. NotebookLM extracts the relevant data and populates the table. Examples:

> *"Generate a table of every named regulation across the sources. For each, include the jurisdiction, the year enacted, the primary subject, and which source(s) discuss it."*
>
> *"Build a comparison table of the three studies. Columns: sample size, methodology, primary finding, claimed effect size, identified limitations."*
>
> *"Extract every quantitative claim across the source set. Columns: claim, value, unit, source, page reference."*

Where Data Tables shine:

Comparing multiple sources side-by-side. When you want to see how three or five sources differ on the same dimensions, a Data Table makes the comparison legible in a way prose cannot.

Extracting structured data from unstructured documents. Reports, regulatory filings, research papers — they're full of structured information that isn't in any structured format. Data Tables extract that structure on demand.

Building reference tables. A table of all named entities, all citations, all referenced studies, all recommendations — useful as a working artifact even when it's not the final product.

Pre-analysis preparation. Before doing quantitative analysis, you often need to extract the data from prose. Data Tables can produce a starting CSV or table you then validate and analyze in a real spreadsheet tool.

The customization that matters: **be specific about columns.** "Extract a table of the studies" produces a table whose columns NotebookLM picks. "Extract a table of the studies with columns for [specific list]" produces exactly the table you wanted.

A note on accuracy: Data Tables are extraction outputs and make the extraction errors you'd expect. A claim ambiguously stated in the source may be mis-extracted. A blurry category boundary may be miscategorized. Always spot-check the table against the source for the entries that matter most. The same citation discipline that applies to chat answers applies here.

When to Use Which

A quick decision matrix for the smaller Studio outputs:

If you want to...	Use
Memorize concepts via active recall	Flashcards
Test understanding	Quizzes
Communicate visually for sharing	Infographic
Compare or extract structured data	Data Table

These four formats fill specific niches. Each is the right tool for its niche and the wrong tool for everything else. Don't use Infographics for what Reports do well, or Quizzes for what Flashcards do well. The variety in the Studio is there because different needs demand different formats.

A Practical Walkthrough

Suppose you're a graduate student preparing for qualifying exams. You have a notebook with 15 papers covering the field you'll be examined on.

A productive use of the four outputs in this chapter:

1. **Generate Flashcards** for each major paper. Use them for daily spaced-repetition review across the weeks leading up to the exam. The flashcards force active recall of the specific findings, methods, and arguments you'll be expected to know.

2. **Generate Quizzes** weekly to test cumulative comprehension. Identify weak spots — topics where you can't reliably answer correctly. Re-study those before the next quiz.

3. **Generate a Data Table** comparing the methodologies and findings across the 15 papers. Use it as a study aid for the kind of cross-paper synthesis qualifying exams typically test.

4. **Generate an Infographic** in Scientific style that visualizes the field's structure — major schools of thought, methodological approaches, contested questions. Print it out, pin it next to your desk. Use it as a daily orientation.

You've now built four complementary study tools from the same source material — each playing to a different cognitive strength, none duplicating the others.

This is the quiet through-line of Part III: not that any single Studio output is transformative, but that the *combination* of outputs, applied thoughtfully to the same source material, can change what's possible.

That closes Part III. You've now covered every Studio output — Audio Overviews, Interactive Audio, Video Overviews, Cinematic Mode, Reports (Briefing Docs, Study Guides, Blog Posts, FAQs, Timelines, Custom), Mind Maps, Slide Decks, Flashcards, Quizzes, Infographics, and Data Tables. That's the full toolbox.

Part IV picks up the threads we've been laying throughout: how to go deeper. Deep Research and Fast Research for bringing the web into your notebook. The detailed customization options for Audio and Video. Interactive workflows. Long-document strategies. Multilingual notebooks. And the often-overlooked mobile experience.

Part IV: Going Deeper

"The expert in anything was once a beginner."

— Helen Hayes

Chapter 16: Deep Research and Fast Research

For most of this book we've described NotebookLM as a tool that works only with the sources you provide. That's still true — by default. But two features bend the rule in controlled ways: **Fast Research** and **Deep Research**. Both let NotebookLM reach onto the open web for information that isn't already in your notebook, then either save the findings as new sources or use them to inform answers in the moment.

These are powerful features. They're also a small philosophical departure from NotebookLM's source-grounded foundation, and they need to be used with awareness of what changes when you let the AI fetch its own sources.

This chapter covers both features, when each is the right tool, and the practices that keep web-augmented work as trustworthy as the rest of NotebookLM.

What Fast Research Does

Fast Research is the lighter of the two. When you trigger it — typically through a button in the sources panel or a contextual option in chat — NotebookLM searches the web for sources on a topic you specify, then offers a curated list of links you can add to your notebook.

You stay in control of what enters the notebook. NotebookLM doesn't auto-add anything. It surfaces candidates; you select. Once added, the new sources behave like any other source — you can chat against them, generate Studio outputs from them, follow citations, the full normal workflow.

A typical Fast Research flow:

1. You're working in a notebook on a topic and realize you need additional context that's not in your existing sources.
2. Trigger Fast Research and describe what you're looking for.
3. NotebookLM returns a list of candidate web sources — typically 5 to 10 links — with brief summaries.

4. You review the candidates, pick the ones that look credible and relevant, and add them to your notebook.
5. NotebookLM ingests the selected sources just like any other web source.

Fast Research is best when:

- **You know what you're looking for.** A specific topic, concept, or piece of context that you can describe in a sentence.
- **You want to evaluate sources before they enter the notebook.** The candidate-list approach lets you reject low-quality sources before they affect retrieval.
- **You're doing focused supplementation.** Adding one or two pieces of context to an existing source set, not building a research base from scratch.

What Deep Research Does

Deep Research is the heavier feature. Instead of returning a list of links for you to evaluate, it executes a research workflow on a topic you specify: searching, reading, synthesizing across multiple sources, and producing a written summary with citations to the web sources it drew from.

Think of Deep Research as commissioning a brief research project. You give it a question. It spends time — a few minutes, sometimes longer — doing the kind of multi-step research a human researcher would: finding sources, reading them, identifying what matters, comparing across sources, and producing a synthesized response.

The output is typically a structured summary, sometimes several pages long, with inline citations to the web sources used. You can save the output as a new source in your notebook, where it becomes available for chat, Studio outputs, and synthesis with your existing sources.

A typical Deep Research flow:

1. You frame a question that goes beyond your existing notebook.
2. Trigger Deep Research and submit the question.
3. Wait. Deep Research takes longer than chat — typically several minutes.
4. Read the resulting synthesis. Click citations to verify.

5. Save the synthesis as a new source if it's worth keeping for future reference.

Deep Research is best when:

- **The answer requires synthesis across multiple web sources.** A question that no single web page would answer well.
- **You don't want to do the searching and reading yourself.** Either time is short or the topic is outside your usual fluency.
- **The topic is reasonably stable.** Deep Research works less well for breaking-news topics where the situation is still evolving — by the time it finishes, things may have changed.
- **You want a working starting point, not the final answer.** The synthesis is a research artifact; you'll typically want to verify and augment with your own judgment.

When to Use Which

The two features overlap in some ways but serve different needs. A useful rubric:

Use Fast Research when:

- You want to add specific sources to your notebook for later use
- You want control over which sources enter your working set
- The information you need is clearly available somewhere on the web, you just need to find it

Use Deep Research when:

- You want a synthesized answer to a research question
- You don't want to do the source-finding and reading yourself
- The question requires comparing across multiple web sources

A common pattern: use Fast Research first to bring high-quality sources into the notebook, then use chat or Studio outputs against those sources for the actual analytical work. Use Deep Research when you need a quick brief on a topic you don't have time to source-build manually.

Quotas and Tier Limits

Both Fast Research and Deep Research are quota-limited, with different caps per tier:

- **Free tier** gets a small daily allotment of Deep Research runs — enough to experiment, not enough for daily reliance.
- **Plus tier** gets meaningfully more — enough that Deep Research becomes a usable daily tool.
- **Pro and Ultra tiers** raise the ceiling further.

Fast Research is less constrained because it does less work per request. Deep Research is the resource-intensive one — each run involves multiple web fetches, multi-step reasoning, and substantial generation, so the per-run cost in compute and quota is higher.

If Deep Research is core to how you'd use NotebookLM, the Plus tier is the practical floor. The Free tier is enough to know whether the feature works for you.

Trust and Source Quality

This is the section to read most carefully.

When NotebookLM works only with sources you've curated, the chain of trust is clean: you chose the sources, you can evaluate them, and the AI's answers are grounded in material you trust. When NotebookLM fetches its own sources, that chain breaks. The AI is choosing what to read. Some of what it reads will be high-quality. Some won't be.

Open-web sources are heterogeneous. A Deep Research run on a contested topic might pull from peer-reviewed journals, reputable news outlets, marketing blogs, biased advocacy sites, AI-generated SEO content, and outright misinformation — all in the same response. The model does its best to weight credible sources higher, but the line between credible and not isn't always clear, and the model isn't a domain expert.

Deep Research outputs need a different kind of verification than chat answers against your own sources:

Always check what sources Deep Research used. The citations point to real URLs. Click them. Look at where the information actually came from. A synthesis built on three peer-reviewed papers and the New York Times is one thing. The same synthesis built on a Wikipedia article, a marketing blog, and someone's Substack is something else.

Be especially skeptical on contested topics. Open-web research on politically charged, scientifically contested, or commercially motivated topics will surface biased sources. The model can't always tell which side of a debate is which. You can.

Don't promote Deep Research output to a source without careful review. A synthesis saved as a source becomes part of your notebook's foundation. If the synthesis has problems, those problems propagate to every subsequent answer that uses it.

Treat Deep Research as a starting point, not a finished answer. The synthesis is useful raw material. It isn't authoritative.

Combining Web Research with Your Sources

The most powerful use of these features is the hybrid pattern: combining your curated sources with targeted web augmentation.

A typical workflow:

1. **Build your notebook from sources you trust** — papers you've read, internal documents, foundational texts.
2. **Identify gaps** — context, current developments, supplementary perspectives that aren't in your existing source set.
3. **Use Fast Research to fill specific gaps** with new sources you've evaluated and accepted.
4. **Use Deep Research for fast briefings on topics adjacent to your work** — not for primary research, but for getting up to speed on something tangential.
5. **Always know which answers are grounded in your trusted sources and which are augmented with web material.** This matters for citation, attribution, and judgment.

The hybrid pattern preserves the trust properties of source-grounded AI while extending NotebookLM's reach into the broader web. It's the right way to use these features for serious work.

What Web Research Doesn't Replace

Two important things Fast Research and Deep Research don't do:

They don't make NotebookLM a general search engine. For real-time information, breaking news, or general queries, dedicated tools are better — Perplexity for cited research, Google Search for everything else.

They don't substitute for primary research. A Deep Research synthesis on a complex topic is not equivalent to reading the actual source material. It's a starting point. Real understanding still requires going to the primary sources, reading them, and forming your own judgment.

This is true of all AI tools but worth stating explicitly. The convenience of Deep Research can be intoxicating — you ask a question, you get a polished summary, you feel like you understand the topic. Polish isn't the same thing as understanding. Use the synthesis to orient. Then go read the actual sources.

A Practical Walkthrough

Suppose you're researching a recent regulatory development for a client briefing. You have a notebook with internal company documents (compliance assessments, current policies, prior briefings on related topics). You need to add context on how the regulation has been received and what other organizations are doing about it.

Two phases:

Phase 1 — Fast Research. Trigger Fast Research with a query like *"news coverage and industry response to [specific regulation], past 90 days, focused on financial services sector implementation."* Review the candidates. Reject anything that looks like marketing content or unreliable opinion. Add the credible sources — typically 3–5 high-quality articles or analysis pieces — to your notebook.

Phase 2 — Deep Research. For a topic where you want a synthesis but don't need to control the source set, trigger Deep Research with a question like *"How are major banks responding operationally to [regulation]? What implementation patterns are emerging in early adopters?"* Wait for the synthesis. Read it carefully. Click through to the cited sources to verify the claims that matter most. If the synthesis holds up, save it as a source for future reference.

You now have a notebook with: your trusted internal documents, a curated set of recent web sources you evaluated yourself, and a Deep Research synthesis you've vetted. From here, the rest of your normal workflow — chat queries, a Briefing Doc for the client meeting, an Audio Overview to listen to in transit — operates against a richer, web-augmented source set.

A Final Note on Currency

Web research is one of the few NotebookLM features where the underlying capability is still rapidly evolving. Google has been steadily expanding what Deep Research can do — adding new search providers, improving synthesis quality, deepening integration with Gemini's own research capabilities.

The features described in this chapter are accurate as of early 2026 but will likely have changed by the time you read this. The principles — when to use which, how to verify, how to combine with curated sources — are durable. The specific UI details may not be.

Now that you can extend NotebookLM beyond your own sources, the next chapter goes deeper on the customization options for the Studio outputs we covered in Part III. The defaults are good. Customization is what turns good outputs into precisely targeted ones.

Chapter 17: Customizing Audio and Video Outputs

Part III walked through every Studio output and the basic mechanics of generating each one. Most of those chapters mentioned the topic focus prompt — the short instruction you can attach when generating an Audio Overview, Video Overview, Report, or Slide Deck. This chapter is about that prompt specifically, and the broader craft of customization.

The reason it deserves its own chapter: a topic focus prompt is often the difference between a generic Studio output and a useful one. Most users never write one. The ones who do find that NotebookLM goes from impressive to indispensable.

Why Defaults Are Generic

Without customization, NotebookLM's Studio outputs are calibrated for the average use case. A default Audio Overview talks about your sources in a balanced, accessible way. A default Briefing Doc summarizes the major points in a neutral structure. A default Slide Deck covers the territory at a default level of detail.

This is reasonable behavior. It's also, by design, generic — the model can't read your mind about what you actually want.

The result, for any specific use case, is almost always slightly off. The Audio Overview spends time on a section you don't care about. The Briefing Doc misses the angle that matters for your audience. The Slide Deck doesn't quite match the framing you wanted. None of these failures are dramatic. None are wrong, exactly. They're just generic.

Customization fixes that.

The Anatomy of a Good Customization Prompt

Topic focus prompts are short — typically a sentence or two, sometimes a paragraph. The good ones share a few features.

They specify what to emphasize. Not just the general topic, but which angle on the topic. Not "summarize this paper" but "focus on the methodology and the empirical findings; treat the literature review as background only."

They specify what to skip or de-emphasize. Equally important. "Skip the methodology details" is as useful as "focus on the methodology." The model needs to know what isn't the point.

They specify the audience. "For an executive audience" produces something different from "for a technical specialist." Audience determines voice, level of detail, what's assumed, what's explained.

They specify the use. "For a 5-minute commute briefing" is different from "for sharing as content with our customer base." Use determines tone, length, structure.

You don't need all four in every prompt. But a prompt with none of them — "make it good" — won't get you much beyond the default.

Customization Patterns That Work

A few patterns that come up constantly.

The Audience Specification

> *"For a [specific audience]. Assume [knowledge level]. Use [tone]. Avoid [things this audience won't connect with]."*

Concrete:

> *"For a hospital CIO. Assume strong familiarity with healthcare IT but no specific knowledge of the AI regulations being discussed. Use direct, executive-level language. Avoid academic framings or extended methodology discussion."*

This kind of prompt produces an output that lands with that audience, because every framing decision is made with them in mind.

The Lens Specification

> *"Discuss this from the perspective of [specific role or lens]. What would a [role] focus on? What would they push back on? What would they want to know that the source doesn't address?"*

Concrete:

> *"Discuss this paper from the perspective of a peer reviewer. What's the strongest part of the argument? Where are the gaps? What would you want to see in a revision?"*

This produces critical analysis the default doesn't.

The Section Spotlight

> *"Focus specifically on [section or sub-topic]. Spend most of the discussion there. Treat the rest as context only."*

Concrete:

> *"Focus specifically on the regulatory implications discussed in chapter 3. Spend most of the audio there. Treat the technical background as context only."*

This produces tighter, more useful output when the source has more in it than you need to surface.

The Comparison Frame

> *"Compare what these sources say about [specific topic]. Where do they agree, where do they disagree, and how do they frame the question differently?"*

Concrete:

> *"Compare what the McKinsey report and the Gartner report say about agent adoption rates. Identify where their numbers conflict and what each one is actually measuring."*

This works particularly well for Briefing Docs and Audio Overviews built across multiple sources.

The Skeptic's Frame

> *"Steelman the argument, then identify its weakest points. What's the strongest possible case for the conclusion? What's the strongest possible case against?"*

Concrete:

> *"Steelman this paper's central claim, then identify where the evidence is weakest. What would a sympathetic critic raise as concerns?"*

NotebookLM has a default tendency toward synthesis and agreement. This frame deliberately disrupts that tendency.

The Reuse Frame

> *"Produce this in the format of [reference]. Match the structure, length, and voice as closely as possible."*

Concrete:

> *"Produce this Briefing Doc in the format of the standard one-pagers our consulting practice uses — single page, three sections (situation, implications, recommendations), no more than 400 words."*

This requires NotebookLM to understand a specific format style, but for common patterns it handles this surprisingly well.

Format-Specific Customization

Different Studio outputs accept different kinds of customization. A few format-specific notes:

Audio Overviews

Audio is the format with the richest customization options. The hosts respond well to direction about:

- **Tone** — "make it casual" vs. "make it analytical"

- **Pacing** — "spend more time on each topic before moving on"
- **Voice register** — "explain everything as you go, don't assume background"
- **Disagreement patterns** — "have the hosts respectfully disagree about [specific question]"
- **Specific moments** — "spend at least 2 minutes on [specific topic]"

You can also direct the hosts to specific structural choices: open with a specific question, end with specific takeaways, return to a specific theme repeatedly.

Video Overviews

Video customization is more constrained because of the visual element. The most consequential variable is **style** (whiteboard, kawaii, watercolor, classic, cinematic). Beyond style:

- **Pacing** — "use slower visual transitions to give viewers time to read"
- **Visual focus** — "include diagrams whenever discussing technical concepts"
- **Narration register** — same controls as audio

Cinematic Mode accepts narrative framing prompts: "treat this as a story arc with a clear beginning, middle, and end" or "open with the surprising finding, then explain the methodology that led to it."

Reports

Reports accept the most structured customization. You can specify:

- **Section structure** — "include sections for: situation, analysis, recommendations, open questions"
- **Length** — "approximately 800 words" or "no more than 2 pages"
- **Voice** — "formal" vs. "conversational"
- **Citation density** — "cite a source for every major claim"

For Custom Reports specifically, the prompt becomes effectively the entire format specification — you describe the output you want and NotebookLM produces it.

Slide Decks

Slide Decks accept slide-count specifications, format selection (detailed vs. presenter), and the same audience and lens framing as other formats. A particularly useful customization:

> *"Specify a logical narrative arc across the deck: opening hook (1 slide), context (2-3 slides), main analysis (the bulk of the deck), implications (2-3 slides), close (1 slide)."*

This produces decks with deliberate dramatic structure rather than the more topic-by-topic default.

Iteration as Customization

Even with good customization prompts, the first generation isn't always the best. The most reliable way to get great Studio outputs is iteration:

1. **Generate** with your initial customization
2. **Listen/read/watch critically** — what works, what doesn't
3. **Refine the prompt** based on what you noticed
4. **Regenerate**
5. **Compare**

Two or three rounds of this typically produce a Studio output meaningfully better than any single shot, no matter how carefully you crafted the initial prompt.

A pattern that works well for Audio Overviews: generate twice with different framings, then listen to both side by side. You'll often notice that one version handles a section better and the other handles a different section better. You might use one as your final output, or — for important deliverables — pull the best framings from each into a third, more deliberate generation.

Style Drift and Consistency

When you produce many Studio outputs over time, you may want consistency across them — a recognizable voice, structure, level of detail. NotebookLM doesn't have a "set my defaults globally" feature beyond basic settings, but two practical approaches help.

Develop a customization template. For any kind of output you produce repeatedly — a weekly briefing, a recurring research summary — write the customization prompt once and save it as a snippet you paste in. Refine it over time. The more you reuse it, the more it captures your specific preferences.

Use consistent source treatment. Style drift across outputs often comes from inconsistent source curation, not from the prompt itself. If your weekly briefing is built from a consistent source pattern — the same internal documents plus the week's new sources — the resulting output tends to feel consistent week to week.

For organizations producing NotebookLM content at scale, developing a small library of templates by use case is one of the highest-leverage things to do. Five well-tuned templates, applied consistently, produce more useful output than dozens of one-off prompts each requiring fresh judgment.

What You Can't Customize

A few things customization prompts won't override:

Source-imposed limits. If your sources don't contain the answer to what you're asking, no prompt will produce a real answer. The model will either refuse or fabricate. This is a source problem, not a prompt problem.

Format-imposed limits. A 5-minute Audio Overview can't have the same depth as a 15-minute one. A 6-slide deck can't cover the same ground as a 25-slide deck. Customization shapes what's covered, not how much.

Underlying model behavior. Some patterns — the tendency toward synthesis, the cautious tone on contested topics, the hedging on causal claims — are baked in by Gemini's training. Prompts can shift these tendencies but rarely eliminate them.

Knowing the limits of customization keeps expectations realistic. You can shape the output substantially. You can't make it produce something the underlying model can't.

A Practical Walkthrough

Suppose you produce a weekly research briefing for an internal team. The team's particular interests are well-defined: they care about specific industries, specific kinds of regulatory developments, specific competitive dynamics.

The default approach: each week, you generate a Briefing Doc with no customization, then heavily edit it to fit the team's interests.

A better approach: invest 30 minutes once in a customization template that captures the team's interests precisely. Something like:

> *"Produce a 600-word internal briefing for our [specific] team. Cover: regulatory developments affecting [specific markets], competitive moves by [specific competitors], and emerging trends in [specific technology areas]. For each topic: 1-2 sentences on what happened, 1 sentence on why it matters to us specifically. Skip generic context. Assume the reader has been following the space and just wants this week's signal. Conversational but tight; not breezy, not stiff."*

Save it as a snippet. Each week, paste it as the customization for your Briefing Doc generation. The output is now tuned to your team — and your editing time drops from 30 minutes per briefing to 5 minutes.

The 30 minutes you spent crafting the template pays back the first week and compounds every week after.

The Habit That Compounds

Customization isn't a one-time setup. It's a habit. Every time you generate a Studio output, take an extra 30 seconds to write the prompt. Notice what works. Refine over time.

Within a few weeks of doing this consistently, your outputs become noticeably better than the defaults — not because you've discovered some hidden setting, but because you've trained yourself to articulate what you actually want.

That habit, more than any specific NotebookLM feature, is what separates power users from people who never quite get past the impressive first demo.

The next chapter goes deeper on Interactive Audio Overviews — the most conversational use of NotebookLM, and one where the customization habits established here pay particularly large dividends.

Chapter 18: Working with Long Documents

Most NotebookLM sources are reasonable in length — research papers running 20–40 pages, reports running 50–100, books occasionally pushing into the hundreds. NotebookLM handles these comfortably. Its 1M-token-per-source ceiling means a typical document fits with room to spare.

But some documents are enormous. The full Code of Federal Regulations. A multi-thousand-page government report. The complete works of an author. A year of meeting transcripts. These don't fit cleanly within the standard limits, and they require workflows that differ from the typical source-and-chat pattern.

This chapter is about the long-document scenario — what NotebookLM can handle, where it strains, and the practical strategies for getting useful work out of source material that pushes the limits.

Understanding the Real Limits

The official ceiling — about 1 million tokens, roughly 500,000 words, or a 1,500-page book — is the hard limit on a single source. In practice, you'll hit softer limits earlier:

Quality drift in very long sources. Even within the 1M-token ceiling, retrieval quality degrades as sources get longer. A specific passage that would be reliably surfaced in a 50-page document might get missed in a 1,500-page one, simply because the model has more haystack to search.

Studio output coherence drift. Audio Overviews and similar outputs work well on focused source material. On enormous sources, they tend toward generality — covering a lot of ground without going deep on any of it.

Generation time creep. Long sources mean longer generation times for Studio outputs, sometimes substantially longer. A Briefing Doc on a 1,000-page report might take five times longer to generate than one on a 100-page report.

In practice, the soft ceiling for individual sources where everything still works smoothly is somewhere around **300–500 pages**. Past that, you get more value from splitting than from keeping the document whole.

The Splitting Pattern

For documents that exceed the soft ceiling, split them into multiple sources within the same notebook. Each chunk becomes its own source, and NotebookLM treats them as related material rather than as one continuous document.

The art is in the splitting. A few patterns that work:

Split by natural sections. Books have chapters. Reports have sections. Long documents almost always have natural divisions you can use as split points. A 1,500-page legal code might split cleanly by title or part. A long technical manual might split by major topic. Use the document's own structure.

Split by length, with context overlap. When a document doesn't have natural sections — long transcripts, sequential narratives — split by length, 200 pages per chunk say, with a few pages of overlap between chunks so the model doesn't lose context at the boundaries.

Split with descriptive naming. Each chunk's source name should make clear which part of the original it is. `Federal Health Code – Title III, Sections 1-150` is much more useful than `Long doc – Part 2`.

Generate per-chunk summaries on upload. As each chunk goes in, write a brief custom summary that captures what's in it. NotebookLM uses these summaries to weight retrieval and frame Studio outputs.

The split-source approach loses some of the benefits of having the whole document as one source — cross-chunk references can get lost, and queries about a specific concept may miss it if it appears in a chunk that wasn't flagged as relevant. But for documents that exceed the workable limits, it's the only practical path.

The Index-Source Pattern

For very large source sets, a powerful pattern is creating an **index source** — a hand-written document that maps what's in your other sources, with descriptions and cross-references.

The mechanics: write a structured document yourself (in a text editor, or directly in NotebookLM as a note that you then promote to a source) like:

```
Notebook contents:

Source 1: Federal Health Code, Title I (Coverage Provisions)
  - Sections 1-50: Basic eligibility frameworks
  - Sections 51-100: Special populations
  - Key terms: "covered entity", "qualifying individual"

Source 2: Federal Health Code, Title II (Privacy Rules)
  - Sections 1-75: Standard privacy requirements
  - Sections 76-150: Breach response and notification
  - Key terms: "protected health information", "minimum necessary"

[continues across all sources]
```

Now when you query the notebook, NotebookLM can use the index to navigate the rest of the source set — finding the right chunk for a question even when the chunk is one of a dozen.

The index source also serves as a navigation aid for *you*, not just for the AI. When you come back to a notebook months later, the index tells you what's there.

Multi-Notebook Strategies

Sometimes a single notebook isn't the right container even with splitting. For source material that exceeds notebook source limits — or material where you'd benefit from organizing subsets for different purposes — consider multiple notebooks.

A few patterns:

One notebook per major section, with a top-level synthesis notebook. For a multi-volume report, have one notebook per volume, plus a top-level notebook that holds synthesis notes and Studio outputs distilled from the per-volume work.

Topic-cut notebooks. For a large corpus where you'll want to investigate multiple distinct questions, build separate notebooks each containing the sources relevant to one question. This produces tighter, more focused output than working out of one giant notebook.

Time-cut notebooks. For large bodies of evolving content — years of meeting notes, ongoing project documentation — one notebook per quarter or per year keeps each one manageable while the topic-cut approach combines across.

The multi-notebook approach trades some convenience (you can't query across notebooks in a single chat) for substantially better quality on each individual notebook. For serious work with large source sets, the trade is almost always worth it.

Pre-Processing Long Sources

Sometimes the right move is to reduce the document before NotebookLM ever sees it. A few pre-processing approaches that pay off for very long source material:

Extract just the relevant sections. If you only care about three chapters of a 30-chapter book, extract those into a focused PDF and upload that instead of the whole thing. PDF editors, Adobe Acrobat, or browser-based PDF splitters do this in minutes.

Remove non-content material. Long government reports often have hundreds of pages of front matter, appendices, regulatory boilerplate, and similar material that isn't the actual content. Stripping these out before upload yields a tighter, more focused source.

Convert tables and data into structured text. A long report with extensive tables may have the data you need locked in formats NotebookLM struggles with. Pre-extracting key tables into clean structured text — in a spreadsheet or as Markdown tables — makes that data more accessible.

Combine related short sources into a single curated source. The opposite of splitting. If you have many related short documents, combining them into a single hand-curated source sometimes produces better results than treating each one separately, especially for Studio outputs.

The pre-processing investment pays off in better retrieval, better Studio outputs, and faster generation. For sources you'll work with intensively, it's worth doing.

When NotebookLM Is the Wrong Tool

For some long-document work, NotebookLM isn't the right answer regardless of which strategies you use.

Real-time live document search. If you need millisecond search across a corpus, NotebookLM is too slow. Dedicated enterprise search tools are built for this.

Production-grade RAG applications. If you're building a product that does what NotebookLM does — RAG over a custom corpus — use the underlying APIs (Gemini, or one of the dedicated RAG platforms) rather than NotebookLM, which is designed for human use rather than programmatic integration.

Massive corpus analysis (hundreds of thousands of documents). NotebookLM is built for tens to a few hundred sources. Analyzing a million emails or every paper in PubMed is a different scale problem requiring different tools.

Highly structured analytical workflows. If you need to run statistical analysis, regressions, or confidence intervals from your sources, NotebookLM isn't the tool. It's a synthesis tool, not an analytics tool.

For all these cases, NotebookLM may still be useful as a complement — a way to explore the qualitative dimensions of material you analyze quantitatively elsewhere — but it shouldn't be the primary tool.

A Practical Walkthrough

Suppose you're researching a 600-page regulatory document for a compliance project. The document is far too long to read end-to-end in the time you have, and it has dense cross-references throughout.

Phase 1 — preparation. Look at the document's table of contents. Decide whether to upload it whole (within the 1M-token limit) or to split. For a 600-page regulatory document with discrete sections, splitting along the natural structure — one source per major title, say — produces better retrieval than one giant source.

Phase 2 — index source. Hand-write a brief index of what's in each section. Promote it to a source so NotebookLM uses it for navigation.

Phase 3 — focused exploration. Use the chat interface to ask questions across the corpus. Click citations. Build understanding section by section, capturing notes as you go.

Phase 4 — Studio synthesis. Once you understand the structure, generate a Briefing Doc with a focus prompt: *"Produce a compliance-focused briefing on this regulation. Identify the obligations that apply to mid-size health insurers specifically. Skip provisions that apply only to providers or to large insurers. For each obligation, note the section it appears in."*

Phase 5 — verification. Read the Briefing Doc against the source. Click every citation that's load-bearing for a compliance recommendation. Where the citations check out, you can rely on the briefing. Where they don't, you've identified the parts that need direct source review.

You've now made tractable a project that would have been a multi-week reading effort. The work is faster but not shallower — because you've combined NotebookLM's strengths (synthesis, retrieval, Studio output generation) with the human judgment long-document work actually requires.

What Long Documents Teach

Working with long documents is a stress test for everything else in this book. Sources you've been treating casually now have to be deliberately curated. Questions you've been asking offhand now have to be specific enough to navigate the haystack. Studio outputs you've been generating without much customization now have to be tightly framed to produce useful results from large source sets.

Every habit that pays off on a normal-sized notebook pays off more on a long-document notebook. Conversely, every habit that doesn't matter much on a small notebook becomes a real problem on a large one.

Get long documents working, and the rest of NotebookLM gets easier.

The next chapter shifts to a different kind of going-deeper: working in multiple languages, including the cross-language workflows that NotebookLM handles uniquely well.

Chapter 19: Multilingual Notebooks

NotebookLM's multilingual support, by early 2026, is one of its quietly remarkable features. The product handles more than 80 languages for chat and most Studio outputs. It will read sources in one language and produce outputs in another. It will mix multiple languages within a single notebook. For international research, multilingual teams, language-learning workflows, and cross-cultural analysis, this is transformative.

It's also a feature most users never explore beyond their native language. This chapter covers what NotebookLM can do across languages, when the cross-language capabilities matter, and the workflows that pay off for users working in more than one.

What Languages NotebookLM Supports

The headline number — 80+ languages — covers the major Studio outputs (Audio Overviews, Video Overviews, Reports), chat, and source ingestion. The list includes:

Tier-1 languages with full quality — English, Spanish, French, German, Mandarin, Japanese, Portuguese, Italian, Russian, Korean, Hindi, Arabic, Dutch, Polish, Turkish, and a dozen or so others. These have been priority languages for the underlying Gemini models, and NotebookLM output quality reflects that.

Tier-2 languages with good quality — most other major European, Asian, and several African languages (Vietnamese, Swahili, Czech, and many others). Audio voice quality may be less natural; chat and reports may occasionally hit awkward phrasings. Still very usable.

Tier-3 languages with usable quality — many less commonly served languages. Performance degrades gracefully but remains workable for many use cases.

Languages with limited or no support — some smaller languages, low-resource languages, and languages NotebookLM (or Gemini) hasn't yet been calibrated for. The product will sometimes work in these but quality is unpredictable.

The list shifts. Google has been expanding language support consistently. By the time you read this, the list may be longer.

Setting Output Language

When generating any Studio output (or in chat), you can specify the output language. The control is typically in the generation settings dialog or in the chat interface preferences.

You don't need to set this every time — there's usually a default based on your account language and the language of your sources. But for cross-language workflows, the explicit language setting is what makes the magic possible.

A few common patterns:

Sources in language A, output in language B. Upload English-language sources, generate the Audio Overview in Spanish. NotebookLM handles the cross-language synthesis natively — it doesn't translate the source first; it reads the source and produces the output in the target language directly.

Mixed-language source set. A notebook can contain sources in many different languages. NotebookLM reads them all and can produce output in any language you specify.

Language-specific Studio outputs from the same notebook. Same source set, multiple outputs in different languages. Useful for international teams who need the same briefing in three languages.

Cross-Language Source Reading

Reading sources in a language other than the output language is one of NotebookLM's most undersold capabilities. For researchers working with international literature, multilingual archives, or content in languages they don't read well themselves, this opens workflows that weren't possible before.

A typical workflow:

1. Add sources in their original languages — Mandarin academic papers, French regulatory documents, German news coverage.

2. Generate Studio outputs in your working language (English, say, or whichever language you'll use for downstream work).
3. NotebookLM produces the output in your working language while the citations point back to the original-language passages.

This isn't a translation tool — translation tools translate the source. NotebookLM does something different: it reads the source in its original language and synthesizes in your target language. The result is closer to what a multilingual research assistant would produce than to what an automated translation would.

Practical caveats:

Quality varies by language pair. English↔Spanish, English↔French, English↔Mandarin all work very well. Less common pairs (Tamil↔Polish, say) work but with more variability.

Cultural and idiomatic context can be lost. Cross-language synthesis handles the literal content of sources better than the cultural framing around them. A source whose meaning depends heavily on cultural context may be reduced to its literal claims.

Citations are still in the source language. When you click a citation in an English Audio Overview built from Mandarin sources, the cited passage is in Mandarin. You'll need to read it (or translate it separately) to verify directly.

For verifying specific claims in cross-language work, keeping a machine translation tool open alongside NotebookLM is often the right setup — NotebookLM for synthesis, dedicated translation for spot-checking.

Multilingual Notebooks for Research

For researchers working with international literature, NotebookLM solves a problem that's plagued cross-cultural and comparative research forever: the language barrier between source corpus and analytical workflow.

Some scenarios where this matters:

Comparative policy research. Comparing how five countries have approached a regulatory question, with primary sources in five languages. Upload all sources in their original languages. Generate Briefing Docs in your working language. The synthesis spans all sources without requiring you to translate each one first.

International literature reviews. A topic where significant work has been done in non-English languages. NotebookLM can synthesize across English and other-language papers without losing the contributions of either.

Cross-cultural analysis. Source material from different cultural contexts — interviews, reports, qualitative data — can be analyzed across language without first being homogenized into a single language. Some nuance is lost; less than would be lost by translating everything first.

Historical archives. Many historical primary sources exist only in their original languages. Researchers who don't read those languages have traditionally had to rely on translations, often partial, often biased. NotebookLM lets them work directly with original-language material in ways that previously required a translator.

Language Learning Workflows

For language learners, NotebookLM offers a few specific affordances that work surprisingly well:

Listen to a Studio output in the language you're learning. Generate an Audio Overview in your target language from sources you already understand in your native language. The result is high-quality, naturalistic audio in the target language about content you already know — making the language easier to follow because you aren't parsing meaning and language at the same time.

Bilingual study notebooks. Add sources in both your native and target languages on the same topic. Cross-language synthesis lets you see the same content from both linguistic angles.

Quizzes and Flashcards in the target language. Generate study aids directly in the language you're learning, from source material in either language. The result is learning material calibrated to your specific sources, in the language you're trying to absorb.

Interactive Audio Overviews for conversational practice. NotebookLM's interactive mode isn't designed as a language tutor, but asking questions and hearing answers in your target language is genuine listening-and-speaking practice on real content.

Multilingual Teams

For multilingual teams, NotebookLM removes a friction that's hard to fix any other way: keeping everyone working from the same source material despite working in different languages.

Shared notebooks with cross-language outputs. A team notebook with shared sources can produce Studio outputs in different team members' preferred languages. Same underlying material, customized presentation for each viewer.

Language-tailored briefings. Generate a Briefing Doc in English for the New York office, in Spanish for Mexico City, in Mandarin for Shanghai — all from the same source set, in minutes.

Cross-language meeting prep. A meeting with stakeholders speaking different languages? Generate Audio Overviews in each language for the relevant participants. Everyone arrives prepared, in their own language, on the same material.

For globally distributed organizations, this is one of NotebookLM's most operationally valuable capabilities — and one that gets little attention because it's invisible until you have a use case for it.

Quality Calibration Across Languages

A few practical notes for managing quality variations:

Spot-check Studio outputs in less common languages. If you're producing output in a language NotebookLM hasn't been heavily optimized for, listen to a sample before relying on it. Usually the audio quality is fine; occasionally a phrase will sound stilted or a term will be mistranslated.

Be explicit about regional variants. "Spanish" is many things — Iberian, Mexican, Argentine. NotebookLM may default to a generic register. For specific audiences, specify the regional variant in the customization prompt: *"Use Latin American Spanish, not Iberian Spanish"* or *"Use Brazilian Portuguese, not European Portuguese."*

Test idiomatic accuracy with native speakers. For high-stakes content — publications, formal communications, customer-facing material — in a language you don't speak, get a native speaker to review before shipping.

Use English as a bridge cautiously. For language pairs NotebookLM handles less well, you can sometimes get better results by going through English as an intermediate language. But this introduces drift. For high-stakes work, direct cross-language synthesis is usually better even if the quality is slightly less polished.

Limitations to Know

A few things NotebookLM doesn't currently do well in multilingual contexts:

Code-switching within a single output. Outputs are generally in one language. If you want bilingual output — alternating between languages, common in some education contexts — you'll need to assemble it from multiple generations.

Voice cloning across languages. The voice models for Audio Overviews handle different languages, but the voices themselves are language-specific. You can't have the same voice persona speak across multiple languages.

Translation per se. NotebookLM isn't a translation tool. It synthesizes across languages, but for direct word-for-word or sentence-for-sentence translation, dedicated tools (Google Translate, DeepL, professional human translation) are more appropriate.

OCR accuracy in non-Latin scripts. OCR for scanned sources works best in Latin scripts. Performance on Chinese, Japanese, Arabic, Thai, and other non-Latin scripts is improving but lags. Pre-processing into clean text formats before upload often pays off for non-Latin source material.

A Practical Walkthrough

Suppose you're a policy researcher studying digital privacy regulation across the EU, the UK, and several non-English-speaking jurisdictions. Your sources include the GDPR text (English), national implementation documents from France (French) and Germany (German), regulatory guidance from Spain (Spanish), and case law from Italy (Italian).

Traditionally, this research required either translating everything or relying on summary commentary from secondary sources.

With NotebookLM:

1. Upload all sources in their original languages — five languages, twelve documents.
2. Generate a Briefing Doc in English with a focus prompt: *"Compare how each jurisdiction has implemented Article 17 right-to-erasure. Note where implementations diverge and where convergence has occurred. For each divergence, identify the underlying policy rationale where the source explains it."*
3. Generate an Audio Overview in English on the same topic for listening on your way to a meeting.
4. For the claims that matter most, click citations to see the original-language passages. Use a translation tool to verify the specific wording.
5. Save the Briefing Doc as a new source. Iterate with follow-up questions.

You've now produced a cross-jurisdictional analysis grounded in primary sources in five languages — without translating any of them yourself, and without relying on secondary commentary. The work is faster and more rigorous than relying on English-language summaries of the non-English sources would have been.

What Multilingual Capability Reveals About NotebookLM

Cross-language work makes one of NotebookLM's deeper strengths visible: it isn't just a chat interface bolted onto a language model. It's a research environment that happens to use a language model as its reasoning engine. The reasoning engine works across languages. So does the research environment.

This is also why NotebookLM is, by some measures, the most consequential AI tool for users outside the English-speaking world. Most AI coverage focuses on English-language workflows. For non-English researchers and knowledge workers, NotebookLM's multilingual capabilities are often the difference between "AI can help me" and "AI doesn't really speak my language."

The next chapter covers the often-overlooked mobile experience — the apps, what they do well, where they lag, and the workflows they enable that the web alone doesn't.

Chapter 20: Mobile and Cross-Platform Use

For most of NotebookLM's history, the product was a web-first tool. You sat at a computer, opened a browser, and worked. The mobile apps — when they finally arrived in 2025 — were, at first, mostly catch-up: ports of the web experience to a smaller screen.

By early 2026, that's changed. The mobile apps have become first-class clients for several specific workflows, and the cross-platform combination (web plus mobile, working from the same notebook on different devices) has become a real productivity multiplier.

This chapter covers what the mobile apps do well, where they still lag the web, and the workflows where mobile is the better client.

The Apps

NotebookLM ships native apps for both major mobile platforms:

- **Android** (requires Android 10 or later)
- **iOS** (requires iOS 17 or later, includes iPadOS)

Both apps share state with the web — sign in, and you have access to the same notebooks, sources, chats, and Studio outputs. Generate a Briefing Doc on your laptop in the morning; read it on your phone during your commute. Capture a source on your phone in the field; query it from your laptop that night.

The apps are free and use your existing NotebookLM tier (Free, Plus, Pro, or Ultra). There's no separate mobile subscription.

What Mobile Does Well

A few specific workflows where mobile beats the web:

Listening to Audio Overviews

This is the killer mobile workflow. Generate an Audio Overview on the web. Open the app on your phone. Play it during a walk, a commute, a workout, while doing dishes. The audio plays in the background like any other podcast app.

For users who do significant amounts of source-based learning or briefing, consuming Audio Overviews during otherwise-unproductive time changes the math on how much research you can absorb. A 30-minute walk plus a 15-minute Audio Overview means you've covered a research paper without sitting down.

The mobile app supports background playback, lock-screen controls, and in some implementations CarPlay/Android Auto integration. It's a good audio client.

Capturing Sources on the Go

You're reading an article on your phone. You see a paper referenced. You take a photo of a page in a book. You're listening to a podcast and want to add the transcript later. All of these are easier on mobile than on the web.

The Android and iOS apps both support:

- **Share-sheet integration.** Share a link from any app — browser, news reader, mail — directly into NotebookLM as a new source. Works with web articles, YouTube videos, PDFs you've received.
- **Camera capture.** Take a photo of a document, a book page, handwritten notes. NotebookLM applies OCR and ingests it as a source.
- **Voice input.** Some implementations let you record audio (a meeting, a thought, an interview) directly in the app and add it as an audio source.

The "capture in the moment, work with it later" workflow is one mobile makes possible in ways the web can't.

Quick Lookups

Sometimes you need to ask a quick question of a notebook while you're away from your computer. A meeting reference. A specific number. A name you can't quite remember. The mobile chat interface is good for this — open the app, navigate to the notebook, ask, get the answer.

It isn't where you do focused work, but for the "I just need to check one thing" use case, mobile is faster than walking back to your laptop.

Reading Studio Outputs

Briefing Docs, Reports, Mind Maps, and similar text-and-visual outputs read well on mobile. For consumption (as opposed to generation or editing), the mobile apps are sufficient.

The iPad version shines for source review. Reading a source on the larger iPad screen with chat in a sidebar is closer to the experience of working with a paper book and a notepad than the laptop equivalent feels.

What Mobile Lags On

The mobile apps still trail the web in several areas:

New Features

The pattern has been consistent: new Studio outputs and major features launch on the web first, then come to mobile weeks to months later. Cinematic Video Mode, Infographics, Data Tables — all appeared on the web before reaching the mobile apps.

If a particular feature is critical to your work, check whether the mobile app has it before relying on it for mobile-first workflows.

Heavy Generation

You can technically generate Studio outputs from mobile, but the experience is slower and the customization controls are sometimes more limited than on the web. For producing outputs, the web is still the right primary client. Mobile is for consumption.

Source Curation at Scale

Renaming sources, reordering, editing summaries, removing sources — the small organizational work that keeps a notebook tidy — is easier on the web than on a phone. The mobile apps support these operations but in a compressed UI that's slower to navigate.

For a single quick edit, mobile is fine. For real source-curation work, do it on the web.

Long-form Writing

Hand-writing notes, especially substantive ones, is easier on a real keyboard than on a phone. Mobile works for short captures — an observation, a question for later. For longer notes, the web is more comfortable.

Side-by-Side Workflows

The web's three-pane layout (sources, chat, Studio) is hard to replicate on a phone screen. Mobile shows one or two panes at a time. For workflows that depend on rapid switching between panes — close-reading a source while chatting about it — the web stays better.

The Cross-Platform Pattern

For users with both mobile devices and a computer, the most productive approach is to think of them as different clients for different phases of the same work.

A typical pattern:

Computer (focused desk work). Source curation, in-depth chat, generating Studio outputs, hand-writing notes, organizing notebooks. The deep work that requires the full UI and a keyboard.

Mobile (capture and consumption). Capturing sources from things you encounter in the world, listening to Audio Overviews during transit or downtime, quick lookups when you're not at your computer, reading shorter Studio outputs on the go.

The two modes complement each other. Mobile turns idle time into productive consumption. Computer time turns the captures and listenings into structured understanding. The combination produces more work than either alone could.

A few cross-platform habits that compound:

Generate before you go. Before a commute or a known block of away-from-computer time, generate the Audio Overviews you want to consume. By the time you're walking, the audio is ready.

Capture freely on mobile, organize on web. Don't worry about getting captures perfect on mobile. Throw sources into a notebook in the moment. When you're back at your computer, rename, organize, decide what to keep.

Make a "captures" notebook for triage. A dedicated notebook for mobile captures lets you keep your main project notebooks clean. Periodically — weekly, say — move good captures into the relevant project notebooks and delete the noise.

Use mobile for review, web for response. A Briefing Doc generated on the web can be read on mobile, in line at the airport or before a meeting. When something prompts a follow-up, capture it as a note from mobile and address it the next time you're at the computer.

Accessibility Implications

The mobile apps deserve specific mention for accessibility. For users with vision impairments, mobile reading impairments, or other accessibility needs, the apps offer:

- **Full screen reader support** (VoiceOver on iOS, TalkBack on Android)
- **Large-text and dynamic-type support**
- **Audio Overviews as the primary medium** — for users who can't easily read screens, the audio-first workflow is transformative
- **Voice input** for source capture and chat

Where these capabilities matter, the mobile apps may be the primary or only viable client. NotebookLM has paid attention to accessibility in ways many AI tools haven't, and the mobile apps reflect that.

Setting Up for Cross-Platform Use

If you're going to use NotebookLM cross-platform, a few setup tips:

Sign in with the same Google account everywhere. Obvious, but easy to mess up if you have multiple Google accounts. Pick one for NotebookLM and use it consistently.

Install the app on whatever phone you actually carry. Not your secondary phone — your primary one. The captures-on-the-go workflow only works if the app is on the device you have with you.

Configure share-sheet integration. On iOS and Android, NotebookLM should appear in the share sheet of any app that exports content. If it isn't showing up, check the share sheet settings and enable it.

Configure background audio playback permissions. For Audio Overview playback to work properly when backgrounded, the app needs the right permissions. Verify these once at setup.

Consider headphones with hardware controls. For the listen-while-walking workflow, being able to pause and skip without taking your phone out of your pocket is a quality-of-life upgrade.

A Practical Walkthrough

Suppose you're traveling for a conference. You'll be away from your normal desk for three days. You want to use the travel time productively while staying on top of work.

Before leaving. On your computer, open the notebooks you'll want to engage with during travel — your conference prep notebook, a current research project, an internal briefing notebook. For each, generate Audio Overviews on the most current material.

On the plane. Phone, headphones, downloaded Audio Overviews. Listen to the conference prep on the way out. By the time you land you've internalized the material for the first day's sessions.

During conference sessions. When something interesting comes up — a referenced paper, a tool you want to look at later, a name you want to remember — capture it on mobile (photo, voice note, web link share) into your conference prep notebook.

Evenings. Brief desk work on hotel-room laptop or tablet. Move good captures into project notebooks. Generate fresh Briefing Docs incorporating new material. Send updated audio to your phone for the next day.

On the way back. New Audio Overviews of what you learned, listened to on the flight home. By the time you land you've already begun synthesizing the conference into something usable.

You return having actually digested the trip, rather than carrying a backlog of material you'll process when you "have time" — which usually means never.

Mobile as a Multiplier

Mobile doesn't replace desk work in NotebookLM. It multiplies it. The deep work — curating sources, writing synthesis notes, generating tightly customized Studio outputs — still happens at a real computer with a real keyboard.

But the productive *time* available for NotebookLM expands enormously when mobile is part of the workflow. Idle time becomes consumption time. Things-encountered-in-the-world become sources without friction. Short blocks of attention become quick chat sessions. Total meaningful engagement with your notebooks goes up, sometimes by a factor of two or three.

For users who treat NotebookLM as a serious working tool, integrating mobile is one of the highest-leverage habits in the workflow.

That closes Part IV. You've now extended your NotebookLM use beyond the basics — into web research with Fast and Deep Research, precise customization of Studio outputs, long-document strategies, multilingual workflows, and cross-platform habits. These are the techniques that turn confident users into power users.

Part V picks up a different thread: the disciplines that make all of this actually work in practice. Source curation as an ongoing practice. Prompting NotebookLM with the rigor the model rewards. And — most importantly — the citation-verification habits that protect you from the failure mode source-grounded AI is uniquely vulnerable to.

Part V: Getting Better Results

"Care is the antidote to violence."

— Saul Williams

Chapter 21: Source Curation Strategy

Source curation has come up throughout this book. In Chapter 4 as the foundational principle — quality beats quantity. In Chapter 6 as a daily habit — the source pane as working memory. In Chapter 9 as an organizational discipline — one topic per notebook. By now the underlying idea should be familiar: in source-grounded AI, the sources are what matter most.

This chapter treats source curation as a deliberate practice rather than a side effect of doing other work. The difference matters. Casual users curate by accident — they upload what they happen to have, work with what's there, and get whatever output the corpus supports. Power users curate on purpose — they think about who's in the room before they ask the room a question. The output difference is enormous.

The Core Principle, Restated

A NotebookLM notebook produces good answers when its sources are:

1. **Relevant** to the questions you'll ask
2. **Credible** enough that their claims are worth synthesizing
3. **Current** enough that their information hasn't been superseded
4. **Coherent** as a set — not a random collection but a deliberate one
5. **Appropriately sized** — enough to support synthesis, few enough to maintain focus

A notebook that meets these criteria produces dramatically better outputs than one that doesn't, regardless of how clever your prompts are. Source curation is upstream of prompting.

The criteria are obvious in the abstract. They're harder to apply consistently in practice. The rest of this chapter is about that practice.

Curation as a Pre-Work Phase

Most NotebookLM users skip the curation phase entirely. They have a project, they grab the documents they can access, they upload them, and they start asking questions. The curation question — *are these the right sources for this work?* — never gets asked.

Treat curation as its own work phase. Before you upload anything, before you ask the first question, spend 15–30 minutes thinking about what should be in the notebook.

A simple checklist:

- **What's the central question or topic?** Be specific. "AI policy" is too broad. "How are healthcare insurers responding to the proposed CMS AI guidance" is workable.
- **What kinds of sources would best inform that question?** Primary documents (the guidance itself), industry analysis, commentary from affected parties, comparative cases from other industries.
- **Which specific sources do you have access to that fit?** Inventory before you upload. Identify what's missing.
- **What sources should be deliberately excluded?** Things tempting to include that would muddy the corpus. Older versions, tangentially related work, low-credibility material.
- **What's the right *size*?** Too few and you can't synthesize. Too many and retrieval gets noisy. For most projects, 5–15 carefully chosen sources is the right zone.

This pre-work pays back many times over. The notebook you build deliberately produces better outputs in the first hour than an accidentally assembled one produces in a day.

Source Quality Markers

"High-quality sources" sounds easy to identify in the abstract. In practice, evaluating sources requires judgment worth making explicit.

A few markers I look for:

Provenance. Who produced this? Are they accountable for accuracy? A peer-reviewed paper, a regulatory document, a respected publication, an internal document with named authorship — all carry different weight than anonymous web content or AI-generated material.

Specificity. Does the source make specific, verifiable claims, or does it traffic in vague generalizations? Sources that deal in specifics — numbers, named events, direct quotations, citations to prior work — are easier to verify and tend to be more trustworthy.

Currency. When was this written? Is the information current? In fast-moving domains — technology, policy, current affairs — even six-month-old material can be substantially outdated. Use the most current credible source available.

Citations. Does the source cite its own sources? A document that grounds its claims in further references is more trustworthy than one that asserts without grounding. Sources that practice good citation discipline tend to have higher signal-to-noise.

Conflicts of interest. Does the source have a stake in what it's claiming? A market-research firm's report on the importance of market research is not neutral. A vendor's case study on their own product is not neutral. Notice these and weight accordingly.

Triangulation. When multiple credible sources independently make similar claims, the claims are more reliable. When a single source asserts something the others don't, that single source needs more verification.

These markers won't always agree. A high-currency source from a vendor with a clear conflict of interest is in tension with itself. Real curation requires weighing the markers against each other, not following a checklist.

Coherence Across the Source Set

A common curation failure isn't that any individual source is bad — it's that the set as a whole isn't coherent.

Some patterns to watch for:

Mixed-purpose sources. A notebook that combines primary regulatory text, news commentary, and marketing material is asking NotebookLM to synthesize across genres with very different epistemic statuses. The output reflects the mix.

Mismatched time periods. A notebook with material from 2019 alongside material from 2026 will produce outputs that conflate two different historical moments. For historical analysis, that's exactly right. For current understanding, it's a problem.

Unbalanced perspectives. If you're building a notebook on a contested topic, a one-sided source set produces one-sided synthesis. NotebookLM will dutifully synthesize what's there; if what's there is biased, the synthesis will be biased.

Conflicting source quality. Five high-quality sources plus three low-quality ones produces output less reliable than the five high-quality sources alone. The model treats them all as inputs and the low-quality material drags down the average.

The fix for all of these is the same: **curate the set as a set, not just as a collection of individual sources.** Look at what you have, ask whether it coheres, and add or remove sources to fix imbalances.

Adding Strategically

Not every gap in a source set needs filling. Some additions improve the notebook; others just add noise.

A gap is worth filling when:

- **A specific question keeps coming up that no source addresses.** The notebook has a topical hole blocking real work.
- **The existing sources are one-sided on a topic where multiple perspectives exist.** A contrasting source improves balance.
- **The existing sources are dated on a topic that's recently evolved.** Current material brings the corpus up to date.
- **A foundational source is missing.** Sometimes the canonical reference everyone in a field knows isn't in your notebook. Adding it grounds the rest.

A gap is *not* worth filling when:

- **It's adjacent but not central.** Resist the urge to add sources for completeness if they don't directly serve your questions.
- **The available sources are low-quality.** Better to leave a gap than fill it with material you don't trust.

- **You're hitting source limits.** When the notebook is at capacity, any addition forces a removal. Make sure the addition is worth more than what it displaces.

"More sources" is rarely the right answer. "The right sources" is the question worth asking.

Removing Strategically

Equally important: knowing when to remove sources you've already added.

Reasons to remove:

- **A source has been superseded.** A newer version exists, and you've added it too.
- **A source has proven unreliable.** As you've worked with the notebook, citations from this source have repeatedly misrepresented things.
- **A source is dragging down output quality.** Studio outputs have been muddier than expected, and you can trace it to a specific source contributing noise.
- **A source has become irrelevant.** The notebook's focus has shifted and a previously central source is now off-topic.

The friction here is psychological. We tend to add sources but rarely remove them. Sources accumulate. Periodically — say, before generating a major Studio output you'll actually share — review the source list and ask: *Is each of these earning its place?*

Source Promotion as Curation

Chapter 8 covered promoting notes to sources. This is a curation operation, not just a notes operation. Promoting a synthesis note adds a curated layer on top of the underlying material — your own synthesis, in your own framing, available for future queries.

Done well, this compounds. After months of work, a long-running notebook contains:

- The original primary sources you started with

- New sources added as the work has evolved
- Promoted synthesis notes from prior sessions, capturing accumulated understanding

NotebookLM treats all three the same way at retrieval time. Your accumulated synthesis sits alongside the original sources, so subsequent queries can build on prior work without re-deriving everything from scratch.

Done badly, this becomes circular. If you promote loose synthesis notes that haven't been verified, NotebookLM may cite your earlier (potentially wrong) framings as if they were sourced material. Be selective. Promote synthesis notes you trust and that capture insights worth carrying forward.

Curation Across Multiple Notebooks

The curation discipline extends to your library, not just to individual notebooks. The principles from Chapter 9 — one topic per notebook, clear naming, periodic pruning — are curation operations at the library level.

A few specific curation habits at the library level:

Periodic pruning. Once a quarter, review the notebook gallery. Archive or delete completed projects. Consolidate stragglers. Keep the active set small.

Cross-notebook synthesis sources. For long-running domains where multiple notebooks contribute related work, occasionally create a synthesis source that distills the most important insights from each. Place it in a top-level reference notebook so future notebooks can reference it.

Cross-pollination. When a source proves valuable in one notebook, consider whether it belongs in others. Don't add it everywhere — add it where it serves a real purpose. But notice which sources have multi-notebook value.

A Walked-Through Curation Session

Suppose you're starting a research project on the impact of generative AI on knowledge work, aiming to produce an internal whitepaper for your organization.

Phase 1 — frame the question. Specifically: "How is generative AI changing the day-to-day work of knowledge workers in [our industry], and what should our organization be doing in response?" That's more focused than "AI in knowledge work."

Phase 2 — identify source categories. You want:

- Primary research on generative AI workforce impacts (academic studies)
- Industry-specific analysis (how *your* industry has been affected)
- Vendor and product perspectives (what tools are actually available)
- Critical perspectives (voices skeptical of the prevailing narrative)
- Internal data (your own organization's prior thinking, current usage)

Phase 3 — inventory. What do you already have? What's missing? Note both.

Phase 4 — gather, but selectively. For each missing category, identify 2–3 high-quality sources. Don't grab everything. Pick the best you can find.

Phase 5 — quality check. Before uploading, look at each source's provenance, currency, and specificity. Reject anything weak. For borderline cases, mark them "tentative" and plan to evaluate after a few queries.

Phase 6 — load and verify. Upload. Read auto-generated summaries to confirm each source ingested correctly. Rename sources clearly. Edit summaries where the auto-generated ones miss what matters.

Phase 7 — first queries. Ask a few exploratory questions to test whether the corpus produces useful answers. If outputs feel scattered or generic, the issue is usually source-side: too many, too few, mismatched, or unbalanced. Adjust before going deeper.

Phase 8 — ongoing curation. As you work, add sources when gaps emerge, remove ones that aren't earning their place, promote synthesis notes when insights crystallize. The notebook evolves deliberately rather than accumulating randomly.

A two-hour curation session up front produces a notebook that delivers value across weeks of work. The investment pays back many times over.

Curation as Thinking

A final framing worth sitting with: **curation is not preparation for thinking. Curation *is* thinking.**

Choosing what to include and exclude. Weighing what's credible. Deciding what perspectives matter. Identifying what's missing. These are intellectual operations of the same kind as the analysis NotebookLM helps with downstream. The curation phase is where you do the thinking the AI can't do for you, because it requires judgment about what counts as truth in your domain.

NotebookLM amplifies the source set you give it. If the set reflects careful judgment, the amplification produces useful work. If the set was assembled carelessly, the amplification produces work that's confidently misleading.

The most important hour you spend in any NotebookLM project is the hour before you upload anything.

The next chapter covers the second discipline of getting good results: prompting NotebookLM well, with the rigor the model rewards.

Chapter 22: Prompting NotebookLM

Chapter 7 covered the basics of asking questions in NotebookLM — scope, specificity, framing, format, and the question patterns that work. This chapter goes deeper. By the end you should have a working library of prompt techniques calibrated for source-grounded AI, distinct from the prompting habits that work for ChatGPT or Claude.

The premise: prompting NotebookLM well is a skill, not a knack. It can be learned, practiced, and refined. The people who get the most out of NotebookLM aren't asking smarter questions on instinct — they've developed prompting habits that produce better results consistently, on any source material.

The Difference, One More Time

Worth restating because it shapes everything that follows: **NotebookLM prompts are not ChatGPT prompts.** General-purpose chatbots reward prompts that elicit knowledge from a model that knows enormous amounts. Source-grounded AI rewards prompts that direct a research assistant who only knows what you've handed them.

Practical implications:

- **Don't ask NotebookLM to draw on outside knowledge.** It can't — not deliberately. Outside-knowledge requests either get refused or produce ungrounded responses.
- **Don't ask NotebookLM to invent.** Creative generation isn't its strength. ChatGPT writes the poem; NotebookLM analyzes the poem you uploaded.
- **Do ask NotebookLM to traverse, compare, extract, and verify.** These are the operations RAG architectures excel at.
- **Do specify scope deliberately.** What part of the corpus? Which sources? Which sub-topic? The more specific, the better.

Once these are second nature, the rest of prompting is craft.

Prompt Templates by Use Case

A library of templates organized by what you're trying to do. None is magical; all of them work. Adapt the bracketed variables to your situation.

For Initial Orientation

When you've just added a source and want to know what's in it:

> *"Summarize [source] in three paragraphs. First paragraph: what is this and who's it written for. Second paragraph: the central claim or finding. Third paragraph: the structure of the document and where the major sections are."*

A useful overview faster than "summarize this."

For Targeted Reading

When you know what you're looking for:

> *"In [source], find the discussion of [specific topic]. Quote the most relevant passage directly, then summarize the surrounding context."*

The quote-and-summarize structure gives you both the source's exact language and the framing around it.

For Cross-Source Synthesis

When you have multiple sources on a related topic:

> *"Across all sources, identify what's said about [topic]. For each substantive claim, note which source(s) support it, where they agree, and where they diverge."*

Stronger than "what do my sources say about [topic]" — it explicitly asks for the comparison structure.

For Identifying Gaps

When you want to know what's missing:

"Across the sources I've selected, what aspects of [topic] are NOT addressed? What questions would a thorough treatment cover that these sources don't?"

NotebookLM is good at noticing absence when you ask explicitly.

For Critical Reading

When you want analysis rather than summary:

"Read [source] critically. Where is the argument strongest? Where is it weakest? What evidence does it offer that's most compelling? What evidence is thin or missing? What would a skeptical reviewer focus on?"

This disrupts NotebookLM's default tendency toward neutral synthesis.

For Steel-Manning

When you want the strongest version of a position:

"Make the strongest possible case for [position] using only what's in the sources. Cite specifically. Address the most likely counter-arguments preemptively."

Useful for understanding contested positions you aren't personally drawn to.

For Tracing Evolution

When you want to see how something has developed:

"How has [concept/topic] been treated across the sources, in chronological order? What changes between earlier and later treatments? Which sources represent shifts in thinking?"

Particularly useful when sources span multiple time periods.

For Extracting Structured Data

When you need facts in a usable form:

> *"Extract all instances where [type of data point] appears across the sources. Present as a table with columns for [specific columns]. Include citations to each source."*

For numerical data, named entities, regulatory citations, etc. Often pairs well with the Data Tables Studio output.

For Verifying a Specific Claim

When you've heard something elsewhere and want to check the source's position:

> *"I've encountered the claim that [specific claim]. Do the sources support this, contradict it, or remain silent? Quote any directly relevant passages."*

Makes the verification work explicit and the answer easier to evaluate.

For Finding Contradictions

When sources may disagree:

> *"Where do the sources contradict each other? Identify specific points of disagreement. For each, note what each source claims and what evidence each offers."*

NotebookLM smooths over disagreement by default. Asking explicitly for contradictions surfaces it.

For Structuring an Argument

When you're writing and need scaffolding:

> *"I'm writing a piece arguing [thesis]. Based on the sources, what would be the most defensible structure? What evidence supports each step? Where would a reader be most likely to push back?"*

Useful for moving from research to writing.

Prompt Patterns That Don't Work

Equally useful: knowing what doesn't work and why.

Vague openers. "Tell me about this." "What do you think?" "Anything interesting?" These produce vague answers. Be specific.

Compound questions. "Summarize the document, identify the weaknesses, suggest improvements, and write a counterargument." Too much in one prompt. Break it into separate turns.

Knowledge requests masquerading as source questions. "Based on the document and your general knowledge, [question]" — NotebookLM will produce ungrounded answers when you invite it to. Don't invite it to.

Extreme open-endedness. "What should I do?" — NotebookLM is a research tool, not a strategic advisor. Use it to understand the landscape; do the deciding yourself.

Vague format requests. "Write something about [topic]." Specify length, structure, audience.

Pseudo-politeness. "Could you possibly perhaps help with..." Wasted tokens. Be direct.

Trying to override source-grounding. "Pretend the sources said [X]." NotebookLM resists this and produces low-quality output when pushed. Use ChatGPT for hypotheticals.

The Iterative Refinement Pattern

A pattern that works regardless of the specific prompt: treat the first answer as a draft, not a finished response.

The basic flow:

1. Ask your question.
2. Read the answer critically.
3. Identify what's missing, what's wrong, what could go deeper.
4. Ask a follow-up that addresses the gap.
5. Repeat until you have what you need.

A typical refinement sequence might look like:

> "Summarize the methodology of [paper]."

(Read the answer.)

"Go deeper on the specific experimental design choices. Why did the authors pick [specific choice]?"

(Read the answer.)

"Quote the exact passage where they explain [that choice]."

(Click the citation. Verify.)

"Now compare that to how [other source] approaches the same question."

Three or four refinement turns produce understanding no single shot — no matter how cleverly phrased — would have. The conversational refinement is where the depth lives.

When to Re-Prompt vs. When to Restart

Sometimes a prompt produces an answer that's just wrong-direction. You have two options:

- **Re-prompt within the same chat.** Add clarification, redirect, narrow the scope. The model retains context and you can usually steer back to useful territory.
- **Start a new chat.** Sometimes the conversation has accumulated assumptions or framings dragging subsequent responses off course. A clean chat with a tighter initial prompt beats continuing to push against a misdirection.

A reasonable rule: re-prompt for one round. If you're still off-direction after the second attempt, start fresh with a more deliberate framing.

Prompting for Studio Output Generation

The customization prompts covered in Chapter 17 are themselves a kind of prompting. The same principles apply: be specific about scope, audience, and use; tell NotebookLM what to emphasize and what to skip; iterate when the first attempt isn't right.

A useful habit: **think of Studio customization prompts as briefs to a producer.** You're not asking the model to do the work; you're directing how the work gets done. The clearer the direction, the better the output.

A Library Worth Building

Over time, the prompts you reach for repeatedly become a personal library. Save them. Refine them. Use them as starting points rather than reinventing each time.

A simple practice that pays off: keep a text file of your best prompts, organized by use case. After every session where a particular prompt produced unusually good results, copy it into the file with a note about what made it work.

Within months you have a personal prompt library that captures your specific working patterns. Within a year, you've built a tool you'd never have on day one — a curated set of phrasings that produce consistently good output across the kinds of work you actually do.

A Final Note on Voice

Different people write prompts differently. Some are terse and command-like. Others are conversational and exploratory. Some use markdown formatting; others write in prose. NotebookLM accommodates a wide range.

The pattern that holds across styles: **the prompt should be clearer than the answer you want.** Whatever style you write in, the prompt should leave less ambiguity than the response you'd accept. A vague prompt that gets a useful response was luck. The reliable path is precision in.

Prompting is where source-grounded AI rewards practice. Early prompts are calibration. The ones after that are increasingly fluent. The skill compounds.

The next chapter is, in some ways, the most important chapter in this book. It covers the verification habit that protects you from source-grounded AI's most consequential failure mode: confident, well-cited, subtly wrong answers.

Chapter 23: Verifying Citations

This is the chapter the rest of the book has been building toward. Throughout the preceding chapters I've asked you to click citations. To verify before trusting. To treat citation links as the moment of truth. This chapter explains why — and lays out the verification habits that make NotebookLM safe to rely on for serious work.

If you remember nothing else from this book, remember this chapter. The single most consequential failure mode of source-grounded AI is the one hardest to notice from the surface: confident, well-formatted answers, with citations that go to real passages, where the answer doesn't actually say what the cited passage says.

It happens. It happens regularly. The habit that protects you is small but non-negotiable.

The Failure Mode

Imagine you ask NotebookLM a question. You get back an answer that reads beautifully — clear, structured, citations scattered throughout. The citations link to specific passages in your sources. You click one. The passage is real. It's in your source. You move on.

Here's the thing: the citation only proves the *passage exists*. It doesn't prove the passage *supports the claim*.

The subtle error is when the answer paraphrases or interprets the cited passage in a way that distorts what the source says. The cited passage might say something close to what NotebookLM claimed. It might say something that, with a particular reading, could imply what NotebookLM claimed. It might say something entirely different that happens to share a few words.

In all these cases, the citation passes the existence test (yes, the passage is in the source) but fails the support test (no, the passage doesn't actually support the claim).

This isn't a NotebookLM bug. It's a property of how source-grounded AI works. The model is doing its best to summarize and synthesize. Sometimes its summary takes liberties the source wouldn't endorse.

The polish hides the problem. A citation that looks legitimate, in a paragraph that reads professionally, in a Briefing Doc with clean formatting, *feels* like authoritative content. The look of authority does more work than it should.

Why This Failure Mode Is Particularly Dangerous

Most AI tools have failure modes you can spot if you're paying attention. ChatGPT will sometimes confidently make up a fact about a person — but you can usually tell something's off because the made-up fact contradicts what you already know, or because there's no way to check.

NotebookLM's failure mode is different. The errors don't contradict anything you already know — you wouldn't be using the AI if you already knew the answers. They come with citations that *look* like proof, wrapped in the format conventions of trustworthy work.

The result: careless NotebookLM use can produce work worse than careful unaided reading would have been, because the AI assistance creates a false sense of grounding. You think you've verified because you saw citations. But you haven't actually verified — you've just seen citations.

The good news: the fix is mechanical. It costs nothing but seconds.

The Habit

The single habit that protects you: **when an answer matters, click the citations and read the cited passages.**

That's it. The whole habit.

Not "scan the citations to confirm they exist." Not "click one or two and trust the rest." Read the cited passages. Compare what the source says to what NotebookLM claimed about it. Confirm the support relation, not just the existence.

For high-stakes content — anything you'll publish, share with a stakeholder, or base a decision on — this verification isn't optional. It's part of the work. Skipping it is skipping the part where you take responsibility for the accuracy of what you're producing.

When to Verify

You can't click every citation in every answer. You'll burn out. The right calibration depends on stakes:

Verify exhaustively when:

- The output will be published or shared externally
- A decision will be made based on the content
- You'll be cited or quoted as the author
- The topic is contested and accuracy matters
- A specific claim is unusual or unexpected

Verify selectively when:

- The output is for personal learning or exploration
- You're using NotebookLM to orient to a topic before deeper reading
- The claims are familiar and triangulate with what you know

Verify lightly when:

- You're using NotebookLM as a search-and-find tool, where the AI's job is mostly to point you to the source
- You're doing rapid iteration where you'll review the underlying sources directly anyway

The principle: **the verification effort should match the consequence of being wrong.** Casual exploration tolerates lighter verification. Published work doesn't.

How to Verify Effectively

A few tactical practices that make verification efficient without skipping the rigor:

Click the citation, don't just look at it. Citation numbers in NotebookLM are interactive. Clicking surfaces the actual cited passage. Looking at the citation number without clicking is not verification.

Read the surrounding context, not just the highlighted span. A passage in isolation can mean something different from the same passage in context. NotebookLM's citation typically highlights a specific span — read the paragraph around it.

Ask: does this passage actually support the claim? Not "is this passage in the source" — that's the easy question — but "does this passage say what the AI said it says?" If the answer is no, you've caught an error.

Check passages that feel surprising. If NotebookLM tells you something that contradicts your prior understanding, the citation is the place to start. Either the passage will surprise you (you've learned something) or the citation won't hold up (you've caught an error). Either way, useful.

Spot-check the boring claims, too. Errors aren't always in the surprising places. Sometimes the most mundane-sounding paragraph is where a subtle distortion lives. Don't only verify the parts that catch your attention.

Use the chat interface for re-verification. When you spot a questionable claim in a Studio output, paste it back into chat with: "Where in the sources does this come from? Quote the exact relevant passages." NotebookLM will surface the relevant material, often more precisely than the original output did.

The Patterns of Subtle Error

A few patterns of error that show up regularly, worth recognizing:

Paraphrase drift. The source says X with a specific qualifier. The summary says X without the qualifier, making the claim broader and stronger than the original.

Inverse implications. The source notes that researchers haven't found evidence of Y. The summary says Y is true. The model flipped the meaning.

Conflation across sources. The source on screen doesn't address the topic, but a different source does. The model conflated, citing the wrong passage.

Selective citation. The source contains a balanced discussion of two positions. The summary cites only the side that supports its narrative, omitting the qualifying material from the same source.

Composite quotes. The summary attributes a "direct quote" to the source, but the quoted phrase is assembled from words appearing in the source rather than a contiguous passage.

Confident interpretation. The source describes something tentatively, with caveats. The summary states it definitively, dropping the hedging.

Plausible filler. The source addresses the topic only briefly. The summary includes substantial detail that *sounds* sourced but is actually generic information the model is confident enough to add.

Once you've spotted these a few times, you'll start seeing them coming. Verification gets faster because you know where to look.

Building the Verification Habit

If verification doesn't come naturally, a few practices help internalize it:

Make it part of the workflow. Every time you generate a Studio output, plan to verify it. Block the time. Don't treat verification as optional or "if I have time."

Track errors when you find them. Keep a brief note when verification catches a real error. Over time you'll calibrate your sense of how often errors happen, which makes verification feel necessary rather than paranoid.

Treat verification as the final 20% of the work. A Briefing Doc isn't done when NotebookLM finishes generating it. It's done when you've verified it. Build that 20% into your time estimates.

Verify in pairs when possible. If you have a colleague or collaborator, a second person spot-checking catches errors that single-reader verification misses.

Verify before sharing, always. "Sent to a colleague unverified" is the moment errors propagate beyond your own work into others' decisions. Verify before you ship.

The Trust Calibration

The right relationship with NotebookLM, after all this, is neither blind trust nor dismissive skepticism. It's calibrated trust:

- **High trust** for what NotebookLM does well: synthesis structure, source identification, finding what's relevant, generating starting drafts.
- **Provisional trust** for specific claims and exact paraphrases: useful as a starting point, requires verification.
- **Low trust** for direct quotations and precise factual assertions: high error rate; verify directly against the source.

This calibration applies to all AI output, not just NotebookLM's. But it matters more for source-grounded AI, because the visible grounding can create a misleading sense that verification is unnecessary.

Why This Discipline Matters

The verification habit isn't a personal preference. It's the discipline that lets AI assistance produce work you can stand behind.

Without verification, you're producing AI output and putting your name on it. You don't know if it's accurate. The polish hides the uncertainty. Eventually errors will get through. Your colleagues, your readers, your clients will catch one. Your professional credibility takes a hit you may not notice until it's eroded badly.

With verification, you're producing accurate work that AI helped you produce faster. The output is grounded in what the sources actually say. When you cite the work, you can defend it. When someone challenges a claim, you can point to the supporting passage. The AI was a tool; the responsibility, accuracy, and judgment are yours.

This is what professional use of NotebookLM looks like. Not "I had AI write it." Not "I trusted the AI's output." But "I used AI assistance, I verified it, and the work is mine."

The discipline costs minutes. The credibility it preserves is everything.

That closes Part V. You now have the three disciplines that turn NotebookLM from a powerful tool into a reliable working partner: source curation as ongoing practice, prompting with the rigor the model rewards, and verification as the non-negotiable final step.

Part VI applies all of this to specific audiences — students, researchers, knowledge workers, content creators. The same principles, calibrated for the shapes of work each audience does.

Part VI: NotebookLM for Your World

"A tool is only as good as the hand that wields it."

— Proverb

Chapter 24: NotebookLM for Students

For a tool that wasn't originally designed as an educational product, NotebookLM has become one of the most consequential study aids of the AI era. Source grounding, automated study materials (Flashcards, Quizzes, Study Guides), Audio Overviews for listening on the go, and the ability to build a working knowledge base from a course's actual readings have made it a daily companion for serious students at every level.

It has also raised real questions about academic integrity, what counts as authentic learning, and where AI assistance helps versus substitutes for the work students are supposed to do themselves.

This chapter covers both: how to use NotebookLM well as a student, and how to think about the lines that matter.

Why NotebookLM Fits Studying

Most general-purpose AI tools — ChatGPT, Claude, Gemini — are tempting for students but problematic in specific ways. They'll write your essay for you. They'll answer your homework problems. They'll often answer them wrong, plausibly enough that you don't notice. They make it easy to substitute AI work for your own learning, which is the opposite of what studying is for.

NotebookLM is different by design. It works from sources you provide — your textbook, your lecture notes, your assigned readings. It can't write your essay because it doesn't know enough outside those sources to do so. It can help you understand the sources, organize them, generate study materials from them, and verify your understanding against them. The structure makes the AI more like a tutor and less like a ghostwriter.

This isn't an accident. Source-grounded AI is the kind of AI that pedagogy can live with.

Building a Course Notebook

The foundational pattern: one notebook per course. Into that notebook go:

- **The textbook** (or chapters from it as you progress)
- **Lecture slides** (uploaded or pulled from your school's LMS as PDFs)
- **Lecture recordings** (where available, as audio sources — NotebookLM transcribes automatically)
- **Assigned readings** (papers, articles, book excerpts)
- **Your own lecture notes** (uploaded as documents or written directly as Notes)
- **Past exams or problem sets** (if available, as primary review material)

What you don't include: solutions to current problem sets, AI-generated answers to current questions, anything that substitutes AI for the assigned work itself.

The result is a notebook containing everything the course expects you to know, organized by your own hand, with citation-grounded synthesis available on demand.

Daily Study Workflows

A few workflows that compound over a semester:

Pre-Reading

Before reading an assigned text, generate an Audio Overview and listen on the way to class or over breakfast. It gives you the lay of the land — main argument, structure, key terms — so when you sit down to read carefully, you have a scaffold to hang the details on.

This isn't a substitute for reading. It's a primer. The actual reading goes faster and sticks better when you're not constructing the whole context from scratch as you go.

Active Review

After reading, generate Flashcards from the text. Use them for active recall — quiz yourself, mark the cards you missed, come back to them. The active-recall research is unambiguous: testing yourself produces far more durable learning than re-reading.

NotebookLM's Flashcards aren't as feature-rich as dedicated spaced-repetition tools (Anki, Quizlet, RemNote) — they don't currently export cleanly to those tools, and they don't implement spaced-repetition scheduling natively. But for in-the-moment review, they work. For students who want spaced repetition, copy the cards into your tool of choice.

Concept Mastery Checks

For dense conceptual material, generate a Quiz to test whether you've absorbed it. Take the quiz. Note which questions you missed. Re-read the relevant sections.

This is one of the highest-leverage study habits NotebookLM enables. Generating a custom quiz from your own course materials used to be friction-heavy enough that nobody did it; now it takes minutes.

Study-Guide Synthesis

Before exams, generate a Study Guide from the relevant course materials. Use a focus prompt to calibrate it: *"Generate a study guide for an undergraduate intro [subject] final exam. Cover all major topics from these sources. Include key terms with definitions, the main concepts and how they connect, and 10 practice discussion questions."*

The output is a structured review document grounded in your actual course material — not a generic AI study guide, but one calibrated to what your professor assigned.

Office-Hours Prep

Before going to office hours, use NotebookLM chat to identify exactly which concepts you don't understand. Ask: *"What are the most subtle or commonly misunderstood points in this material? Where would a student typically get tripped up?"*

This produces a list of likely confusion points. Identify which ones map to your own. Bring those specific questions to office hours instead of the vague "I don't get this." Your professor will give you better help, and you'll get more out of the time.

Lecture Capture and Review

If you can record lectures (with appropriate permission — check your school's policy), upload the audio as a source. NotebookLM transcribes it. You can then chat across multiple lectures, identify themes, and build Study Guides that span a whole semester rather than a single class.

For students with attention or note-taking challenges, this can be transformative. The transcription captures what you missed in the moment, and the chat interface lets you find specific moments later ("when did the professor talk about [topic]?").

Subject-Specific Patterns

Different subjects reward different uses:

Humanities and social sciences. NotebookLM is excellent for synthesis across primary and secondary sources. Build a notebook for each major topic or paper assignment, with the primary texts plus your secondary sources. Use chat for cross-source comparison and Briefing Docs for paper outlines.

STEM coursework. NotebookLM is less helpful for problem-solving (use ChatGPT or Claude for that, with appropriate care about academic integrity) but strong for conceptual understanding. Build notebooks for the conceptual material; use Quizzes and Study Guides aggressively. For problem sets, work the problems yourself first, then use NotebookLM to verify your understanding by asking it to explain the underlying concepts.

Languages. Audio Overviews in your target language, drawn from sources you understand in your native language, are a remarkable language-learning tool. Generate Quizzes in the target language for vocabulary review. Use the cross-language synthesis features to compare how a concept is expressed across different linguistic traditions.

Professional school (law, medicine, business). NotebookLM shines for case-based learning. Build notebooks for each course's case set or core readings. Generate comparative Briefing Docs across cases. Use Mind Maps to visualize the case law or framework you're learning. Generate Study Guides per course unit.

The Academic Integrity Question

This is the section to read carefully.

Different schools, different programs, and different professors have different rules about AI assistance. Some prohibit it outright. Some require disclosure. Some accept it for some uses and not others. *Know your specific rules.* What follows is general principles, not a substitute for your school's policy.

The principles I'd argue for:

AI for understanding is generally fine. Using NotebookLM to summarize, explain, generate Study Guides and Flashcards, and prepare for exams — these are tools for learning, not substitutes for it. They're not meaningfully different from reading a different summary, joining a study group, or using flashcards a friend made. The intellectual work — taking the exam, writing the paper, doing the problem set — is still yours.

AI for substitution is generally not fine. Using ChatGPT to write your essay, AI to do your homework, NotebookLM to generate the answers you'll submit as your own — these substitute AI work for the work you're supposed to do. They constitute academic dishonesty under most reasonable interpretations of the term.

The line is not always clean. Some uses are ambiguous. If you use NotebookLM to generate an outline and then write the paper yourself from it, is that AI assistance or AI substitution? Reasonable people disagree. The conservative answer is to disclose, ask, and err on the side of doing the work yourself.

Disclosure is your friend. If you're using NotebookLM in a way that might be questionable, disclose it. "I used NotebookLM to generate study materials from the assigned readings" is a defensible disclosure. "I used AI to help me organize my thinking, then wrote the paper myself" is a defensible disclosure. Hidden AI use is the dangerous kind — even when the use itself was acceptable.

Age-Appropriate Use

NotebookLM is, by Google's terms, intended for users 13+. For younger students (with parental supervision), the source-grounded nature makes it less risky than general chatbots — but parental supervision still matters.

A few age-appropriate principles:

Younger students benefit most from passive consumption. Audio Overviews of age-appropriate source material can be excellent learning tools. Younger learners shouldn't be the primary curators; an adult should be.

Middle and high school students can curate their own notebooks with guidance, especially for project-based learning. Help them think about source quality. Help them build the verification habit early.

The verification discipline (Chapter 23) matters more for students, not less. The professional consequences of trusting AI output uncritically are eventually painful. The educational consequences are formative — bad habits internalized at 16 are hard to unlearn at 30.

What NotebookLM Doesn't Replace

A few things NotebookLM is not, even at its best:

A substitute for reading. Audio Overviews and Briefing Docs are useful, but the deep reading required for real understanding still has to happen. Treat NotebookLM outputs as scaffolding for reading, not a replacement.

A substitute for thinking. Studying isn't just absorbing information; it's working through it, struggling with it, building your own mental models. NotebookLM can support that work but can't do it for you.

A substitute for human teachers. Office hours, study groups, conversations with professors and TAs — these are where confused students become unconfused. NotebookLM is helpful between those conversations, not instead of them.

A substitute for writing your own work. What you turn in has to be yours — in voice, in argument, in the actual sentences. NotebookLM can help you understand source material; what you do with that understanding is still your job.

A Practical Walkthrough: Preparing for an Exam

Suppose you're an undergraduate facing a final exam in a content-heavy course. You have three weeks. You have the textbook (15 chapters), lecture slides for 30 lectures, assigned readings (12 papers), and your own notes.

Week 1 — build the notebook. Set up a course notebook. Upload everything in batches as you review each unit. Rename sources clearly. Verify auto-generated summaries.

Week 2 — active study cycle.

For each major unit: 1. Read the relevant material directly. 2. Generate Flashcards on the unit. Use them for active recall. 3. Generate a Quiz on the unit. Take it. Note misses. Re-study weak spots. 4. Use chat to ask "What are the most subtly tricky points in this material?" — adjust your study based on the answer. 5. Capture confusions as Notes for later.

Week 3 — synthesis and exam prep.

1. Generate a comprehensive Study Guide across the whole course with a focus prompt: *"Generate a final exam study guide. Cover all major topics. For each, include key concepts, common misconceptions, and the kinds of questions that would test deep understanding."*
2. Generate Audio Overviews of the major units. Listen to one per day on your commute or workouts.
3. Re-take the per-unit Quizzes to confirm retention.
4. Use chat to do exam-style practice: *"Give me three essay-style exam questions on [topic] and grade my responses."*
5. The day before: scan the Study Guide one final time. Sleep.

You've turned a content-heavy course into a structured study system, with multiple complementary review modes anchored to your actual course materials. The work is still yours — you're the one absorbing, recalling, applying. NotebookLM is the scaffolding that made it tractable.

What This Adds Up To

For students serious about learning (as opposed to students serious about credentials), NotebookLM is one of the most valuable tools to emerge from the AI era. It rewards the habits that have always made for good students — careful sourcing, active recall, deliberate review, real engagement with the material — and amplifies them.

For students focused only on getting the assignment done, NotebookLM is a poor cheat code. It won't write your essays well. It won't reliably do your problem sets. It will help you fake some kinds of understanding superficially — and fail you when the real exam comes.

The good news: serious learning has always been the more rewarding path, and NotebookLM makes it more accessible than it's ever been.

The next chapter applies the same principles to the closely related world of academic research, where the stakes shift from passing exams to producing original contributions to a field.

Chapter 25: NotebookLM for Researchers and Academics

If students were the unexpected early-adopter audience for NotebookLM, researchers and academics were the predicted one. The product's pitch — read your sources, synthesize across them, ground every answer in citations — describes what working researchers do every day. The moment NotebookLM appeared in stable form, academic Twitter, research-method newsletters, and graduate-student forums lit up with workflows, tips, and use cases.

By early 2026, NotebookLM is changing how some kinds of research get done. Literature reviews that took months can be scaffolded in days. Cross-paper synthesis that required hours of careful side-by-side reading can be drafted in minutes (then verified in hours, but the time savings remain substantial). Exploratory work in adjacent fields — historically gated by the cost of catching up — has gotten meaningfully cheaper.

This chapter covers what works, what doesn't, and the patterns that have emerged in the research community.

Where NotebookLM Fits in the Research Workflow

Research is a multi-stage process: identify a question, survey existing work, design and execute new investigation, analyze results, write up. NotebookLM helps most with the survey and write-up stages, less with the new-investigation stage.

Strong fits: - Literature review (drafting, not finishing) - Cross-paper synthesis and gap-finding - Building structured understanding of unfamiliar adjacent fields - Generating draft sections from your own source material - Citation-traceable summaries for grant proposals or related-work sections - Conference and journal scanning — staying current on a field without reading everything end to end

Weak fits: - Original empirical work (NotebookLM doesn't do experiments or analysis) - Mathematical and formal work (use ChatGPT/Claude for that, with care) - Real-time collaborative writing (NotebookLM has some collaboration, but it's not Google Docs) - Citation management as a publication tool (use Zotero, Mendeley, or your institutional tool)

The right way to think about it: NotebookLM is a research *thinking* tool, not a research *production* tool. It helps you understand the literature; you still write the papers, run the experiments, and do the analysis.

Literature Reviews

This is NotebookLM's killer use case for academic work. The traditional literature review is one of the most time-intensive parts of research. You collect papers. You read each one. You take notes. You compare across them. You identify themes. You spot gaps. You synthesize. A serious review can take weeks or months.

NotebookLM compresses the synthesis steps dramatically while preserving the rigor that makes a real literature review valuable.

A workflow that's emerged across many research communities:

Phase 1: Source assembly. Collect papers as you normally would. The set should be reasonably complete (enough to be representative) and reasonably curated (high-quality work, not everything that mentions your keywords). Fifteen to fifty papers is the sweet spot for a single notebook.

Phase 2: Notebook construction. Upload all papers to a dedicated notebook. Rename sources with `Author (Year) — Short title` patterns. Verify auto-generated summaries.

Phase 3: Cross-paper exploration. Use chat to traverse the literature: - *"What are the main theoretical frameworks across these papers? Which papers represent each?"* - *"How has [specific concept] been operationalized across different studies? Where do operationalizations diverge?"* - *"What methodologies dominate this literature? What methodologies are conspicuously absent?"* - *"Which papers cite each other? What does the citation pattern reveal about how the literature has developed?"*

Each query produces a structured answer with citations to the relevant papers. Save the useful answers as Notes.

Phase 4: Gap-finding. Use chat specifically for what's missing: - *"What questions does this literature consistently fail to address?"* - *"What populations* *or contexts are underrepresented?" - "Where is the evidence weakest, and what kind of new study would strengthen it?"*

This is powerful. NotebookLM's pattern-finding across sources extends to patterns of absence — and gap-finding is where new research questions come from.

Phase 5: Synthesis writing. Generate Briefing Docs or Custom Reports for specific sections of the eventual review: - *"Generate a 1500-word literature review section covering [theme], grounded in the relevant sources. Match the conventions of [target journal or field]. Cite specifically."*

Treat these as drafts to be substantially revised — not finished prose, but scaffolding that captures the structure and the citations.

Phase 6: Verification. Every claim that will appear in your final review needs verification. Click citations. Read the cited passages. Confirm the support. The discipline from Chapter 23 is non-negotiable here.

The end result: a literature review that took weeks rather than months, with the same rigor — because the time-intensive synthesis steps were AI-scaffolded while the rigorous verification stayed human.

Cross-Paper Synthesis

Beyond formal literature reviews, NotebookLM is excellent for the everyday cross-paper work that academics constantly do. Comparing methods across two new papers in your area. Reconciling apparently conflicting findings from three studies. Tracking how a specific debate has evolved across recent issues of a journal.

For these smaller, ongoing tasks, the workflow is faster still:

1. Add the relevant papers to a topic-specific notebook (or a "current reading" notebook for general scanning).
2. Ask the synthesis question directly.
3. Verify any claims that will inform your work.

The cumulative effect is substantial. Over a year, a researcher who uses NotebookLM regularly will have read across more papers, in more depth, with better cross-comparison, than would otherwise have been possible.

Generating Draft Section Text

For working researchers writing papers, NotebookLM can produce drafts of certain section types — related-work sections, methodology summaries, background sections — that are faster to revise than to write from scratch.

The pattern:

1. Build a notebook with the relevant sources for the section you're writing.
2. Generate a Custom Report with a precise specification: *"Generate a related-work section for a [field] paper on [topic]. Approximately [length]. Match the conventions of [target journal]. Cite the sources I've provided. Use [voice characteristics]."*
3. Treat the output as a starting draft. Edit substantially — for voice, for argument, for the specific points NotebookLM didn't capture.
4. Verify every citation before submitting.

This is faster than writing from a blank page. It also carries real risks — to authorial integrity (you're presenting AI-drafted text as your own) and to accuracy (AI-generated paragraphs can subtly misrepresent the cited work). The "edit substantially" and "verify every citation" steps are non-negotiable.

For sections requiring original argument or analysis — the discussion section of an empirical paper, the contribution-framing of an introduction, the interpretive work in a humanities paper — write from scratch. NotebookLM doesn't do original argument well. It synthesizes; it doesn't argue.

Citation Tracing for Accountability

A surprising secondary use of NotebookLM in research: it makes citation tracing dramatically easier.

When reading a paper that makes a claim grounded in another work, the traditional process — find the cited paper, read the relevant section, check whether it actually supports the claim — has historically been costly enough that most readers skip it. They trust the citation.

With NotebookLM, the workflow shrinks: add the cited paper to a notebook, ask "does this paper support the claim that [X]?" — and you have a usable answer in seconds. For high-stakes citation work — peer review, replication assessments, anything that depends on accurate sourcing — this enables a level of rigor that was previously impractical.

Working Across Languages and Disciplines

NotebookLM's multilingual capabilities (Chapter 19) matter especially for cross-disciplinary and international research. A few specific use cases:

Cross-language literature. Researchers reading work in languages other than English can build notebooks with original-language sources and produce English-language synthesis without first translating each paper.

Cross-disciplinary translation. A researcher in one field reading work from an adjacent field often struggles with disciplinary jargon and conventions. NotebookLM can produce explanations calibrated to the reader's home discipline: *"Explain this paper's argument in terms a [other-field] researcher would understand, mapping the key terms to [other-field] equivalents."*

Historical research. Primary source material in older languages or registers becomes more tractable. NotebookLM can synthesize across historical sources without losing temporal context, and can produce contemporary-language summaries that preserve what the originals actually said.

The 2026 Voice-Cloning Lawsuit and What It Means

In 2026, journalist David Greene filed a lawsuit alleging that NotebookLM's Audio Overview voice models reproduced his voice without consent. Google has denied the claim. As of this writing the case is unresolved.

For academic users, this matters in a few ways:

Voice attribution. If you're using Audio Overviews in any context where the voices might be perceived as belonging to specific individuals (a course you teach, a research presentation, a publication), be aware that the legal status of the underlying voice models is still being worked out. Standard disclosure is wise.

Source representation. The lawsuit is, in part, about whether AI representations of source material accurately represent the source. For research use, this connects directly to citation-verification discipline. The same care you take with text outputs should apply to audio.

Institutional policy. Some universities and research institutions have begun developing policies on AI tool use in research. These policies are evolving rapidly. Check what your institution requires for disclosure, attribution, and permitted uses.

The general principle: use NotebookLM in ways you can defend openly. If a use would be embarrassing if it became public, reconsider.

Disclosure and Attribution

Different research communities handle AI disclosure differently. Some require explicit disclosure of any AI assistance. Some require disclosure only for substantial assistance. Some leave it to authorial judgment.

A baseline practice that holds up in most contexts:

- **Disclose AI tool use in your methods section** (or equivalent): which tools, for what purposes, at what stages of the work.
- **Don't list AI tools as authors.** They aren't.
- **Verify AI-assisted content against primary sources.** What's in your paper is your responsibility.
- **Be conservative about hidden use.** When in doubt, disclose.

For the kind of research-support use this chapter has covered — building a notebook of papers, using NotebookLM for synthesis and exploration — disclosure is simple and low-stakes. For more ambitious uses (drafting substantial portions of papers, generating analytical content, producing publication-ready outputs), the disclosure obligation is heavier and the verification obligation heavier still.

A Practical Walkthrough: Starting a Literature Review

Suppose you're a graduate student starting a dissertation literature review on a moderately specific topic. You've identified roughly 40 papers as the core literature.

Week 1. Build the notebook. Upload all 40 papers. Rename sources clearly. Spend two days reading the auto-generated summaries to confirm each ingested correctly and start building familiarity.

Week 2. Cross-paper exploration. Ask systematic questions across the literature — methodologies, theoretical frameworks, empirical findings, contested points, historical evolution. Save useful answers as Notes. Identify the major themes the review needs to cover.

Week 3. Per-theme deep work. For each major theme, generate a Custom Report drafting that section of the eventual review. Edit each draft substantially, weaving in your own argument and context. Verify every citation.

Week 4. Gap analysis and contribution framing. Use NotebookLM to identify what's not in the literature. Compare to what your own work will contribute. Draft the contribution framing in your own voice (NotebookLM is a poor tool here — it can describe what's there, not argue for what should be).

Week 5. Verification pass. Click every citation in your draft. Confirm support. Catch the subtle paraphrase errors. Fix.

Week 6. Polish, get feedback from your advisor, revise.

What used to be a six-month project becomes a six-week project, with comparable rigor — because the rigor was preserved at the verification stage while the synthesis stage was scaffolded.

What Working Researchers Are Actually Doing

A few patterns from the academic NotebookLM community as of early 2026:

- **Reading group notebooks.** Shared notebooks where research groups upload the week's readings and chat collaboratively.

- **Conference notebooks.** Notebooks built around the proceedings of a conference, used for catching up rapidly afterward.
- **Topic notebooks.** Long-running notebooks on specific research interests, accumulating sources over time.
- **Journal-scanning notebooks.** Notebooks refreshed monthly with the latest issue of key journals, with Audio Overviews generated for commute listening.
- **Method notebooks.** Notebooks dedicated to specific methods (multilevel modeling, qualitative coding, specific computational approaches), built up across many methodological papers.

These are all variations on the same underlying workflow: source-grounded AI as research support, calibrated to specific kinds of academic work.

What This Means for the Field

NotebookLM is changing what's possible in research, in ways that haven't fully shaken out yet. Some likely effects:

- **Higher baseline literature awareness.** Researchers who use NotebookLM well will track more literature than was previously possible.
- **Faster cross-disciplinary work.** The cost of engaging with adjacent fields drops substantially.
- **Higher pressure on novelty.** When more is read, the bar for genuine contribution rises.
- **More attention to citation quality.** As verification gets cheaper, the carelessness with which some published work has cited supporting sources becomes more visible.
- **New questions about what counts as authorship.** As AI assistance gets more capable, the boundary lines will continue to evolve.

These effects are happening with or without any individual researcher's input. The question isn't whether to engage with the shift but how to do so in a way that supports — rather than undermines — the integrity of research.

The next chapter shifts from the academic context to the broader knowledge-worker context — analysts, consultants, internal researchers, anyone whose job involves making sense of large amounts of source material on a recurring basis.

Chapter 26: NotebookLM for Knowledge Workers and Analysts

Most of the people who get the most value from NotebookLM aren't students or academics. They're knowledge workers — analysts, consultants, internal researchers, strategy leads, compliance officers, product managers, lawyers, anyone whose job centers on turning piles of source material into briefings, recommendations, and decisions.

The job has a recognizable shape across industries: read a lot of documents, synthesize what they say, produce something useful from the synthesis (a brief, a memo, a recommendation, a decision-support document), repeat. NotebookLM is exceptionally well-suited to this shape.

This chapter covers the patterns that work for knowledge work specifically — different from student or academic patterns, different from content-creator patterns, calibrated to the realities of corporate, consulting, and internal-research contexts.

The Knowledge Worker's Source Reality

Most knowledge workers don't have the luxury of curating their source set carefully. The sources arrive: a stakeholder sends a 60-page report. A regulator publishes a 200-page proposed rule. A vendor delivers a stack of materials. A leader asks for a perspective on whatever just happened in the news. Input is fast and varied; the output expectation is fast and high-quality.

This means the curation discipline from Chapter 21 has to compress. Instead of spending hours carefully selecting sources, the typical pattern is:

- The sources come with the assignment
- You evaluate them quickly for credibility and relevance
- You add supplementary sources only when clearly necessary
- You move to synthesis fast because that's what's being asked for

NotebookLM accommodates this rhythm well. The speed at which you can move from "here's a stack of documents" to "here's the key insight" is one of its highest-value capabilities for working professionals.

Common Knowledge-Worker Workflows

A few patterns that come up repeatedly:

The Briefing Pipeline

Recurring scenario: you need to brief someone (a manager, a client, an executive, a colleague) on something they don't have time to read. The briefing has to be accurate, structured, and calibrated to the audience.

Workflow:

1. Build a focused notebook with the source material the briefing is about.
2. Identify the specific audience: what do they care about, what do they already know, what level of detail do they want?
3. Generate a Briefing Doc with a precise focus prompt that captures the audience: *"For [specific person/role]. Focus on [their specific concerns]. Skip [things they don't need]. Length: [target]."*
4. Verify every load-bearing citation.
5. Edit for voice, add your own framing where the AI's framing doesn't quite fit.
6. Optionally generate an Audio Overview of the same material for them to listen to in transit.

Done well, this takes 30–60 minutes for source material that would otherwise eat a half-day. Done badly (skipping verification, using the AI output without editing), it produces briefings that look polished and contain subtle errors that eventually surface.

The Comparison Analysis

Scenario: you need to compare options, vendors, approaches, frameworks, jurisdictions, or time periods. Source material exists for each. The task is structured comparison.

Workflow:

1. Build a notebook with sources covering each option being compared.
2. Use chat to ask explicit comparison questions: *"Compare options A, B, and C on dimensions [X, Y, Z]. For each dimension, note where each option stands and which sources support that assessment."*
3. Generate a Data Table for the structured comparison: *"Build a comparison table across the options, with columns for [specific dimensions]. Cite each cell."*
4. Generate a Briefing Doc that frames the comparison narratively: *"Produce an analysis of these options for [decision-maker]. Identify the trade-offs. Make a defensible recommendation if the sources support one."*

This turns scattered source material into structured analysis fast, while preserving the citation chain back to the originals.

The Postmortem and Retrospective

After a project, outage, incident, or campaign, knowledge workers often produce structured retrospectives. The source material — meeting notes, decision documents, communications, logs — is typically scattered and voluminous.

Workflow:

1. Build a notebook with all the relevant source material.
2. Generate a Timeline to organize events chronologically.
3. Use chat to identify decision points, key turning moments, what went well and what went badly.
4. Generate a Briefing Doc with the standard retrospective structure (situation, what happened, what worked, what didn't, recommendations).
5. Iterate based on the conversations the draft prompts.

NotebookLM is particularly useful here because retrospectives often span more material than any one person remembers in detail. The AI doesn't have memory issues — it sees all the source material equally.

The Recurring Industry Brief

Many knowledge workers produce recurring briefings — a weekly market update, a monthly competitive scan, a quarterly regulatory tracker. The work is repetitive but high-stakes; readers come to depend on the briefings being current and accurate.

Workflow:

1. Build a notebook for the recurring brief. Add foundational sources that don't change (key reference documents, baseline analyses).
2. Each cycle, add the new source material that's emerged.
3. Use a saved customization template to generate the brief in your established format.
4. Verify and edit; ship.

The notebook accumulates over time. The template captures the format. The marginal effort per brief drops dramatically once the system is set up.

The Quick Lookup

Sometimes you just need to know what some specific document says about some specific topic. Open the notebook, ask the question, get the answer with citations. Verify if it matters; move on.

This is the most underrated NotebookLM workflow for knowledge work. The cumulative time savings — across hundreds of small lookups a month that no longer require finding and skimming the source — is substantial.

Internal Documents Specifically

A particular case that matters for many knowledge workers: working with internal documents — handbooks, runbooks, postmortems, decision records, internal research, prior briefings.

For organizations standardized on Google Workspace, NotebookLM offers a particularly clean fit. Workspace accounts get stronger data protections; Google Drive integration means internal docs can be added without leaving the ecosystem; the audit and admin controls common in enterprise Workspace deployments apply.

Patterns that have emerged in some organizations:

Departmental knowledge notebooks. A shared notebook (Plus tier or higher) containing the department's reference materials. New employees chat with it during onboarding. Existing employees reference it for institutional knowledge.

Project history notebooks. Long-running notebooks that accumulate across the lifetime of a project — initial scoping documents, decision records, status reports, postmortems. New team members joining mid-project can get up to speed quickly.

Compliance and policy notebooks. Notebooks containing the organization's regulatory and policy material, queried by compliance officers, legal teams, and product managers as questions come up.

The risks: organizational data going into AI tools is sensitive, often subject to internal policies and sometimes to regulatory constraints. Before adopting NotebookLM as part of your workflow at work, check your organization's AI policy. For Workspace-managed accounts, your administrator may have already established parameters; for personal accounts used for work, the question is more open.

Industry-Specific Notes

A few specific notes for common knowledge-work contexts:

Consulting. NotebookLM is excellent for engagement-specific notebooks — client materials, market data, prior deliverables. Build one notebook per engagement; archive at engagement end. Use it to compress the read-in phase of new projects.

Legal. NotebookLM handles long legal documents (contracts, regulations, case law, depositions) well. Citation discipline matters here — legal interpretation depends on precise language, and AI paraphrase can lose the legal significance. Use NotebookLM for orientation and synthesis; verify rigorously before relying.

Financial analysis. Earnings reports, analyst reports, regulatory filings, market commentary — all are excellent NotebookLM material. The Data Table output is useful for extracting structured financial data across reports. Be cautious about treating extracted data as analysis-ready without verification.

Compliance and risk. Regulatory documents are dense, often interrelated, and frequently revised. NotebookLM excels at cross-regulation comparison, identifying where requirements overlap or diverge, and producing audit-friendly briefings. Verification discipline is non-negotiable for compliance work.

Product management. Customer research, competitor analysis, internal data, user interviews — all benefit from NotebookLM-style synthesis. Use it to maintain awareness of what's known across your team without requiring everyone to read everything.

Strategy and corporate development. Market reports, M&A targets, internal strategic documents — NotebookLM enables faster orientation and deeper cross-document analysis than was previously practical.

The Verification Discipline at Work

The citation-verification habit (Chapter 23) takes a specific shape in knowledge work: it has to be calibrated to stakes.

For a quick internal lookup, light verification is fine. For a briefing that will inform an executive decision, exhaustive verification is mandatory. For a client deliverable, verification is part of the professional responsibility you're being paid to provide.

A useful framing: imagine the worst plausible outcome of an error in your output. Brief your CEO on a competitive trend that turns out to be misreported? Embarrassing, recoverable. Recommend a vendor based on a misreading of their compliance posture? Bigger problem. Misinterpret a regulatory requirement and ship policy guidance based on it? Career-defining problem.

The verification effort should match the worst plausible consequence. For high-stakes work, treat AI-assisted output as a draft that needs editorial validation, not as a finished product.

Time Calibration

A common knowledge-worker mistake: assuming NotebookLM speeds up the *whole* process equally. It doesn't.

It speeds up: - Initial source ingestion and orientation - Cross-document synthesis - Generating draft outputs in standard formats - Quick lookups and reference questions

It doesn't (much) speed up: - Verification (which still takes the time it takes) - Editing for voice and final framing - Original analysis and judgment - Stakeholder communication and revision cycles

A realistic estimate for AI-assisted knowledge work: 30% time savings on initial absorption and synthesis, modest savings on draft production, none on verification and revision. The net effect is significant — often 25–40% total savings on the kinds of work AI can scaffold — but not the 80–90% that less-grounded users sometimes claim.

A Practical Walkthrough: Pre-Meeting Briefing

Suppose you're an analyst preparing for a strategy meeting in two hours. Your manager has just sent you 80 pages of materials — a competitor's earnings report, two analyst notes about that competitor, and an internal market update. You need to produce a one-page briefing for the meeting.

0–15 minutes: setup. Build a focused notebook. Upload all four sources. Rename clearly. Check the auto-generated summaries to confirm correct ingestion.

15–30 minutes: exploration. Use chat to identify key facts and themes. Ask: *"What's the most important takeaway from each source? Where do the sources agree, where do they diverge? What signals matter most for our positioning?"* Save useful answers as Notes.

30–50 minutes: drafting. Generate a Briefing Doc with the focus prompt: *"One-page strategic briefing for the [team] meeting today. Focus on competitive implications, what we should be watching for, and any decision points that emerge from the materials. Skip background — assume the audience knows the company. Punchy and specific."*

50–90 minutes: verification and editing. Click every citation. Confirm support for every load-bearing claim. Edit for voice; add your own framing where the AI's is generic. Tighten.

90–105 minutes: optional Audio Overview. Generate a brief Audio Overview to listen to on the way to the meeting, reinforcing what you've internalized.

105–120 minutes: walk to meeting, mentally rehearse.

You've turned 80 pages of source material into a meeting-ready briefing in two hours, with the verification discipline that makes it trustworthy. Without NotebookLM, the same work would have meant skimming, missing things, and showing up under-prepared. With it, you arrive ready.

The Long Game

For working knowledge workers, the highest-leverage NotebookLM use isn't any single workflow — it's the cumulative effect of building the habits over months and years.

Source curation discipline. Verification discipline. Customization templates that capture your team's patterns. A library of notebooks that accumulates organizational knowledge. The compounding effect of every brief, every analysis, every recommendation being a little faster and a little better than it would have been without the scaffolding.

A year of consistent NotebookLM use, applied to real knowledge work, doesn't just save time. It changes what's possible — in the volume of material you can engage with and the depth at which you can engage it. For knowledge workers, that compounding is the actual value.

The next chapter looks at the audience that has, in some ways, gotten the most public attention from NotebookLM's launch: content creators, podcasters, and the producers building public-facing material with AI assistance.

Chapter 27: NotebookLM for Content Creators

When NotebookLM's Audio Overviews went viral in late 2024, the loudest celebrants were content creators. Podcasters posted about generating episode-length audio in minutes. Newsletter writers showed off briefings produced from research stacks they hadn't touched yet. Educators demonstrated lesson plans built from textbook chapters with one click. The hype cycle was, briefly, intense.

The reality has been more nuanced. NotebookLM is transformative for some content workflows. For others, it's a useful tool that needs heavy human work on top. For still others, it's tempting but ultimately the wrong choice — producing AI-generated content that adds to the slop flooding the open web.

This chapter is for creators who want to use NotebookLM well: where it actually helps, where the line is between assistance and substitution, and how to think about disclosure, attribution, and the ethics of AI-assisted content.

What "Content Creator" Means Here

Broad audience: podcasters, video creators, newsletter writers, educators producing course material, internal corporate communicators, agency content teams, social media producers, marketers, anyone whose primary output is content meant to be consumed by an external audience.

The shared shape: source material exists. Output material needs to be produced from it. Audience expectations about quality, voice, originality, and attribution apply.

Where NotebookLM Genuinely Helps

A few specific creator workflows where NotebookLM is unambiguously useful:

Research-to-Episode Pipelines for Podcasters

A common podcaster workflow: research a topic deeply, then record an episode discussing it. The research phase traditionally meant reading papers, articles, and books, taking notes, then organizing those notes into a script or outline.

With NotebookLM, the pipeline compresses dramatically:

1. Build a notebook of research sources for the episode topic
2. Use chat to explore the territory, identify the most interesting threads, find the contested points
3. Generate a Briefing Doc as the foundation for your episode outline
4. Generate an Audio Overview as a starting point — and then either use it as a reference for your own recording or, in some cases, edit and incorporate excerpts (with appropriate disclosure)
5. Record your episode with the AI-assisted research as scaffolding

The "use it as a reference for your own recording" path is safer. Recording your own audio means the episode has your voice, your perspective, your judgment — even though the underlying research was AI-scaffolded. The "incorporate excerpts" path requires more careful disclosure and runs into watermarking and the audio-quality limits of AI-generated voice.

Newsletter and Blog Production

For writers producing recurring written content (newsletters, blogs, internal communications), NotebookLM accelerates the research-and-draft cycle:

1. Build a notebook for the topic
2. Generate a Briefing Doc as a starting research summary
3. Use chat for cross-source synthesis on the angles that interest you most
4. Write the actual piece in your own voice, using the AI synthesis as scaffolding rather than as content

The output is a piece written by you — informed by research that was substantially faster than reading everything end to end yourself.

The alternative — publishing AI-generated drafts with light editing — produces the generic, characterless content that has become the bulk of the open web in the AI era. Don't do that.

Educational Content

Educators producing course material — slide decks, video lessons, study guides — can use NotebookLM as a structural scaffold:

1. Build notebooks for each course unit with the foundational source material
2. Use NotebookLM to generate Study Guides, Mind Maps, and Slide Decks as starting structures
3. Heavily customize for your specific teaching voice, framing, and audience
4. The AI provides the scaffolding; the teaching judgment is yours

For educators whose value-add is teaching judgment (sequencing, framing, examples drawn from experience), this is straightforwardly beneficial. For "courses" that are essentially AI-generated content with a thin instructor layer, the result isn't really education and shouldn't be sold as such.

Translating Long-Form Content into Other Formats

A creator with a long article, video, or podcast episode often wants derivative content for other platforms — short videos, social posts, summaries, infographics.

NotebookLM is good at this:

1. Add the original long-form content as a source
2. Generate format-specific outputs: an Infographic for Instagram, a Briefing Doc for an email summary, a Slide Deck for a Twitter thread, a short Audio Overview for a podcast tease
3. Edit for the platform's voice and length

This use is straightforwardly assistive — you're not generating new content, you're recasting existing content into different formats. The original creative work stays yours.

Where to Be Careful

A few content workflows where NotebookLM is tempting but the line is harder to walk:

Publishing Audio Overviews as Podcasts

It's technically possible to publish a NotebookLM Audio Overview as a podcast episode. Some creators do. But:

- **Watermarking.** Free, Plus, and Pro tier outputs include the NotebookLM watermark. Only Ultra produces watermark-free audio for commercial use.
- **Voice attribution.** The AI hosts' voices have been the subject of legal action (the 2026 Greene case mentioned in earlier chapters). The legal status is unsettled.
- **Disclosure.** Publishing AI-generated audio without disclosure is increasingly treated as misrepresentation. Most platforms now require AI disclosure for synthetic media.
- **Quality.** Even at its best, NotebookLM audio doesn't quite match what a thoughtful human host produces. Audiences notice over time.

This doesn't mean don't do it. It means: do it deliberately, with clear disclosure, and recognize that you're making different tradeoffs than producing your own audio.

Video Content for Public Platforms

The same considerations apply to Video Overviews used as published content. Cinematic Mode in particular produces video polished enough to pass without disclosure — which makes the disclosure obligation more important, not less.

Drafting Content You'll Sign

Generating a Briefing Doc, Blog Post, or Report and publishing it under your name without substantial editorial work raises both authenticity and accuracy concerns:

- **Authenticity.** The voice isn't yours. Readers eventually notice when "your" writing doesn't sound like you.
- **Accuracy.** AI drafts contain subtle errors. Without close editing, those errors propagate to your audience under your byline.

Treat AI drafts as scaffolding, not finished work. The editing is the work.

The Disclosure Question

Should you disclose that you used AI in producing your content? The norms are evolving rapidly. A few principles that hold up:

Disclose when the AI is doing creative work that affects audience perception. AI-generated audio, video, or images the audience might mistake for human work — disclose.

Disclose when accuracy is the audience's concern. Briefings, recommendations, analyses — the audience cares whether you've personally verified the content. Disclose AI assistance so they can calibrate their trust.

Disclose for educational and informational content. Audiences seeking to learn deserve to know whether the source is human expertise or AI synthesis.

Disclosure matters less when the AI is purely supportive. Using NotebookLM to research a piece you wrote in your own voice, with your own verified citations, doesn't necessarily require explicit disclosure (though some publications now require it). Using it to generate the actual published text does.

Hidden use is the dangerous use. The cases where AI assistance has caused reputational damage have generally been cases where the use was hidden, then discovered. Open use, even of substantial AI assistance, doesn't carry the same risk.

When in doubt, disclose. The downside of disclosing assistance you didn't need to disclose is small. The downside of failing to disclose assistance that turns out to matter can be large.

Producing Watermark-Free Audio and Video

For creators who do want to publish NotebookLM-generated audio or video commercially, the practical mechanics:

- **Ultra tier** ($249.99/month) is the only tier that produces watermark-free Studio outputs.
- **Output formats** are standard MP3, MP4 — usable directly in any podcast or video distribution platform.

- **Editing externally** is possible — the audio and video files behave like normal media files.
- **Post-production polish** (intro music, outros, branded segments) needs to be added externally.

For occasional use, the Ultra subscription is hard to justify financially. For creators producing significant volumes of commercial AI-generated content, the math works.

A practical alternative for many creators: use Audio Overviews as research and reference, then record your own audio. You get fast research synthesis without the watermark, voice attribution, or quality concerns of publishing AI audio directly.

The "AI Slop" Problem

A real risk for creators using AI tools, NotebookLM included: producing content that's technically usable but creatively weightless. The open web in 2026 is increasingly full of it — articles that summarize without insight, videos that present without perspective, podcasts that discuss without conviction. The phrase "AI slop" has emerged to describe it.

The risk for individual creators is reputational. Audiences are getting better at recognizing AI-flavored content. Once they associate your output with the slop pile, the association is hard to reverse.

The protection is voice. Your specific perspective, your specific examples, your specific framings — the things that make your content yours — have to stay prominent in any AI-assisted workflow. If you can't tell whether a piece is yours by reading the first paragraph, your audience can't either.

This is why "edit substantially" and "use as scaffolding" keep recurring throughout this chapter. It isn't pedantry. It's the difference between creators who use AI as a tool and creators whose work disappears into the slop.

Specific Recommendations by Creator Type

Podcasters. Use NotebookLM heavily for research and prep. Record your own audio. Disclose AI assistance even when you're recording yourself. Don't publish unedited Audio Overviews as your podcast.

Newsletter writers. Use NotebookLM for synthesis and research. Write the newsletter in your voice. Verify citations rigorously — newsletters have a high accuracy expectation. Disclose per your platform's norms.

YouTube creators. Use NotebookLM for script research and outlining. Record your own video. Video Overviews are useful as reference, not as published work for serious channels.

Educators. Use NotebookLM extensively for course material scaffolding. Customize heavily for your teaching voice. Disclose AI-assisted material to students; show them the verification habits as part of teaching responsible AI use.

Internal corporate communicators. Use NotebookLM for briefings and synthesis material. Apply your organization's disclosure policies. Verify per stakes — executive communications get exhaustive verification, broad internal updates get reasonable verification.

Agencies and content teams. Develop team-wide standards for NotebookLM use, customization templates, and disclosure norms. Build verification into the workflow as a non-skippable step.

A Practical Walkthrough: A Podcast Episode

Suppose you're a podcaster producing a 30-minute episode on a complex topic — say, a recent regulatory development. You've collected eight sources: the regulation itself, three analyst pieces, a press release, a critical commentary, and two recent news reports.

Phase 1: Research notebook. Build the notebook. Upload all eight sources. Verify ingestion.

Phase 2: Exploration. Use chat to map the territory. Ask: *"What are the three most important things a listener needs to understand about this regulation? What's contested? What's misunderstood? What angles haven't been covered well in mainstream coverage?"* Save useful answers as notes.

Phase 3: Episode structure. Generate a Briefing Doc with a focus prompt for podcast structure: *"Generate a 30-minute podcast episode outline on this regulation. Structure: hook (2 min), background context (5 min), the central* *tension (10 min), implications (10 min), close (3 min). For each section, include the specific points to cover and the most relevant supporting material."*

Phase 4: Reference Audio Overview. Generate an Audio Overview with the same focus prompt. Listen to it. Notice what works and what feels off — useful for refining your own framing.

Phase 5: Script and record. Write your own script using the outline as scaffolding. Record yourself, in your voice, with your perspective. The research synthesis informed your prep but the episode is yours.

Phase 6: Disclosure. In the show notes, mention that you used NotebookLM for research. Explain the use briefly. Audiences who care can calibrate their trust accordingly.

You've produced a research-grounded episode in a fraction of the time it would have taken without AI assistance. The episode is still yours. The disclosure is honest. The verification was rigorous.

This is what responsible content-creator use of NotebookLM looks like.

The Path Forward for Creators

NotebookLM, like all AI tools, will keep evolving. Audio quality will improve. Video production will get more sophisticated. The line between AI-generated and human-generated content will keep blurring in ways that affect every creator's craft.

The skills that hold up as the technology evolves: voice (yours, distinctly), verification (always), disclosure (honest), and judgment about which uses cross the line from assistance into substitution.

For creators who internalize those skills, NotebookLM and tools like it are extraordinary additions to the workflow. For creators who don't, the tools accelerate the slide into commodity content that audiences tune out.

The choice between those paths is yours to make, every time you sit down to create something.

That closes Part VI. You've now seen how NotebookLM applies to four very different audiences — students, researchers, knowledge workers, and content creators — all using essentially the same underlying capabilities, calibrated to the specific shapes of their work.

Part VII covers a topic that runs across all four audiences: sharing notebooks, collaborative workflows, and the team-tier features that turn NotebookLM from a personal tool into a shared one.

Part VII: Sharing and Collaboration

"Many hands make light work."

— John Heywood

Chapter 28: Sharing Notebooks

For most of NotebookLM's history, the product was a personal tool. You built notebooks for yourself. You worked in them alone. The outputs you generated lived in your account.

That changed when sharing arrived. A notebook can now be shared with other people — read-only, editable, or somewhere in between — and the outputs you produce can be sent to colleagues, clients, classmates, or the public. By 2026, NotebookLM is shareable in ways the original product wasn't.

This chapter covers what sharing means in NotebookLM, the modes available, what the recipient sees when you share, and the practical considerations that come up once your notebooks become artifacts other people see.

Two Kinds of Sharing

Distinguish two different sharing operations:

Sharing a notebook. You give another person access to the notebook itself — its sources, its chats, its notes, its Studio outputs. They can view (and possibly edit) the notebook in the NotebookLM interface, the way you do.

Sharing an output. You generate a Studio output (an Audio Overview, a Briefing Doc, an Infographic) and send the resulting file. The recipient consumes the output but has no access to the underlying notebook.

The implications differ. Sharing a notebook is intimate — the other person sees how you work, what you've asked, what you've saved. Sharing an output is bounded — they get the artifact, nothing else.

For most use cases, sharing outputs is the safer default. Sharing notebooks is for collaboration where the inside view matters.

Sharing a Single Output

The simplest sharing operation: generate a Studio output, then share the resulting file or link.

For most outputs:

- **Audio Overviews** can be downloaded as MP3 and shared like any audio file (email attachment, message, link to cloud storage).
- **Video Overviews** download as MP4. Share via the same paths as any video.
- **Briefing Docs and Reports** can be exported as DOCX or PDF.
- **Slide Decks** export as PPTX, openable in PowerPoint, Keynote, or Google Slides.
- **Mind Maps** export as PNG or, in some interface versions, as importable mind-map files.
- **Infographics** download as image files.
- **Data Tables** can be copied as text or exported as CSV.

In each case, the recipient sees the artifact but has no view into the source material, the chat history, or the notebook itself. This fits most professional sharing — your colleague gets the briefing without seeing your messy work-in-progress notebook.

A practical note: shared outputs carry any watermarks present at generation. If you generated on Free, Plus, or Pro and the output has the NotebookLM watermark, that watermark goes with it. Only Ultra produces unwatermarked audio and video.

Sharing a Link to an Output

Some outputs (notably Audio Overviews in many interface versions) can be shared as a link rather than a downloaded file. The recipient clicks the link and plays the audio (or views the output) in their browser, without downloading.

This is convenient for casual sharing — a quick podcast link to a colleague, an Audio Overview pasted into a Slack message — but the recipient is still subject to whatever access controls and watermarking apply to the underlying file.

One subtle implication: if you regenerate the output (replacing the file on Google's servers), the link may serve the new version. For point-in-time sharing where the artifact should be stable, download the file and share it directly.

Sharing a Notebook

Sharing the notebook itself is a heavier operation. You give another person access to:

- All sources in the notebook
- The chat history
- All saved notes
- All generated Studio outputs
- The ability to ask new questions and generate new outputs (depending on permission level)

NotebookLM offers (typically) three permission levels for shared notebooks:

Viewer. The recipient can read sources, view chats and notes, and consume Studio outputs. They can't modify anything or generate new chats. Read-only access.

Commenter. Some interface versions add a commenter role between viewer and editor — the recipient can add notes or comments but can't modify sources or generate new outputs.

Editor. Full collaboration — add and remove sources, ask new questions, generate Studio outputs, modify notes. The equivalent of handing someone a key to the workspace.

The right permission level depends on the relationship and the use case. The next chapter covers collaboration patterns in detail; this one focuses on the narrower sharing-as-distribution case.

The Privacy Dimension

Sharing a notebook is more revealing than sharing an output. The chat history, in particular, is a candid record of how you engaged with the material — the questions you didn't quite know the answer to, the dead ends, the moments where you pushed back against something the AI said.

For shared workspaces with trusted colleagues, this is fine and even useful. For shared notebooks where the recipient is an evaluator — a manager assessing your work, a client reviewing your engagement, an instructor grading you — the candid record may not be what you want them seeing.

Practical guidance:

Before sharing a notebook with anyone outside your trusted circle, review what's in it. Skim the chat history. Look at the saved notes. Check whether any of it would be embarrassing or misleading taken out of context.

Consider creating a "share-ready" copy. If you've done heavy exploratory work and now want to share a clean version, duplicate the notebook — copy sources to a new notebook, optionally re-run the key chats — and share the clean version. The exploratory work stays private.

Use output-only sharing when possible. A polished Briefing Doc shared as a PDF reveals nothing about your process. The same notebook shared as a workspace reveals everything.

Sharing Permissions and Access Control

A few mechanical details that matter for serious sharing:

Collaborator sharing requires the recipient to have a Google account. NotebookLM uses Google identity for access control. Recipients without Google accounts — or with accounts outside your organization, depending on your settings — may not be able to open shared notebooks.

Workspace administrators can restrict sharing. Organizations on Google Workspace often have policies governing external sharing. If you try to share a notebook with someone outside your organization and it doesn't work, your administrator may have blocked it.

Sharing is revocable. You can remove someone's access at any time. Local copies of files they downloaded persist, but they lose access to the notebook itself.

Some output types have limited sharing. As Google adds new Studio outputs, the sharing mechanics lag. Check what's actually shareable before promising someone an output type.

Sharing With the Public

A few interface versions support truly public sharing — a link anyone with the URL can open without a specific account. This capability is more limited than its Google Docs equivalent (where public sharing is fully baked-in) and may require specific tier or organizational settings.

For public sharing of NotebookLM outputs:

Distribute the output, not the notebook. Public sharing of a notebook exposes far more than most situations warrant. Public sharing of a polished output is bounded and clear.

Know what the watermark communicates. A public-facing piece of content with a NotebookLM watermark signals "AI-generated." Sometimes that's the point — the disclosure matters. Sometimes it undercuts the perceived authority of the content. Decide deliberately.

Watch for evolving terms of use. Google's terms around public distribution of NotebookLM-generated content have evolved and will continue to. For commercial public distribution, check the current terms.

Embedding and Distribution

Some outputs can be embedded in other contexts — an Audio Overview on a website, a Mind Map dropped into a slide deck, an Infographic posted to social media. The mechanics vary by output type and platform; NotebookLM has been adding capabilities here steadily.

Two practical considerations for embedding workflows:

Embeds may not respect access controls. A privately generated Audio Overview embedded on a public website is, effectively, public. If you wouldn't want the content public, don't embed it on a public surface.

Embed reliability depends on Google's continued support. Embedded content lives on Google's servers. For long-lived content — a permanent webpage, a course you'll teach for years — prefer downloaded files over live embeds.

Sharing in Education

Educators have a particular set of sharing needs worth calling out:

Sharing course notebooks with students. A read-only notebook containing course readings, assignments, and study aids is a useful resource. Plus tier or higher; review what's in the notebook before students see it.

Sharing student work with educators. Less common but worth knowing — students can share their notebooks with instructors as evidence of their study process. This is closer to a portfolio than a finished assignment.

Using NotebookLM for class discussions. Some educators have begun running seminar discussions in shared collaborative notebooks — adding the week's readings, then having the class annotate and discuss together. This is real collaboration, covered in the next chapter.

Disclosure norms. Educators sharing AI-assisted course materials with students should disclose that fact — both as a model of responsible AI disclosure and so students can calibrate their engagement.

Sharing in Professional Contexts

For professional sharing — clients, stakeholders, external collaborators — a few additional considerations:

Use Workspace accounts when possible. The data protections, audit controls, and admin features of Google Workspace make professional sharing safer and cleaner.

Make sharing intentional. Document who has access to what, especially for client-related notebooks where access lists may need to be auditable.

Share outputs by default, notebooks by exception. Most client and stakeholder relationships are well-served by polished outputs; full notebook sharing is for actual collaboration partners.

Plan for the end of the engagement. When a client engagement ends, decide what happens to the shared notebook. Archive? Delete? Hand off? Have a default and follow it consistently.

Versioning and Stability

NotebookLM doesn't currently support formal versioning of notebooks or outputs. A few implications:

A shared notebook is the live notebook. If you keep working in it after sharing, your collaborators see the changes. There's no "share this version" snapshot.

Outputs are point-in-time snapshots. When you generate one, it captures the sources and chat context at that moment. If sources change later, the output doesn't.

For stable distribution, download the artifact. A downloaded MP3 or PDF is stable in a way an in-app reference isn't.

For workflows that depend on stable, citable artifacts — academic publications, regulatory submissions, audit trails — download and archive the relevant outputs at known points in time. Don't rely on NotebookLM to preserve the exact state.

A Practical Walkthrough: Sharing a Briefing With a Stakeholder

Suppose you've produced a strategic briefing in NotebookLM that needs to go to your VP. You've done the work — built a focused notebook, asked the right questions, generated a Briefing Doc with the right framing, verified the key citations.

What you do next:

1. **Export the Briefing Doc as a PDF or DOCX.** Treat this as the deliverable — it's stable, recipients can annotate it, and it doesn't expose the underlying workspace.
2. **Edit the export for final voice.** Adjust the framing, add your own commentary, fix anything the AI got slightly off in tone.
3. **Optionally generate an Audio Overview as a companion artifact.** For a busy executive, a 10-minute audio file may get more attention than a 5-page PDF.

4. **Send the artifacts** through your normal channels — email, Slack, whatever your team uses.
5. **Don't share the underlying notebook unless the VP asks to see your work.** The polished artifacts are the deliverable; the messy workspace was the process.

If the VP later wants more detail — a specific question the briefing didn't cover, a follow-up analysis — go back to the notebook, do the work, generate a follow-up output, send that. The notebook stays your workspace; the outputs flow outward.

When Sharing the Notebook Is Right

The default for sharing should be outputs, not notebooks. But notebook-sharing isn't a corner case — it has clear uses:

Real collaborators. Co-authors, research partners, project teammates who are doing the work with you and need the same workspace.

Handoff situations. When someone is taking over your work, sharing the notebook — with all the context built up in chats and notes — is more useful than sharing just the outputs.

Teaching and mentorship. Sharing a notebook with a junior colleague or student so they can see how the work was done — the chat patterns, the citations followed, the synthesis built up.

Knowledge preservation. When you're leaving a role and want to hand off relevant work to whoever comes next, sharing the notebook is more durable than sharing only the outputs.

In each case, the recipient benefits from seeing the inside of the workspace, not just the polished exterior. That's when notebook sharing earns its keep.

The next chapter goes deeper on the case where multiple people are working in the same notebook at once — the collaboration that NotebookLM's Plus-tier features enable, and the team workflows that have emerged in early adopter organizations.

Chapter 29: Collaborative Notebooks (Plus Tier)

The previous chapter covered sharing — distributing notebooks and outputs from a workspace that's still essentially yours. This chapter covers the harder, more interesting case: when a notebook is the shared workspace for multiple people working in it together.

True collaboration in NotebookLM became practical with the Plus tier in late 2024 and matured through 2025 and into 2026. By early 2026, collaborative notebooks are usable for research teams, course discussions, project groups, and small organizations using NotebookLM as a shared knowledge tool.

But collaboration in source-grounded AI has a different shape than collaboration in document tools, project management software, or general-purpose chat. This chapter is about that shape — what works, what breaks, and the team practices that make collaborative notebooks productive.

What Collaboration Looks Like

In a shared collaborative notebook, multiple users (with appropriate permissions) can:

- **Add and remove sources**
- **Ask questions in chat** — though typically each user sees their own chat history; some interface versions support shared chats
- **Save notes** that other collaborators can see
- **Generate Studio outputs** that the whole notebook benefits from
- **See each other's contributions** — who added which source, who wrote which note

The model is closer to a shared lab notebook than a shared chat room. People come and go, contribute their own work, build on each other's contributions, and end up with a workspace richer than any single person could produce alone.

The core asymmetry: **chats are typically per-user; sources, notes, and Studio outputs are shared.** This fits most uses — chat is exploratory and personal, sources and notes are the durable record. But it means collaboration is more about the workspace artifacts than about the conversational layer.

Tier Requirements

Collaborative notebooks generally require Plus tier or higher. The free tier supports limited read-only sharing but not full multi-user editing.

For teams considering NotebookLM as a shared tool, this is a significant input to the tier decision. A team of five doing real collaboration is looking at five Plus subscriptions — about $40/month total. Pro becomes attractive for heavy users; Ultra makes sense only at team scale.

A practical pattern for organizations: one or two designated power users on Pro or Ultra handle the heavy generation work, with everyone else on Plus or Free depending on contribution level. This minimizes total subscription cost while keeping the team functional.

Common Collaborative Patterns

A few patterns that have emerged in early-adopter teams:

The Reading Group Notebook

Research labs, book clubs, study groups, and learning communities have adopted NotebookLM for shared reading. The pattern:

1. The coordinator creates a notebook for the topic or for a specific reading session.
2. Sources (papers, book chapters, articles) get added before the meeting.
3. Group members preview the sources and chat with the notebook on their own time.
4. During the meeting, the notebook is open as a shared reference. Questions get asked live; Studio outputs generated as needed.
5. After the meeting, key insights get saved as shared notes for the group's persistent record.

This works well for groups that meet recurrently on the same body of material. Over time the notebook becomes a shared knowledge base that captures both the source material and the group's accumulated thinking about it.

The Project Team Notebook

For project teams working on something complex — a strategic analysis, a regulatory response, a product launch — a shared project notebook can serve as the team's central reference:

- Initial source material (research, briefs, data) gets added at project kickoff
- New material gets added as it arrives
- Team members add observations and synthesis as notes
- Studio outputs (briefings, status updates, decision documents) get generated and saved as the project evolves

Done well, this produces a project archive that captures not just the deliverables but the underlying thinking — useful for the project itself, for retrospectives, and for new team members joining mid-project.

The Consulting Engagement Notebook

For consulting teams, a per-engagement collaborative notebook is increasingly common:

- Client materials get loaded at engagement start
- Engagement team members work in the notebook together
- Studio outputs (briefings, deliverables) get generated, edited externally, shared with the client as polished documents
- At engagement end, the notebook becomes part of the firm's knowledge base — or, depending on client confidentiality requirements, gets archived with appropriate handling

The key: the notebook is the team's working environment, not the client's deliverable. The client gets polished outputs. The notebook stays internal.

The Knowledge-Hub Notebook

Some organizations use long-running collaborative notebooks as shared knowledge hubs for specific functions or domains. A "regulatory tracking" notebook for compliance. An "engineering architecture" notebook for the platform team. A "competitive intelligence" notebook for strategy.

These differ from project notebooks — they're not bounded by a single deliverable. They accumulate over time, get refreshed periodically, and serve as institutional memory for whatever they cover.

What Makes Collaborative Notebooks Work

A few practices that distinguish productive collaborative notebooks from chaotic ones:

Designated Curator

Even in collaborative notebooks, someone has to own the curation discipline — keeping the source list focused, removing what's no longer relevant, enforcing naming conventions, archiving when appropriate. Without a designated curator, collaborative notebooks drift into the same accumulating chaos as shared folders.

The role can rotate, but it should always be someone's explicit responsibility.

Shared Naming Conventions

In a personal notebook, your idiosyncratic naming patterns are fine. In a shared notebook, the team needs conventions. Agree on a naming pattern for sources. Agree on one for notes. Agree on a structure for the Studio outputs that get saved.

The conventions don't need to be elaborate — just consistent enough that any team member can find what they need without asking.

Note Authorship Conventions

When multiple people are writing notes, mark authorship — at least informally, by starting each note with initials or a name. This makes the notebook navigable as a record of who contributed what.

For more formal conventions, some teams prefix notes with category markers: `[SYNTHESIS]`, `[QUESTION]`, `[TODO]`, `[OBSERVATION]`. This makes it easy to scan a long notebook and find specific kinds of contributions.

Asynchronous-First Communication

NotebookLM isn't built for real-time collaboration the way Google Docs is. Multiple people editing the same notebook simultaneously can lead to conflicts and lost work.

Treat collaboration as asynchronous-first: each person works in the notebook on their own time, leaves clear notes about what they did, and the team coordinates the bigger questions through other channels — Slack, email, meetings.

Periodic Synthesis Sessions

For long-running collaborative notebooks, periodic synthesis sessions keep the work coherent. Once a week — or once a month, depending on activity level — a designated team member reviews what's been added, generates a summary of the recent work, and saves it as a synthesis note.

This is the single biggest difference between collaborative notebooks that grow in value over time and ones that become unnavigable graveyards of contributions nobody can find.

Roles and Permissions in Practice

For teams using collaborative notebooks at scale, thinking about roles formally helps:

Owner. The person responsible for the notebook overall. Usually the curator. Has full access; controls who else has access.

Editors. Active contributors. Can add sources, write notes, generate outputs. Most team members in a productive collaborative notebook are editors.

Viewers. Stakeholders or interested parties who need to see the notebook but aren't contributing. Read-only.

External collaborators. Outside-the-team participants — clients, consultants, partners — who need access but with limits. Usually viewer or commenter; rarely editor.

A team that gets this clear up front avoids the awkward conversations later about why someone has more or less access than they expected.

Managing Conflict and Drift

Some predictable issues come up in collaborative notebooks:

Source conflicts. Two people add the same source in different formats or different versions. The notebook ends up with redundant material. Fix: a curator who handles deduplication.

Note conflicts. Two people write notes that contradict each other or take different positions. This isn't a bug — team members will see things differently — but the notebook should make the disagreement visible rather than smooth it over. Consider notes like `[SYNTHESIS – POV 1]` and `[SYNTHESIS – POV 2]` to mark divergent perspectives explicitly.

Drift in scope. What started as a focused notebook expands as people add tangentially related sources. Fix: periodic review and pruning.

Stale collaborators. People who had access for a previous phase of work but aren't active anymore. Fix: a regular access review — quarterly is reasonable — where the owner removes anyone who no longer needs access.

Most of these issues are organizational, not technical. NotebookLM gives you the tools; the team has to use them deliberately.

When Collaborative Notebooks Aren't the Right Tool

A few cases where the team's use case doesn't fit NotebookLM's collaboration model:

Real-time co-editing of documents. Use Google Docs. NotebookLM isn't built for the simultaneous editing Docs handles natively.

Rich threaded discussion. Use Slack, Discord, or a forum tool. NotebookLM's chat is per-user; it isn't designed for threaded team conversation.

Project management. Use a project management tool. NotebookLM doesn't track tasks, deadlines, or assignments well.

Formal document version control. Use Git, SharePoint, or a document management system. NotebookLM has no proper versioning of outputs.

A common mistake: trying to use NotebookLM as the team's everything-tool. It's not built for that. It's built for shared synthesis of source material. Use it for that, use other tools for what they're built for, and the combination works far better than either alone.

A Practical Walkthrough: A Five-Person Research Team

Suppose you're leading a five-person research team running a quarterly literature scan in your domain. The work is recurring (quarterly), shared (everyone contributes), and produces both internal artifacts and external outputs.

Setup (one-time). Create a shared collaborative notebook. Invite the team as editors. Establish naming conventions for sources (`Author (Year) – Short title`) and notes (initials prefix). Designate a curator, rotating quarterly. Decide on the artifact pattern: synthesis brief at the end of each quarter, plus per-paper notes.

Weekly cadence. Each team member adds the papers they've encountered in the prior week, with per-paper notes capturing the most important points. The curator does light deduplication and naming cleanup.

Monthly cadence. A designated team member generates a synthesis Briefing Doc covering the month's additions. The team reviews it together — probably in a meeting where the notebook is on screen — and edits as needed.

Quarterly cadence. A larger synthesis: a comprehensive review of the quarter's literature, generated as a Briefing Doc with custom focus. The team edits and refines together. The polished version becomes an external deliverable; the raw notebook stays internal.

End of year. The notebook gets archived. Key insights from the year get promoted into a top-level reference notebook for the team. A new notebook starts for the next year.

This produces a workflow that compounds — the notebook grows in value as the team's work accumulates in it. New team members can read through the historical notebook and get up to speed on the team's domain in a way that would otherwise require months of reading.

The Long-Term Picture

Teams that adopt NotebookLM as a shared workspace tend to follow the same trajectory. The first month is awkward — people are working out the conventions, the curation discipline, the right cadences. The second and third months are productive. By month six, the notebook has become the team's central knowledge artifact, and it's hard to remember what work was like before.

The question isn't whether collaborative notebooks work. They do. The question is whether your team commits to the practices — designated curation, shared conventions, periodic synthesis — that distinguish productive shared workspaces from accumulating graveyards.

For teams willing to make that commitment, NotebookLM becomes a transformative addition to how the team works.

That closes Part VII. You now know how to share NotebookLM outputs and notebooks responsibly, and how to operate collaborative notebooks as productive shared workspaces.

Part VIII covers the topics every NotebookLM user needs to think about even when things are going well: what NotebookLM gets wrong, how to think about privacy and data, and the ethical questions that source-grounded AI raises in ways general-purpose AI doesn't.

Part VIII: Safety, Ethics, and Limitations

"With great power comes great responsibility."

— Voltaire (and, later, Spider-Man)

Chapter 30: What NotebookLM Gets Wrong

This is the chapter every honest book about an AI tool needs and most don't include. NotebookLM is a remarkable piece of software. It's also wrong, sometimes, in ways that matter. Knowing the failure modes is the difference between using the tool well and being burned by it.

Chapter 23 covered citation verification as the protective habit. This chapter goes wider — covering the full set of failure modes, not just the citation-related ones. The goal isn't to scare you away from the tool. It's to give you a calibrated view of where it can fail so you know where to apply the verification discipline most aggressively.

Citation Drift

We've covered this throughout the book, but it's worth restating in the context of failure modes generally: **NotebookLM's citations confirm that the cited passage exists, not that it supports the claim.** This is the most consequential failure mode of source-grounded AI. The polish of citations creates an authority signal the underlying accuracy doesn't always earn.

Specific patterns to watch for, drawn from Chapter 23 and from real-world experience:

- **Paraphrase that drops qualifiers**, broadening claims beyond what the source actually said
- **Inverse implications**, where the source's hedge or caveat gets read as the underlying assertion
- **Conflation across sources**, where a citation points to one source but the actual content was synthesized from another
- **Selective citation**, where a balanced source is cited only on the side that supports a narrative
- **Composite quotes**, where a "direct quotation" assembles fragments from non-contiguous passages

- **Confident interpretation**, where a tentative source becomes a definitive summary
- **Plausible filler**, where the summary contains generic content the model added on top of what was actually in the source

The discipline: click citations, read the cited passages, confirm the support relation. For high-stakes work, do this exhaustively.

Subtle Domain Errors

NotebookLM is built on Gemini, a general-purpose model. Gemini is broadly competent across domains but has uneven domain depth. For specialized fields — subspecialties of medicine, narrow areas of law, niche scientific disciplines, technical domains with their own jargon and conventions — NotebookLM may produce summaries that *sound* authoritative but contain subtle domain errors.

The pattern: the model summarizes a paper from a specialized field. The summary is grammatically clean and structurally reasonable. To a non-specialist it looks fine. To a specialist, something is off — a term used in a way the field wouldn't use it, a methodology mischaracterized, an implication no one in the field would assert.

This failure mode is dangerous for two reasons:

First, you may not catch it. If you're using NotebookLM to learn a field you don't know, the expertise needed to spot the error is the expertise you don't have.

Second, it propagates. Subtle domain errors in your synthesis become subtle domain errors in whatever you produce. If you're presenting to people in the field, they'll catch them. If you're presenting to people outside the field, the errors propagate further.

Mitigations:

- **For specialized work, have a domain expert review.** Even a quick review by someone who knows the field can catch errors that careful citation verification misses — some errors aren't in the citations, they're in the framing.
- **Cross-reference with authoritative sources.** Use NotebookLM as one input, not the only input.

- **Be cautious in fields you don't know.** The convenience of fast synthesis is also the danger of confident error.

Hedging and False Balance

NotebookLM has a default disposition toward synthesis and balance. Usually a virtue. But on topics where the evidence isn't balanced, the default can produce false equivalence.

If your sources are 90% on one side and 10% on the other, NotebookLM may summarize the dispute as roughly even. The synthesizing impulse smooths the asymmetry the sources actually reflect.

This matters most for:

- **Scientific consensus questions.** A notebook of climate-science papers and a few contrarian pieces may produce summaries that present the science as more contested than it is.
- **Empirically settled questions.** Some debates have answers; the model may treat them as ongoing because that's the safer rhetorical default.
- **Clearly weighted evidence.** When one position has overwhelming support and the other has weak support, NotebookLM may not signal the asymmetry clearly.

Mitigations:

- **Ask explicitly about evidence weight.** "How strong is the evidence on each side? Are these positions held by comparable proportions of experts, or is one substantially better-supported?"
- **Don't accept implicit balance as accurate balance.** Treat balanced-sounding summaries on contested topics as a starting point that needs further interrogation.
- **Curate sources that reflect actual proportions.** If the field is 90/10, your notebook should reflect that, not a 50/50 sample chosen for "balance."

Hallucinations Past the Source

Even though NotebookLM is source-grounded, it isn't perfectly grounded. Occasionally the model produces content that goes beyond what the sources support — adding generic information, drawing conclusions the sources don't quite state, providing context the sources don't quite include.

When this happens, the response may have no citation for the unsupported portion, or a citation that doesn't actually anchor the unsupported claim.

This is rarer than in pure chat models like ChatGPT, but it isn't zero. "RAG reduces hallucination" is true on average; it isn't true categorically.

Mitigations:

- **Be alert for paragraphs without citations.** Substantive claims without citation support are flags.
- **Be alert for citations that look like decoration.** A citation that doesn't quite map to the surrounding claim is doing decorative work, not supporting work.
- **For load-bearing claims, demand citation explicitly.** "Quote the exact passage that supports this." If the model can't, the claim isn't grounded.

Long-Context Decay

NotebookLM's per-source context window is large (1M tokens), but quality isn't uniform across that range. Passages buried deep in very long sources may be missed by retrieval; nuances at the edges of the context window may be summarized less accurately than nuances at the center.

For most sources of typical length (20–100 pages), this isn't an issue. For very long sources (300+ pages, especially when they approach the upper end of the context window), retrieval quality degrades. Important information in the long tail of a long document may be effectively invisible to the model.

Mitigations:

- **Split very long sources strategically.** As covered in Chapter 18, a 600-page document split into focused chunks often produces better retrieval than the same document as one source.
- **Ask explicitly about specific sections of long sources.** "Look specifically at section 7. What does it say about [topic]?" forces the model to retrieve from the section you specify.
- **Verify against the source directly for content from long documents.** Don't trust that a brief mention in a 1,500-page source was found and incorporated. Check.

The Studio Output Visibility Cliff

A failure mode specific to Studio outputs: once an output is generated, errors in it are hard to spot without going back to the underlying material.

A Briefing Doc looks clean. An Audio Overview sounds smooth. A Slide Deck presents well. The polish creates a barrier to noticing errors — you read or listen for the gist rather than verifying line by line.

This is most dangerous when:

- The output will be shared with others who can't verify against the sources
- The output is consumed casually (the audience trusts you, you trust the output)
- The output will be cited or referenced elsewhere, propagating any errors

Mitigations:

- **Verify Studio outputs as carefully as you'd verify a chat answer.** The polish doesn't change the verification obligation.
- **Build verification into the output workflow.** The output isn't done when generation finishes. It's done when you've verified it.
- **For outputs you'll share or publish, be exhaustive.** Click every citation. Read every cited passage. Confirm every load-bearing claim.

Limitations of Web Research Features

Fast Research and Deep Research (Chapter 16) extend NotebookLM beyond your curated sources. They also import the failure modes of open-web research:

- **Source quality varies dramatically** in web-fetched material
- **AI-generated content may be in the source pool** without you knowing it
- **Bias in source selection** propagates into Deep Research outputs
- **Currency is uneven** – recent, evolving topics may be inadequately covered

The verification discipline applies even more strongly to web-augmented work than to work with curated sources, because the trust chain is broken at the source-selection step.

Mode Limitations

Some failure modes are about what NotebookLM doesn't even attempt:

- **Original argument and analysis.** NotebookLM synthesizes; it doesn't argue. Asking it to make a novel case for or against something usually produces synthesis-of-existing-arguments rather than new analysis.
- **Quantitative analysis.** NotebookLM can extract numbers from sources but doesn't do statistical work, modeling, or computation. Pretending it does produces nonsense.
- **Forecasting and prediction.** NotebookLM can summarize what sources say about the future. It can't predict the future. Don't treat its predictions as forecasts.
- **Real-time information.** Even with Deep Research, NotebookLM is not built for breaking news or real-time data.
- **Voice and idiosyncratic writing.** NotebookLM produces competent prose. It doesn't produce *your* prose. Drafts need substantial editing for voice.

These aren't bugs. They're scope limits. Knowing what NotebookLM doesn't do – and not asking it to – is part of using it well.

Visual and Multimodal Limitations

A few specific weaknesses worth noting:

- **OCR errors in images.** Scanned PDFs, photographed documents, and images with text can have OCR errors that propagate into NotebookLM's understanding. Quality is good, not perfect.
- **Charts and diagrams in PDFs are largely invisible.** A document whose argument depends on its figures may be substantially misunderstood by NotebookLM, which sees only the surrounding text.
- **Video content is transcript-only.** YouTube videos and uploaded video sources are processed by their transcripts. Visual content — demonstrations, expressions, on-screen text — is missed.
- **Audio quality affects transcription.** Noisy recordings, multiple speakers, heavy accents — all degrade transcription quality. Errors in transcription become errors in synthesis.

For sources where these dimensions matter, treat NotebookLM's output as covering only the parts it can access. Visual content needs visual review. Audio nuance needs human listening.

Cumulative Failure Patterns

A few failure modes that emerge from how the parts interact:

Subtle errors compound across iterative work. A small error in an early synthesis note, promoted to a source, gets cited in a later synthesis, gets cited in a Studio output, gets shared with stakeholders. Each step looks clean. The end result has an error grounded in your own previous work, with no clear way to trace it back to the original mistake.

Verification fatigue. People who use NotebookLM intensively often hit verification fatigue — the discipline that's straightforward in your first ten uses gets harder to maintain in your hundredth. The errors that get through tend to come at the end of a long working session.

Trust calibration drift. As you accumulate good experiences with NotebookLM, your default trust level rises. Good experiences stay well-calibrated only as long as the verification discipline persists. Once trust drifts upward without continued verification, the errors that eventually surface are the ones you stopped checking for.

The mitigations for these are organizational, not technical:

- **Build verification into the workflow.** Don't rely on willpower. Rely on process.
- **Calibrate trust deliberately.** When you find yourself trusting NotebookLM more than the verification record warrants, recalibrate.
- **Periodic audits.** For long-running notebooks, sample notes and citations for accuracy on a schedule.

What Failure Looks Like in Practice

A composite of the kinds of NotebookLM failures that have shown up in real-world reports as of early 2026:

The misframed academic citation. A graduate student generates a literature review with NotebookLM. The review summarizes a paper as supporting hypothesis X. The actual paper carefully argues X is unlikely. The student doesn't catch the error because the citation looks fine. The review goes to the advisor. The advisor catches it (this time). Embarrassment, lesson learned.

The misleading executive briefing. A consultant generates a briefing for a client meeting. The briefing summarizes a regulatory document as imposing a specific obligation. The actual regulation imposes a different obligation. The consultant doesn't notice. The client makes a decision based on the briefing. The error surfaces three weeks later when a compliance team reviews it. Awkward conversation, possible engagement consequences.

The audio summary that sounded right. A researcher listens to an Audio Overview of a paper while commuting. The overview asserts the paper found a specific effect size. The paper actually found something different (or didn't find a clear effect). The researcher cites the asserted finding in a presentation. A colleague who knows the paper raises the discrepancy. Public correction needed.

The propagated synthesis error. A team's collaborative notebook has accumulated synthesis notes over months. One early note contained a subtle misreading. Subsequent work built on it. By the time the error surfaces, dozens of downstream notes and outputs are affected. Untangling takes substantial effort.

These failures aren't hypothetical. Variations of all of them have happened to real users. They're the predictable failure modes of trusting AI output without verification.

What Doing It Right Looks Like

The same composite, with the verification discipline:

The graduate student clicks the citations in the literature review. Reads the cited passages. Notices the misframing. Fixes it. Submits clean work.

The consultant verifies the regulatory citations before the client meeting. Catches the error. Corrects the briefing. Goes into the meeting with accurate material.

The researcher spot-checks a few claims from the Audio Overview before relying on them. Notices the effect-size discrepancy. Checks the paper directly. Cites the actual finding in the presentation.

The team has a designated curator and periodic synthesis review. Errors get caught early, before they propagate. The notebook stays trustworthy as it grows.

The difference between the failure cases and the success cases isn't smarter prompting or better source curation, though both help. It's the verification discipline. The minutes spent clicking citations save hours of recovery later.

NotebookLM Is Not Your Excuse

This chapter has cataloged a lot of ways NotebookLM can fail. None of those failures are NotebookLM's responsibility. They're yours. The model is a tool. The verification, the curation, the calibrated trust — those are the user's job.

This sounds harsh; it isn't meant to be. It's the reality of working with any tool that produces work product on your behalf. A spreadsheet that produces an incorrect total because of a formula error is your responsibility, not the spreadsheet's. An AI that produces an inaccurate summary because of paraphrase drift is your responsibility, not the AI's.

The professional standard is the same one that's always applied to tool-assisted work: you're accountable for what you produce, regardless of how it was produced. NotebookLM doesn't change that standard. It just makes the work faster — for users who maintain the verification discipline, dramatically faster.

The next chapter shifts from technical failure modes to a different set of considerations: privacy, data handling, and what happens to the material you put into NotebookLM.

Chapter 31: Privacy, Data, and Trust

NotebookLM is a Google product, which means everything you put into it lives, in some form, on Google's servers. For a tool whose primary use is uploading documents and asking questions about them, that's a meaningful fact. The documents you upload — research papers, internal memos, personal records, client materials, intellectual property — sit somewhere in Google's infrastructure. So do the questions you ask, the notes you write, and the Studio outputs you generate.

Most users don't think carefully about this. Convenience overrides considered analysis of what's happening to the data. For low-stakes use, that's fine. For higher-stakes use, it isn't.

This chapter covers what happens to your data in NotebookLM, the practical privacy choices available to you, the regulatory and institutional dimensions that matter for some users, and the 2026 voice-cloning lawsuit that has put NotebookLM's data practices under legal scrutiny.

What Google Stores

When you use NotebookLM, Google stores:

- **The sources you upload** (PDFs, documents, images, audio, video, text, links to web sources)
- **The chat history** of every conversation you have with the AI
- **The notes you write or save**
- **The Studio outputs you generate** (Audio Overviews, Reports, Slide Decks, etc.)
- **Metadata** about your usage (when you accessed what, what features you used, for how long)

This data lives on Google's infrastructure and is, in principle, available for Google's operational purposes — running the product, responding to legal process, improving the service.

What Google does *with* it depends on the type of account you're using.

Personal Account Data Practices

For personal Google accounts (typical Gmail addresses), Google's posture as of early 2026 is:

- **Source documents are not used to train general-purpose Gemini models.** Google has made this commitment explicitly.
- **Your interactions (prompts, generated outputs) may be used for product improvement** – including some level of human review for quality assurance and model training related to NotebookLM specifically.
- **Aggregate usage data informs product development** without identifying individual users.

The practical implication: for personal accounts, treat NotebookLM as a Google product whose data practices may evolve and whose operations may include human review. Don't put anything in a personal-account NotebookLM you'd be uncomfortable with a Google reviewer occasionally seeing.

You can reduce some of this through Google account privacy settings (myaccount.google.com → Data & Privacy), where you can control whether your activity is used for personalization and product improvement. The controls are real but not absolute – even with maximum privacy settings, Google still has operational access to your data.

Workspace and Education Account Practices

For Google Workspace and Google Workspace for Education accounts, the data picture is meaningfully different:

- **Your data is not used for training Gemini models.** This is a contractual commitment to Workspace customers.
- **Administrators have additional controls** over retention, sharing, and external access.
- **Audit logs are typically available** to administrators for compliance and oversight.
- **Data residency and processing locations** can be specified for organizations with regulatory requirements.

For organizations doing serious work with NotebookLM — confidential research, client materials, internal strategic documents — Workspace is the right account type. Stronger contractual data protections plus admin-level controls make Workspace usable for material that personal accounts shouldn't touch.

If you're a graduate student with a university Google account, your research notebooks have stronger protections than they would on a personal Gmail. If you're an employee at a Workspace organization, work-related notebooks belong on the Workspace account, not your personal one.

What Counts as Sensitive

Some categories of source material warrant special care, regardless of which account type:

- **Personal health information** (medical records, prescription information, health histories)
- **Financial information** (bank statements, tax records, account numbers)
- **Legal materials** (privileged communications, confidential settlements, sealed records)
- **Intellectual property** (unpublished research, trade secrets, proprietary processes)
- **Internal business documents** (strategic plans, financial forecasts, personnel matters)
- **Information about identifiable individuals** subject to GDPR, CCPA, HIPAA, or similar regulations
- **National security or export-controlled material**

For these categories:

- **Personal Gmail account: don't.** The data protections aren't strong enough.
- **Workspace account: probably okay, with administrator awareness.** Make sure your administrator has configured the account appropriately and approved this use.

- **Highly sensitive subcategories: consult.** Some material requires explicit institutional approval (HIPAA-covered data, certain legal materials) before going into any cloud AI tool. When in doubt, ask.

The principle that holds across categories: **the same care you'd apply to uploading material to any other cloud service applies to NotebookLM.** It's not categorically more or less safe than Google Drive, Dropbox, or any other major cloud service. It's one more place your data lives, with the implications that follow.

Data Retention and Deletion

NotebookLM retains your data indefinitely by default — your notebooks persist until you delete them. Mostly a feature (your work is preserved), but it has implications:

- **Forgotten notebooks accumulate.** A notebook you created two years ago for a one-off project still contains whatever sources you uploaded then.
- **Stale sources retain their content.** A source uploaded years ago is still in NotebookLM, in the version it had then.
- **Account access is total access.** Anyone who gains access to your Google account has access to everything in your NotebookLM library, going back to the beginning.

Practical hygiene:

- **Delete notebooks for completed projects** you don't need to reference further. Especially important for notebooks containing sensitive material.
- **Delete sources containing material you no longer need.** A source uploaded for a specific question that no longer matters can be removed.
- **Periodic library audits.** Once a quarter, review your notebook library. Archive what's still relevant. Delete what isn't.

For Workspace accounts, your administrator may have retention policies that affect this — automatic deletion after specified periods, retention for compliance reasons. Know your organization's policy.

The 2026 Greene Voice-Cloning Lawsuit

In 2026, journalist David Greene filed suit against Google, alleging that NotebookLM's Audio Overview voice models reproduced his distinctive voice without consent. Greene's argument, simplified: the AI hosts that NotebookLM uses to generate Audio Overviews share characteristics — vocal cadence, phrasing patterns, intonation — sufficiently distinctive that listeners familiar with Greene's work have identified the AI as sounding like him. Google has denied that its voice models were trained on Greene's voice and has moved to dismiss.

The case was unresolved as of this writing. Whatever the outcome, it has implications for NotebookLM users:

Voice attribution is a contested area. The legal status of AI-generated voice that resembles real individuals' voices is being worked out across multiple jurisdictions and multiple cases. NotebookLM users producing audio content should be aware of the unsettled legal terrain.

Disclosure matters more, not less. If the legal status of AI voice generation tightens, users who clearly disclosed AI generation will be better positioned than users who passed AI audio off as human production.

Source representation has a separate legal dimension. The lawsuit raises broader questions about what AI representations of source material can and can't do — implications that extend beyond voice to text and visual outputs.

For most users, the practical effect is: continue to be careful about disclosure (you should have been anyway), watch the evolving legal landscape around AI-generated content, and consult counsel for high-stakes commercial use.

Regulatory Considerations

Some users have specific regulatory frameworks that affect their use of NotebookLM:

GDPR and similar privacy regimes. For users in the EU and other jurisdictions with comprehensive privacy laws, what data is being processed where matters substantially. Workspace accounts can be configured for EU data residency; personal accounts have less explicit control.

HIPAA in the US. For healthcare-related material in the US, NotebookLM is not, as of early 2026, generally considered a HIPAA-covered tool. Don't put protected health information in personal-account NotebookLM. For Workspace accounts with appropriate Business Associate Agreements, the picture is more complex; consult your organization's compliance team.

Financial services regulations. SEC, FINRA, and similar frameworks have implications for the storage and processing of certain financial communications and data. Don't assume NotebookLM is a permitted tool for regulated financial workflows. Check.

Educational records (FERPA in the US). For educators handling student records, the same caution applies — don't assume NotebookLM is FERPA-compliant for that material without specific institutional guidance.

Export-controlled material. Some research, technical, and defense-related material has export-control implications that affect which cloud services can be used. NotebookLM is generally not appropriate for export-controlled work without explicit institutional clearance.

These considerations don't make NotebookLM a bad tool. They make it a tool that, like any cloud service, has to be used within the regulatory frameworks that apply to your specific work.

Trust as a Continuum

The right way to think about trust in NotebookLM isn't binary (trust it or don't) but as a continuum calibrated to use case:

High trust — appropriate uses: - Public source material (published papers, news articles, websites, books) - Personal exploratory work where data sensitivity is low - Educational use of publicly available materials - General professional research where institutional policies permit

Medium trust — appropriate with care: - Internal organizational documents on Workspace accounts - Client materials with appropriate engagement-level access controls - Research materials with conventional confidentiality - Personal materials you'd share with a trusted colleague

Lower trust — significant caution: - Any material subject to regulatory frameworks (HIPAA, GDPR, financial regs) - Genuinely sensitive personal information (health, finances, relationships) - Privileged legal communications - Pre-publication research with intellectual property implications - Internal business material with confidentiality obligations

Should not be in NotebookLM: - Classified or export-controlled material - Trade secrets - Material subject to attorney-client privilege you haven't been authorized to upload - Material whose disclosure would cause specific known harm - Anything you wouldn't be comfortable seeing leaked

The calibration isn't about NotebookLM being uniquely risky. It's about applying the same data-handling care to NotebookLM that you'd apply to any cloud tool in your workflow.

Threat Modeling Your Use

A useful exercise for serious users: think through what could plausibly go wrong with the data you put in NotebookLM, and how bad it would be.

The plausible scenarios:

Google has a security incident. Cloud breaches happen. Google's security is strong but not perfect. Material you've uploaded could, in principle, be accessed by parties you didn't authorize.

Your account gets compromised. Phishing, credential reuse, malware — your Google account is the keys to your entire NotebookLM library. If it's compromised, everything is exposed.

Legal process compels disclosure. Government legal process, civil litigation discovery — your NotebookLM data could be subpoenaed.

Internal Google employee access. Google has internal controls, but a determined or malicious employee could potentially access your data. Workspace contractual protections reduce this risk; personal-account use doesn't have the same protections.

Product change. Google could change its terms or its data practices. Material put in under one set of terms is, in principle, governed by future terms unless you delete it.

Acquisition or business change. Google products have been discontinued before. NotebookLM probably won't be — it's strategically important to Google — but the possibility isn't zero.

For each scenario, the question is: how bad would it be? For most users, for most material, the answer is "not very bad" and the convenience of NotebookLM clearly outweighs the data risks. For some users, for some material, the answer is "very bad" and the calculation flips.

The honest assessment is yours to make. Defaulting to "it's fine, it's just Google" is the convenient answer. It's not always the right one.

Practical Recommendations

For most users, the practical playbook:

1. **Use the right account type.** Personal Gmail for personal-stakes work; Workspace or Education for work-related material; consult before putting regulated material anywhere.
2. **Curate what you upload.** Don't upload material that doesn't need to be in NotebookLM. Especially for sensitive categories, ask whether the AI assistance value justifies the data exposure.
3. **Practice library hygiene.** Delete notebooks for completed projects. Remove sources you no longer need. Audit your library periodically.
4. **Strong account security.** Two-factor authentication, strong unique passwords, care on shared devices. Your Google account is the gateway.
5. **Know your institution's policies.** Workspace administrators may have configured restrictions you should know about. Comply with them.
6. **Document NotebookLM use for compliance-relevant work.** If your professional context requires audit trails for AI tool use, maintain them.
7. **Be conservative when uncertain.** When in doubt about whether something belongs in NotebookLM, don't put it in.

These aren't paranoid practices. They're the basic data discipline any cloud service warrants in 2026 — calibrated to the specific properties of NotebookLM.

The Trust-with-Verification Frame

The same frame that applies to NotebookLM's content (calibrated trust, verified at high stakes) applies to its data handling. You can trust the product to do roughly what it claims, including its data protections. But for high-stakes data, that trust should be backed by verification — administrator review, institutional policy, legal counsel where appropriate.

The combination — calibrated trust plus stakes-appropriate verification — is what makes NotebookLM safe across the range of professional contexts where it's being used. The casual user can be casual. The regulated-industry user has to do the work.

The next chapter takes the privacy and trust questions in this chapter and broadens them to the ethical questions AI-assisted research raises generally — questions every NotebookLM user, casual or serious, should work through.

Chapter 32: The Ethics of AI-Assisted Research

If you've read this far, you have the technical and operational knowledge to use NotebookLM well. You know how to curate sources, ask questions, verify citations, share appropriately, and think about data privacy. You can produce work with NotebookLM that's faster, more thorough, and more rigorous than you could produce without it.

But knowing how to use a tool isn't the same as knowing when to use it, how to disclose it, and how to think about what it's doing to the practice of work that depends on it. The questions in this chapter are the harder ones — not technical questions with technical answers, but ethical questions where reasonable people disagree.

This is the last full chapter of the book. It's worth reading even if — especially if — you've been using NotebookLM for a while. The ethical questions about AI-assisted research aren't going away; they'll intensify as the tools get more capable.

Disclosure: The Default Question

The most consequential ethical practice for AI-assisted work is disclosure. Different contexts have different norms, but the underlying question — should the audience know AI was used — comes up everywhere AI gets used.

A useful framework for thinking about disclosure:

Disclose when AI is doing creative or evaluative work. If the AI is producing the actual content — the writing, the synthesis, the analysis — and you're sharing it under your name, the audience has a legitimate interest in knowing.

Disclose when accuracy is the audience's concern. Briefings, recommendations, claims of fact — the audience cares whether you've verified the content personally. Knowing AI was involved lets them calibrate trust.

Disclose when the medium might mislead. AI-generated audio, video, or images that the audience might mistake for human-generated work — disclose, regardless of context.

Disclosure is less critical when AI is purely supportive. Using NotebookLM to explore literature you then summarize in your own voice doesn't necessarily require explicit disclosure (though some venues now require it). Using it to generate the published text does.

Hidden use is the dangerous use. The cases where AI assistance has caused reputational damage have almost always been cases where use was hidden, then discovered. Open use, even of substantial AI assistance, doesn't carry the same risk.

When in doubt, disclose. The downside of disclosing assistance you didn't need to disclose is small. The downside of failing to disclose assistance that turns out to matter can be severe.

Authorship and Attribution

Beyond disclosure, there's the deeper question of what authorship means when AI is involved.

A useful position: **AI tools, including NotebookLM, are not authors.** They're tools. The author is the human who decided what to ask, evaluated the output, made editorial decisions, and put a name on the result.

This means:

- **Don't list AI tools as co-authors.** They aren't.
- **Don't credit them in author bylines or attribution lines.** The work is yours; the assistance was tooling.
- **Do disclose the assistance** in methods sections, footnotes, or acknowledgments as appropriate.
- **Take full responsibility for the output.** Errors in AI-assisted work are still your errors.

This frame puts the author squarely in the accountability seat. AI assistance doesn't reduce your responsibility for what you produce; it shifts it from "I wrote this" to "I produced this with AI assistance, and I stand behind its accuracy and quality."

Academic Integrity

For students and academics, the ethical landscape is shifting rapidly. Institutions, programs, professors, and journals all have different rules, and the norms are still being established.

A few principles hold up across most contexts:

Know your specific rules. Institutional policies, course policies, journal policies. Don't guess; check.

When the rules permit AI assistance, document your use. Methods sections, acknowledgments, course-specific disclosure mechanisms. Document so that your use can be evaluated.

When the rules prohibit AI assistance, don't use it. Even if you think the rule is wrong, using AI is still a violation. Argue for changing the rule openly; don't violate it covertly.

For ambiguous cases, ask. Most professors, advisors, and reviewers would rather answer a clarifying question than catch an undisclosed use. Asking demonstrates good faith.

Consider the educational point. When a course assigns you to write an essay analyzing a text, the educational purpose is your engagement with the text — not the production of an essay. AI that substitutes for the engagement undermines the purpose, even when it produces a passable essay.

The general principle: AI assistance is appropriate when it amplifies your engagement with the work; it's inappropriate when it substitutes for the engagement the work is meant to require.

The Effect on Skills

A subtler question: what does relying on AI assistance do to the skills you're supposed to be developing?

For students, this is acute. Research, writing, analysis, and synthesis aren't just about producing outputs; they're about developing the cognitive skills the work exercises. A student who outsources synthesis to AI may produce equivalent outputs in the short term while developing far less synthesis capability over time.

The same dynamic applies to working professionals, less acutely. A research analyst who uses NotebookLM to draft every briefing may produce briefings faster and develop briefing skills more slowly than one who drafts manually with NotebookLM as a supporting tool.

This isn't an argument against using NotebookLM. It's an argument for using it deliberately:

- **For skills you're trying to develop, do the work without AI assistance regularly.** Even when AI-assisted work is the production norm, manual work keeps the skills sharp.
- **For skills you've already developed, AI assistance lets you produce more output at quality you can evaluate.** Use the tools freely once the underlying skills are reliable.
- **For students especially, the skill-building stakes are higher than the output stakes.** Resist the temptation to optimize for output quality at the expense of skill development.

The Slop Problem

Throughout this book I've used the term "AI slop" — the generic, characterless content that has flooded the open web in the AI era. It deserves a more direct treatment.

When AI-assisted content production becomes ubiquitous, the median quality of output drops. Articles summarize without insight. Videos present without perspective. Podcasts discuss without conviction. Information density per unit of content stays roughly constant, but the ratio of human voice to AI-flavored generality drops.

The slop problem has two dimensions for individual users:

The aggregate-harm dimension. Every AI-slop output contributes to a degraded information environment. The collective effect: finding human thinking online gets harder, the value of human creative work gets diluted, and the platforms hosting content get worse at distinguishing signal from noise.

The personal-credibility dimension. Audiences are getting better at recognizing AI-flavored content. Once your output is associated with the slop pile, the association is hard to reverse. Reputation, once degraded, is expensive to rebuild.

The protection — for yourself and the broader information environment — is voice. Your specific perspective, your specific examples, your specific framings. The things that make your work yours have to stay prominent in any AI-assisted workflow.

This is why "edit substantially" and "use as scaffolding" keep appearing throughout this book. They aren't pedantry. They're the practices that separate creators who use AI as a tool from creators whose work disappears into the slop.

Power Dynamics

A broader ethical dimension that gets less attention: AI tools concentrate certain kinds of power in the organizations that build and operate them.

For NotebookLM specifically:

- **Google decides what the model can and can't do.** Capabilities can be added or removed by product decision.
- **Google decides what the data practices are.** Privacy protections evolve with corporate priorities, regulatory pressure, and market conditions.
- **Google decides what the pricing is.** Tools that become essential to your workflow can become more expensive over time.
- **Google decides whether the product continues to exist.** Google has discontinued products before.

Using NotebookLM intensively means depending on Google's continued operation, goodwill, and strategic interest in the product. For most users, this dependency is acceptable — the value clearly exceeds the cost. For some users, particularly those building organizational workflows around NotebookLM, the dependency warrants more deliberate thought.

A few mitigations:

- **Don't put critical work product only inside NotebookLM.** Export important outputs. Keep copies of source material outside the tool.
- **Maintain workflows that can survive tool change.** If NotebookLM disappeared tomorrow, what would you lose? Make sure the answer isn't "everything."
- **Consider open-source alternatives where they exist.** For some workflows, open RAG tools (LangChain, LlamaIndex, others) provide similar capabilities with different dependencies. The convenience trade-off is real, but the dependency trade-off shifts.

The Equity Question

A different power dimension: who has access to NotebookLM, and what does that access enable that lack of access doesn't?

NotebookLM's Free tier is capable. The more powerful tiers — particularly Pro and Ultra — are priced at levels that put them out of reach for many potential users globally. Students, researchers, and professionals who can afford Pro tier are doing different work than those who can't.

This isn't NotebookLM's fault — the entire AI tool landscape has the same dynamic — but it's worth noticing. The productivity gap between those with access to powerful AI tools and those without is widening, with implications for which research gets done, which content gets produced, and which professional work scales.

For individual users, this is mostly a matter of awareness. You're benefiting from access not everyone has; the people you're competing with may have less; the people you're collaborating with internationally may have very different tool environments. The equity dimension shapes what's reasonable to expect, what counts as good practice, and how to think about your own privileged position.

For institutional users — universities, research institutions, employers — there's a more direct question about how to make AI tool access equitable. Some institutions are negotiating bulk access to NotebookLM and similar tools to reduce the access gap among their members. Worth advocating for if your institution hasn't.

The "Synthesizer's Responsibility"

A frame that's emerged in academic discussions of AI-assisted research: the *synthesizer's responsibility*. The idea is that when AI does much of the synthesis work, the human's responsibility shifts upstream and downstream of the synthesis itself — to the choice of sources (upstream) and the verification of synthesis quality (downstream).

The synthesizer is now you, even if the synthesis text was generated by NotebookLM. You picked the sources. You're going to use the synthesis. You're putting your name on the resulting work. Synthesis quality is your responsibility, regardless of who or what produced it.

This frame resists two common abdications:

The abdication to the AI. "I can't be expected to verify everything; the AI did it." No — you used the AI; the use was your choice; the verification is your responsibility.

The abdication to the sources. "The errors are in the sources, not in my use of them." Sometimes true, but the responsibility for what you produce always includes responsibility for the source set you chose.

The synthesizer's responsibility is, in some ways, harder than the traditional researcher's — you're accountable for more dimensions of the work, even though you produced fewer of them yourself.

The Long View

Stepping back from the specific questions: NotebookLM and tools like it represent a shift in how some kinds of intellectual work get done. The shift is real, large, and probably irreversible. The ethical questions of how to do AI-assisted work well will be central to many professional and academic practices for the foreseeable future.

A few predictions about how the ethical landscape will evolve:

Disclosure norms will tighten. As AI use becomes more common, expectations of disclosure will become more explicit. Hidden use will become correspondingly more costly to reputation.

Verification expectations will rise. As tools improve, the bar for "you should have caught this" rises. Errors that are clearly AI-introduced will be less excusable as verification tools and practices mature.

Authorial responsibility will be reasserted. Some of the early breeziness about "the AI wrote it" will give way to clear restatement that authorship implies responsibility for the work.

New genres of work will emerge. Some kinds of work — long literature reviews, certain kinds of synthesis, certain genres of educational content — will be reshaped by AI assistance into formats that look different from their pre-AI ancestors.

Equity questions will become political. As AI access ties more directly to professional success, equitable access will become an institutional and policy concern.

You're working in the early years of a new period in how knowledge work gets done. The ethical questions you're working through aren't abstract; they're actively shaping what counts as competent, responsible practice in your field.

A Personal Synthesis

The ethical posture I've tried to model throughout this book: NotebookLM is a powerful tool, useful for many kinds of work. Used well — with curation discipline, verification habits, deliberate disclosure, and continued human judgment — it makes work faster and often better. Used badly — with credulity, hidden use, and abdication of authorial responsibility — it produces work that looks polished but contains subtle errors, contributes to a degraded information environment, and eventually damages the reputation of users who rely on it without care.

The choice between these isn't determined by the tool. It's determined by you, every time you use it.

The good news: doing it right isn't much harder than doing it badly. The verification discipline costs minutes; the disclosure habit costs nothing; the curation habit becomes second nature. The marginal cost of using NotebookLM responsibly is small. The marginal cost of using it irresponsibly stays hidden until the day it isn't.

That closes Part VIII, and with it the substantive content of the book. Part IX is reference material — the epilogue, plus appendices covering shortcuts, prompt templates, troubleshooting, glossary, what's-new-in-2026, and resources for further learning.

What you've learned across the preceding eight parts — the mechanics, the workflows, the disciplines, the ethical posture — is enough to use NotebookLM well, for years, across the kinds of work you actually do.

The rest is practice.

Epilogue: The Quiet Revolution

The loud AI story of the last few years has been about chatbots. ChatGPT. Claude. Gemini. The conversational AI that talks to you about anything, knows about everything, and writes whatever you ask it to write.

NotebookLM is a different story. Quieter. Narrower. Bounded by the sources you give it. It doesn't know the world; it knows your folder of PDFs. It doesn't write your essay; it helps you understand the papers your essay is about. It doesn't replace expertise; it amplifies the work of people who already know what they're trying to learn.

This is, in some ways, the more important AI story. The chatbot revolution made AI conversational, which mattered. The source-grounded revolution is making AI *trustworthy*, which matters more. A tool whose answers come with citations you can verify, that refuses to invent when the source is silent, that surfaces the underlying material rather than burying it — this is AI that knowledge work can live with.

NotebookLM isn't the only source-grounded AI tool, and it won't be the only one for long. The pattern it represents — RAG architectures, citation-traceable answers, source-as-truth — is becoming the default for any AI tool that takes accuracy seriously. The chatbots are adapting in this direction, too: ChatGPT's web search, Claude's long-context document handling, Gemini's grounding modes. The era of "AI that confidently states things" is giving way to the era of "AI that confidently states things and shows you where they came from."

That shift won't fix every problem AI has caused. But it's a real shift, and one knowledge workers, students, researchers, and creators should participate in deliberately rather than passively.

What You've Built

If you've read this book and used NotebookLM alongside it, you've built something concrete. Maybe a course notebook that's getting you through finals. Maybe a literature review notebook that's saving you weeks. Maybe a project notebook that's becoming your team's institutional memory. Maybe a personal-research notebook that captures something you've been chasing for years.

Whatever it is, it's yours. Built deliberately, source by source, question by question, note by note. Verified at the points where verification mattered. Shared at the points where sharing made sense. Calibrated to your specific work and your specific stakes.

That's the value NotebookLM actually delivers. Not the impressive Audio Overview demo. Not the polished Briefing Doc. The accumulating, deliberate workspace that supports real intellectual work over months and years.

What Comes Next

NotebookLM will keep evolving. New Studio outputs will appear — formats nobody has thought of yet, capabilities the current product doesn't have. The underlying Gemini models will get better. The pricing will shift. The mobile apps will catch up to the web; the web will pull ahead again. Some features described in this book will be deprecated; some new features will warrant chapters of their own.

The principles will hold up longer than the specifics. Source curation as deliberate practice. Prompting as a learnable craft. Verification as the habit that protects the work. Disclosure as the default. The synthesizer's responsibility to the underlying material. These aren't NotebookLM-specific principles. They're how to do AI-assisted intellectual work well, regardless of which tool you're using or how that tool evolves.

Beyond NotebookLM, the broader AI landscape will keep shifting too. Other source-grounded tools will emerge. Open-source RAG systems will get good enough that some users move off cloud products entirely. Regulatory frameworks will develop. Disclosure norms will tighten. The role of AI in research, education, journalism, and knowledge work will keep being contested.

You're not at the end of a technology curve. You're in the middle of one — early enough that your habits and instincts are still being formed, but late enough that the tools are mature enough to use seriously. The choices you make about how to use NotebookLM and tools like it will shape what kind of professional, scholar, or creator you become as the curve continues.

A Personal Note

If this book has done its job, you have the technical and operational knowledge to use NotebookLM well, the discipline to use it responsibly, and the ethical posture to use it with integrity.

You also have the most important capability the book can give you: the ability to evaluate, on your own, whether a particular use of NotebookLM is the right use. Not because the book told you the answer for every situation — it didn't, because no book could — but because the principles, frameworks, and habits the book covered let you reason about new situations as they come up.

That's the value of any well-written reference book on a fast-moving topic. The specific features will change. The screen layouts will be redesigned. The pricing tiers will be restructured. But the way of thinking about the tool and the work it supports — the verification discipline, the curation craft, the calibrated trust, the ethical clarity — carries forward, intact, across whatever changes the underlying technology goes through.

You're equipped. Now do the work.

Where to Go From Here

If you've found this book useful, you may want to look at the other books in the Finnoybu Press AI for Everyone series. *ChatGPT: The Definitive Guide* and *Claude: The Definitive Guide* cover the general-purpose chatbots NotebookLM complements rather than replaces. *AI Prompt Engineering* covers the deeper craft of prompting across all the major AI tools. *AI Governance for Practitioners* takes the ethical and institutional questions raised in Chapter 32 and develops them into a full framework for organizations adopting AI responsibly.

For staying current with NotebookLM specifically, Google maintains a help center, a community forum, and a blog that announces new features. Several independent newsletters and YouTube channels track NotebookLM developments closely. Appendix F has a curated list.

For the broader practice of AI-assisted research and knowledge work, you'll do better building your own habits than reading more books on the subject. The skills compound through use, not through study. Pick a workflow from Part VI that fits your work, try it for a month, refine it based on what you learn.

That's the end of the book. The rest is reference material — keyboard shortcuts, prompt templates, troubleshooting, glossary, what's new, further resources. Use them when you need them. Come back to them as the product evolves.

Thanks for reading. Now: open NotebookLM, build something useful, and verify your citations.

Part IX: Reference

"Knowing where to look is half the battle."

— Anonymous

Appendix A: Keyboard Shortcuts and Interface Tips

NotebookLM's interface is mostly mouse-driven, but a working set of keyboard shortcuts and interface conventions speeds up daily work substantially. Specific shortcuts evolve as Google iterates on the UI; this appendix covers the categories stable enough to learn, with the caveat that you should check current documentation when shortcuts seem to have changed.

Web App — General Navigation

- **Tab / Shift+Tab** — move focus through interactive elements (sources, controls, chat)
- **Enter** — activate the focused element
- **Esc** — dismiss dialogs, panels, and overlays
- **/ (slash)** — focus the chat input from anywhere in the notebook (most interface versions)

Chat Input

- **Enter** — send your message
- **Shift+Enter** — new line within the message (without sending)
- **Up arrow** in an empty chat box — recall your previous message
- **Ctrl+K / Cmd+K** — open the chat focus mode in some interface versions

Source Pane

- **Click source** — open the source detail view
- **Checkbox toggle** — include or exclude the source from the next query (the underused control from Chapter 6)
- **Right-click on source name** — most interface versions surface a context menu (rename, remove, summarize)

Studio Output Generation

There aren't hotkeys for triggering Studio output generation. You'll click through the Studio panel for these operations.

A few efficiency tips:

- **Pin frequently used Studio outputs** to the top of the Studio panel where the option exists.
- **Use the source-selection checkboxes deliberately before generating** to avoid having to wait for output across an unwanted source set.
- **Save the generation parameters as part of your workflow notes** so you can reproduce a successful Studio output later without re-deriving the customization prompt.

Mobile App Gestures

- **Swipe between panes** — most mobile views support swipe navigation between sources, chat, and Studio panels.
- **Long-press on a source** — context menu for source operations.
- **Pull to refresh** — sync the notebook with the current state on Google's servers.
- **Share-sheet integration** — system share menu surfaces NotebookLM as a destination for adding sources from other apps.

Audio Overview Playback (Mobile)

- **Play/pause from lock screen** — standard media controls work as expected
- **Skip forward/backward** — typically 15- or 30-second jumps via standard controls
- **Background playback** — keeps playing when you switch apps or lock the screen
- **CarPlay/Android Auto** — supported in some implementations for in-vehicle listening

Power-User Patterns

A handful of small habits compound into substantially faster daily use:

- **Name notebooks the moment you create them.** Untitled notebooks accumulate; named notebooks stay navigable.
- **Rename sources immediately after upload.** Auto-generated names are noise; deliberate names are signal.
- **Save useful chat answers as notes immediately.** "I'll come back to this" almost never happens.
- **Use source-selection checkboxes before every Studio output.** Default-everything is rarely what you actually want.
- **Verify citations at generation time, not later.** Verification fatigue is real; do it while you're already in the relevant material.
- **Pin your two or three active notebooks.** Keep the gallery navigable.

Appendix B: Prompt Template Library

Sixty-plus prompt templates organized by use case. Adapt the bracketed variables to your situation. Most of these are drawn from or expanded versions of patterns introduced in Chapters 7, 17, and 22.

Initial Orientation

1. *"Summarize [source] in three paragraphs. First paragraph: what is this and who's it written for. Second paragraph: the central claim or finding. Third paragraph: the structure of the document and where the major sections are."*
2. *"What's the main argument or finding in [source]? What kind of evidence does it offer? What does it hedge on?"*
3. *"List the five most important things a reader needs to know about [source] before engaging with it."*
4. *"What's the one-sentence pitch of [source]? Now expand that to a paragraph. Now to a page."*
5. *"For someone unfamiliar with [topic/field], what do they need to know to follow [source]? Define key terms as needed."*

Targeted Reading

6. *"In [source], find the discussion of [specific topic]. Quote the most relevant passage directly, then summarize the surrounding context."*
7. *"What does [source] say about [specific question]? Quote rather than paraphrase where possible."*
8. *"Walk me through [section] of [source] in plain language. Explain the choices the author made and why."*
9. *"What's the strongest piece of evidence [source] offers for [claim]? Quote it. What's the weakest?"*

10. *"How does [source] define [specific term]? Where does this definition appear, and is it consistent throughout the source?"*

Cross-Source Synthesis

11. *"Across all selected sources, identify what's said about [topic]. For each substantive claim, note which source(s) support it, where they agree, and where they diverge."*

12. *"Compare what [Source A] and [Source B] say about [specific topic]. Where do they agree, where do they disagree, and how do they frame the question differently?"*

13. *"What's the consensus view across these sources on [topic]? Which sources represent the consensus and which dissent?"*

14. *"How has [concept] been treated across the sources, in chronological order? What changes between earlier and later treatments?"*

15. *"Build a synthesis of what these sources collectively say about [topic]. Note where individual sources contribute uniquely and where they reinforce each other."*

Identifying Gaps

16. *"Across the selected sources, what aspects of [topic] are NOT addressed? What questions would a thorough treatment cover that these sources don't?"*

17. *"What populations, contexts, or perspectives are underrepresented in these sources?"*

18. *"What does this literature consistently fail to engage with? What's the elephant in the room?"*

19. *"If a critical reviewer were to identify gaps in [source's] argument, what would they target first?"*

20. *"What evidence would be required to test or extend [claim from source] that doesn't currently exist in these sources?"*

Critical Reading

21. *"Read [source] critically. Where is the argument strongest? Where is it weakest? What evidence is most compelling? What evidence is thin or missing?"*

22. *"Identify the implicit assumptions in [source]. What does the author take for granted that might not hold?"*

23. *"What's the weakest part of [source]'s methodology? What would a skeptical peer reviewer focus on?"*

24. *"Where does [source] generalize beyond what its evidence actually supports?"*

25. *"What conflicts of interest or biases might shape [source]'s framing? Note specific places where these might be visible."*

Steel-Manning and Debate

26. *"Make the strongest possible case for [position] using only what's in the sources. Cite specifically. Address the most likely counter-arguments preemptively."*

27. *"Steelman both sides of the debate over [contested question]. Make the strongest case for each. Identify what the disagreement actually hinges on."*

28. *"Where in the sources do the strongest counter-arguments to [claim] appear? Quote them directly."*

29. *"If you had to defend [position] in front of a hostile audience, what evidence from these sources would you use?"*

30. *"What's the most defensible position someone could hold given only this source set? What does it require them to discount?"*

Tracing Evolution

31. *"How has [field's] understanding of [concept] evolved across these sources? Identify the major shifts and what drove them."*

32. *"What was the dominant view before [pivotal source/event] in this literature? What did it shift to afterward?"*

33. *"Trace [author's] thinking on [topic] across the sources by them I've included. Where does it remain consistent? Where does it change?"*

34. *"What questions did this literature start with? What questions does it ask now? What changed?"*

Structured Extraction

35. *"Extract all instances where [type of data point] appears across the sources. Present as a table with columns for [specific columns]. Include citations to each source."*

36. *"List every named entity of type [type] across the sources. For each, note what's said about it and which source(s) discuss it."*

37. *"Build a comparison matrix of [items] across the sources. Columns: [specific dimensions]. Cite each cell."*

38. *"Extract every quantitative claim across the source set. Columns: claim, value, unit, source, page reference."*

39. *"List every recommendation across the sources, organized by priority. Tag each with which source(s) made it."*

Verifying Specific Claims

40. *"I've encountered the claim that [specific claim]. Do the sources support this, contradict it, or remain silent? Quote any directly relevant passages."*

41. *"Where does [source] say [paraphrased claim]? Quote the exact passage so I can verify the wording."*

42. *"Is [claim] a direct claim of [source], or is it being paraphrased or interpreted? Quote what the source actually says."*

43. *"How confident is [source] in [claim]? Quote the hedging language, if any."*

44. *"Does any source push back on [claim]? Quote the strongest counter-arguments, with citations."*

Finding Contradictions

45. *"Where do the sources contradict each other? Identify specific points of disagreement. For each, quote the conflicting passages."*

46. *"What does [Source A] assert that [Source B] would dispute? Quote both positions."*

47. *"Are there places where [source] contradicts itself, or where its later claims sit uneasily with its earlier ones? Quote specifically."*

48. *"Identify where the consensus across these sources hides genuine disagreement. What's being smoothed over?"*

Structuring Arguments and Writing

49. *"I'm writing a piece arguing [thesis]. Based on the sources, what would be the most defensible structure? What evidence supports each step?"*

50. *"Suggest a structure for an essay on [topic] based on these sources. What would be the major sections? What would each cover?"*

51. *"Draft the introduction to a paper on [topic], framed as [angle], grounded in these sources. Cite specifically."*

52. *"Generate an outline for a [target length] piece on [topic]. Each section should have a clear claim and the supporting evidence from the sources."*

53. *"What would a critical reviewer of [piece I'm writing] push back on? What sources would they cite to do so?"*

Studio Output Customization

54. *"Generate an Audio Overview focused on [specific aspect]. Skip [things to skip]. Audience: [specific audience]. Tone: [characteristics]."*

55. *"Generate a Briefing Doc for [audience]. Length: [target]. Structure: [specific sections]. Skip [things to omit]."*

56. *"Generate a Slide Deck for a [target audience] presentation. [N] slides. Format: [presenter-focused / detailed]. Include [specific elements]."*

57. *"Generate a Mind Map of how [topic] decomposes across these sources. Emphasize [specific dimension]."*

58. *"Generate Flashcards covering [specific scope]. Difficulty: [level]. Quantity: [N]. Focus on [terms / concepts / relationships]."*

Reflection and Refinement

59. *"Looking back at the answer you just gave, what's the weakest claim in it? What would I need to verify most carefully?"*

60. *"You said [previous claim]. I'm not sure that's quite right. Re-check the cited passages and tell me whether the claim holds up."*

61. *"What questions should I be asking that I haven't asked yet, given what's in these sources?"*

62. *"Summarize what I've learned from this notebook so far. What's still unresolved or worth investigating further?"*

Notes and Synthesis

63. *"Generate a synthesis note capturing what we've established in this conversation. Format suitable for promoting to a source."*

64. *"What are the three most important takeaways from the recent chat history? Phrase as standalone notes I can save."*

65. *"Identify any tensions or unresolved questions from the chat history that warrant follow-up."*

Appendix C: Troubleshooting Common Issues

Quick-reference solutions for the issues NotebookLM users hit most often. Organized by symptom.

Source Upload Issues

"Upload failed" or stuck progress indicator. - Check file size — very large files (approaching the 1M-token ceiling) take longer than smaller ones - Check file format — confirm the type is supported (PDF, DOCX, TXT, CSV, PNG/JPG, MP3/WAV, MP4, etc.) - Check network connectivity - For very large files, try reloading the page after a few minutes — ingestion may have completed even if the UI didn't update - If the file genuinely won't upload, try splitting it (Chapter 18) or converting to a different supported format

Web URL fetch failed or returned wrong content. - The site may have a paywall, JavaScript-only rendering, or aggressive bot detection - Try saving the page as a PDF in your browser, then uploading the PDF instead - Check the auto-generated source summary — if it says "page not found" or similar, the fetch failed silently

YouTube source missing content. - NotebookLM uses the video's transcript (auto-generated or creator-uploaded) - If the video has no transcript available, the source will be empty - For visual content (cooking demos, art tutorials, etc.), the transcript may capture only a fraction of what matters - Try copying the transcript manually if YouTube provides one and uploading as text

OCR errors in scanned documents. - NotebookLM applies OCR to scanned PDFs and image sources - Quality varies — clean scans work well; faded, skewed, or low-resolution scans degrade - For important sources, run a higher-quality OCR pass externally (Adobe Acrobat, dedicated OCR tools) and upload the cleaner text

Audio/Video Generation Issues

Audio Overview generation stuck or queued. - Generation typically takes 2–10 minutes depending on source size - High-demand periods can extend this - If it's been more than 30 minutes, refresh the page and try again - If it consistently fails, try generating with a smaller source selection

Audio Overview cuts off mid-sentence. - This occasionally happens with very long generations - Regenerate; the issue is usually transient

Voice quality sounds off compared to previous outputs. - Voice models have been upgraded periodically; differences across sessions may be intentional - If voice quality is consistently poor for a particular language, that language may be in a less-developed tier

Video Overview generation taking very long. - Video generation is slower than audio — 5–15 minutes for typical sources, longer for Cinematic Mode - Very long sources push this further - If it's been more than 45 minutes, refresh and check status

Citation and Accuracy Issues

Citations point to the wrong passage. - Click through to the cited passage and verify - If the citation is genuinely wrong (passage doesn't support the claim), this is a model error — re-prompt or use different framing - Sometimes the highlighted span is right but the surrounding context is more relevant — read the paragraph

Answer says "I don't know" but the information is in the sources. - Try rephrasing the question using terms more likely to appear in the source text - The relevant passages may have been missed by retrieval — try a more specific question - Try selecting just the source that contains the information and re-asking

Answer asserts something not in the sources. - This is a hallucination — surfacing during a process designed to prevent them - Be specific: "Where in the sources does this come from? Quote the exact passage." - If NotebookLM can't produce a supporting passage, the claim is ungrounded

Studio output contains errors not present in chat answers. - Studio outputs and chat use the same model but different prompting; outputs can drift in ways chat doesn't - For high-stakes outputs, generate, then verify via chat by paste-and-asking for citations

Notebook and Library Issues

Can't find a notebook I created. - Check the gallery search — search filters by title only - Check sort order — recently modified is the default; alphabetical or recently created may surface older notebooks - Confirm you're signed into the correct Google account

Sources missing from a notebook I haven't touched. - Sources don't typically disappear — confirm you're in the right notebook - If sources truly are missing, this is a Google product issue; report through the help center

Shared notebook not accessible to a collaborator. - Check the recipient's Google account is the one you shared with - Workspace organizations may restrict external sharing — check with your administrator - Confirm the link or share invitation was correctly sent

Mobile App Issues

Mobile app missing a feature available on web. - New features launch on web first and roll out to mobile over weeks to months - For features critical to your workflow, use the web app

Mobile sync seems out of date. - Pull to refresh in most interface versions - Force-quit and relaunch the app - Verify network connectivity

Audio Overview won't play in the background. - Check app permissions for background audio - Some operating system battery-saving modes may prevent background playback - For in-vehicle use, confirm CarPlay/Android Auto pairing

Account and Tier Issues

Hitting daily quotas faster than expected. - Quotas reset on a 24-hour rolling window in most implementations - Check your tier's specific limits - For consistent quota issues, the next tier may be the right answer

Plus features not available even though I'm subscribed. - Sign out and back in to refresh subscription state - Check that the Google account you're signed into is the one with the subscription - Subscription propagation can take a few minutes after upgrading

Can't access Plus collaboration features. - Both you and your collaborators need Plus tier or higher for full collaboration features - Free-tier users can typically view shared notebooks but not edit them

When to Contact Google Support

Most issues resolve through the troubleshooting above. For issues that persist:

- **Account access problems** — use the standard Google account recovery flow
- **Billing or subscription issues** — Google AI subscription support
- **Bug reports for NotebookLM specifically** — the help center includes a feedback channel
- **Workspace administrator issues** — your IT or admin team is the right first contact

For most everyday problems, the fix is one of: refresh the page, sign out and back in, regenerate the failed output, or rephrase the failed query. The product is reliable enough that persistent issues warrant deeper investigation.

Appendix D: Glossary of Terms

A reference for the key terms used throughout this book and across NotebookLM's interface, documentation, and broader source-grounded AI discourse.

Audio Overview. A generated audio track in which two AI hosts discuss the contents of selected sources in podcast-style conversation. Default Studio output type. Released September 2024.

Briefing Doc. A Studio output type producing an executive-style structured summary of source material. Most-used Report format for knowledge work.

Chat. The conversational interface for asking questions of your sources. Per-user; chats persist within a notebook but are not (by default) shared across collaborators.

Cinematic Video Mode. A Studio output type producing more produced, narrative-driven video output than the standard Video Overview. Released July 2025.

Citation. A reference back to a specific passage in a source that supports a claim in NotebookLM's output. Clickable in the chat interface and Studio outputs.

Citation drift. The failure mode where a citation points to a real passage but the cited passage doesn't actually support the claim being made. The most consequential failure mode of source-grounded AI; covered extensively in Chapter 23.

Collaborator. A user with access to a shared notebook. Permission levels typically include viewer, commenter, and editor.

Context window. The amount of text the model can consider at once. NotebookLM's per-source context window is approximately 1 million tokens.

Custom Report. A Studio output where you specify the format and structure rather than selecting a pre-defined Report type.

Data Table. A Studio output that extracts structured tabular data from sources based on a prompt specifying the desired columns. Released December 2025.

Deep Research. A NotebookLM feature that performs multi-step web research on a specified question, returning a synthesized answer with citations to the web sources used.

Editor. A collaboration permission level granting full ability to add and remove sources, ask questions, generate Studio outputs, and modify notes in a shared notebook.

Fast Research. A NotebookLM feature that searches the web for sources relevant to a topic and returns candidate links you can selectively add to your notebook.

FAQ. A Studio Report format that restructures source material as questions and answers.

Flashcards. A Studio output type generating question-and-answer cards from source material for active recall study.

Gemini. Google's flagship large language model family. NotebookLM is powered by Gemini, with the underlying model upgraded periodically (most recently to Gemini 3 in March 2026).

Google AI subscription. Google's bundled AI subscription tier (Plus/Pro/Ultra) that includes NotebookLM among other AI capabilities.

Hallucination. When an AI model generates content that isn't grounded in its training or in source material — confident but unsupported claims. NotebookLM's source grounding reduces but doesn't eliminate hallucination.

Index source. A handwritten document added as a source that serves as a navigation map of other sources in a notebook. Useful for very large source sets (Chapter 18).

Infographic. A Studio output producing visual summaries in one of 10 available styles (Sketch Note, Kawaii, Professional, Scientific, Anime, Clay, Editorial, Instructional, Bento Grid, Bricks). Released November 2025.

Interactive Audio Overview. A mode of Audio Overview where you can interrupt the AI hosts to ask questions of your own. Released December 2024.

Mind Map. A Studio output producing a visual hierarchical diagram of concepts from source material.

Notebook. The primary organizational unit in NotebookLM. Contains sources, chats, notes, and Studio outputs related to a specific topic or project.

Notebook gallery. The home screen showing all notebooks you've created. Includes search, sort, and (in some interface versions) pinning.

NotebookLM Plus. The paid tier that unlocks expanded quotas, collaborative features, and higher-tier Studio output access. Bundled into Google AI subscriptions starting at $7.99/month.

Note. A small text artifact within a notebook used to capture insights, hypotheses, observations, or saved chat answers. Can be promoted to a source.

Notebook owner. The user who created a notebook and has primary control over its access permissions.

Plus tier. See NotebookLM Plus.

Pro tier. A higher Google AI subscription tier providing expanded NotebookLM quotas. $19.99/month, or $9.99/month for verified students.

Project Tailwind. The original (May 2023) name for what became NotebookLM. Internal Google Labs experimental project.

Promoting a note. Converting a saved note into a source so future queries can reference it directly. Enables cumulative synthesis within a long-running notebook.

RAG (Retrieval-Augmented Generation). The technical approach underlying NotebookLM. The model retrieves relevant passages from sources, augments its context with those passages, then generates an answer grounded in them.

Report. A Studio output category producing structured written documents. Includes Briefing Doc, Study Guide, Blog Post, FAQ, Timeline, and Custom Report formats.

Slide Deck. A Studio output producing complete presentations from source material. Available in detailed (information-dense) and presenter-focused formats. Exports as PPTX. Released November 2025.

Source. Any document, web page, video, audio file, or text added to a notebook for the AI to read. The foundation of everything NotebookLM does.

Source-grounded AI. AI that produces answers based exclusively on a specified set of sources, with citations back to those sources. NotebookLM is the most prominent consumer source-grounded tool in 2026.

Source pane. The left side of the NotebookLM interface, where sources are listed and managed.

Source selection. The checkbox-based control for including or excluding specific sources from a query or Studio output generation. Underused; covered in Chapter 6.

Source summary. An auto-generated overview of a source, displayed when you click the source in the source pane. Editable.

Studio. The right side of the NotebookLM interface, where Audio Overviews, Video Overviews, Reports, Mind Maps, Slide Decks, Flashcards, Quizzes, Infographics, and Data Tables are generated.

Study Guide. A Studio Report format producing structured learning aids with key concepts, themes, and discussion questions.

Synthesis note. A note that captures accumulated insights across multiple chats or working sessions. Often promoted to a source for ongoing reference.

Timeline. A Studio Report format that extracts events from sources and organizes them chronologically.

Token. The unit of text the underlying model processes. Roughly three-quarters of a word in English. NotebookLM's per-source context window is approximately 1 million tokens.

Topic focus prompt. A short text instruction provided when generating a Studio output, telling NotebookLM what to emphasize, what to skip, and who the audience is. The single most underused customization control.

Ultra tier. The highest Google AI subscription tier. $249.99/month. Maximum quotas across all features and watermark-free Studio outputs.

Video Overview. A Studio output combining AI-generated narration with visuals (in styles including Whiteboard, Watercolor, Kawaii, Classic). Released 2025.

Viewer. A collaboration permission level granting read-only access to a shared notebook.

Watermark. A small NotebookLM identifier applied to Audio Overview and Video Overview outputs on Free, Plus, and Pro tiers. Removed only on Ultra tier.

Workspace (Google Workspace). Google's enterprise/organizational account type. Provides stronger data protections than personal Gmail accounts and admin-level controls. Recommended for any sensitive or work-related NotebookLM use.

Appendix E: What's New in 2026

A timeline of the major NotebookLM developments leading up to and through early 2026, focused on what's changed since the product's stable launch in October 2024.

The Pre-2026 Foundation

For context, the changes that set up the 2026 product:

May 2023 — Project Tailwind launches as an experimental Google Labs product.

2024 — Tailwind rebrands to NotebookLM and graduates from experimental to stable status (October 17, 2024).

September 2024 — Audio Overviews launch. The feature goes viral. Spotify Wrapped 2024 partnership puts NotebookLM-generated podcasts in front of hundreds of millions of users.

December 2024 — Interactive Audio Overviews launch. NotebookLM Plus launches for enterprise customers.

February 2025 — NotebookLM Plus extended to individual users via Google AI subscriptions.

Mid-2025 — Video Overviews launch.

July 29, 2025 — Cinematic Video Mode launches.

November 2025 — Infographics (with 10 visual styles powered by Nano Banana Pro) and Slide Decks (with PPTX export) launch.

December 2025 — Data Tables launch.

Early 2026 Developments

January 2026 — Mobile app updates push toward closer feature parity with the web (versions 2026.01.06 on Android, 1.21.0 on iOS).

February 2026 — Reports of legal action begin. The Greene voice-cloning lawsuit (formally filed earlier) enters public discussion.

March 2026 — Google upgrades the underlying model to **Gemini 3**, dramatically improving long-document reasoning, multilingual outputs, and the audio voice models that drive Audio Overviews. The pricing tiers restructure from a two-tier (Free/Plus) into a four-tier model (Free, Plus, Pro, Ultra), bundled with Google AI subscriptions.

Spring 2026 — Continued Studio output refinements; new visual styles added to existing output types; mobile feature parity continues to close.

Through early 2026 — Steady expansion of language support (now 80+ languages for Audio and Video Overviews), continued improvements to Deep Research and Fast Research capabilities, growing collaborative notebook adoption among research teams and small organizations.

Trends That Will Likely Continue

A few patterns to watch for as the product continues to evolve:

Closer mobile parity. The historical pattern: web-first feature launches with mobile catching up over weeks to months. Google has been narrowing this gap.

More Studio output formats. Each year has brought new ways to transform source material — Audio, Video, Cinematic, Reports, Mind Maps, Slide Decks, Infographics, Data Tables. The pattern likely continues.

Deeper Gemini integration. As Gemini's capabilities grow (reasoning, multimodal understanding, agentic behavior), NotebookLM inherits them. The line between "general-purpose Gemini" and "source-grounded NotebookLM" may continue to evolve.

Expanding tier capabilities. Google's tendency has been to push capabilities downward over time (features that started in Plus eventually appear in Free; features that started in Pro eventually appear in Plus). Free-tier capability has grown substantially since 2024.

More integration with Google Workspace. The collaborative and enterprise features for Workspace customers have been expanding. Expect this to continue.

Evolving disclosure norms. As AI-generated content becomes more sophisticated, expect both regulatory and platform-level requirements around disclosure to tighten.

What to Watch For

For users wanting to track NotebookLM's continued evolution:

- **Google's NotebookLM blog and help center** for official feature announcements
- **Steven Johnson's writing** for product perspective from one of the original team members
- **Independent NotebookLM newsletters and YouTube channels** (see Appendix F for specific recommendations)
- **Academic and industry use case discussions** as established practices accumulate
- **Legal developments** around AI-generated content, voice models, and disclosure obligations

The product as described in this book is accurate as of early 2026. Significant changes will appear before the next edition. Use the principles and frameworks in the book to evaluate new features as they arrive — most of what makes NotebookLM useful (or problematic) doesn't change with new features.

Appendix F: Resources and Further Reading

A curated list of resources for staying current with NotebookLM specifically and source-grounded AI more broadly. URLs and specific recommendations were accurate as of early 2026 but evolve quickly; treat this as a starting point, not a permanent reference.

Official Google Resources

NotebookLM Help Center — Google's official documentation. Authoritative on current features, pricing, and account-related questions. The first stop for any specific operational question.

NotebookLM Blog — Product announcements, feature deep-dives, and team perspective. Updated periodically. Worth subscribing for early notice of new capabilities.

Google AI Subscription Documentation — For tier comparison, pricing, and bundled-feature questions across the broader Google AI product line.

Google Workspace Admin Documentation — For administrators configuring NotebookLM for organizational use, including data handling, sharing controls, and compliance settings.

People to Follow

Steven Johnson — Author and one of the original NotebookLM team members. His writing provides product perspective from someone who has shaped the tool's vision since Project Tailwind.

Raiza Martin — NotebookLM product manager. Periodically posts about product direction and decisions.

Independent voices in the AI tools space — A rotating set of writers and analysts who track AI tool development closely. The specific names change over time; identify a few whose perspective you trust and follow.

Communities

Academic Twitter and Mastodon (academic communities) – Particularly active around new feature releases and research workflow discussions.

r/NotebookLM and related subreddits – Mixed quality but useful for spotting common issues and emerging workflows.

Discord communities – Several AI-tool-focused Discord servers have active NotebookLM discussion channels.

Academic conferences and workshops – Increasingly include sessions on AI-assisted research methodologies. Worth seeking out in your field.

Newsletters Worth Following

The newsletter landscape changes quickly, but in early 2026 the strongest options for AI-tool tracking generally include:

- **Specialized AI-tool newsletters** that cover NotebookLM alongside other tools
- **Education-focused newsletters** that track AI tool adoption in academic and learning contexts
- **Knowledge-management newsletters** (PKM, "tools for thought") that often cover NotebookLM as part of their broader coverage

Pick two or three that match your specific interests; subscribing to too many produces noise without insight.

Recommended Reading on Source-Grounded AI Generally

For readers who want to understand the broader context of what NotebookLM represents:

- **Foundational papers on RAG** (Retrieval-Augmented Generation) provide the technical underpinnings. Searchable on arXiv and Google Scholar.

- **Research on AI-assisted writing and research** is a growing literature with both empirical findings (how does AI assistance affect work quality?) and ethical analysis (what does authorship mean in an AI-assisted era?).
- **Historical work on tools for thought** (from Vannevar Bush's "As We May Think" forward) provides the intellectual context for what NotebookLM is trying to do.

Other Books in the Finnoybu Press AI for Everyone Series

For readers who found this book useful, the broader series covers complementary topics:

- *ChatGPT: The Definitive Guide* — General-purpose AI chatbot. Different from NotebookLM in fundamental ways; covers what NotebookLM doesn't try to do.
- *ChatGPT: The Power User Guide* — Advanced techniques for ChatGPT specifically.
- *Claude: The Definitive Guide* — Anthropic's general-purpose AI. Strong on long documents and nuanced reasoning.
- *Claude Code: The Power User Guide* — Claude's agentic coding tool.
- *Gemini: The Complete Guide* — Google's general-purpose AI assistant. Shares the underlying model with NotebookLM but with very different framing.
- *Gemini: The Advanced Guide* — Power-user techniques for Gemini.
- *Copilot: The Workplace AI Guide* and *Copilot: The Advanced Workplace Guide* — Microsoft's enterprise AI assistant.
- *Perplexity: The Research Playbook* and *Perplexity: The Advanced Research Playbook* — Perplexity's search-and-research focused AI.
- *DeepSeek: The Complete Guide* — Open-weight AI models with frontier capability at a fraction of the cost.
- *Cursor: The Complete Guide* — AI-native code editor.
- *OpenClaw: The Complete Guide* — Personal AI assistant.
- *AI Systems Playbook* — Cross-platform patterns for working with multiple AI tools.

- *AI Prompt Engineering* — The deeper craft of prompting across all major AI tools.
- *AI for Developers* — AI tool use for software developers specifically.
- *AI for Business* — AI tool adoption for business teams.
- *AI for Students* — AI tool use across academic contexts.
- *AI Governance for Practitioners* — Frameworks for organizations adopting AI responsibly.
- *Securing Agentic AI* — Security considerations for autonomous AI systems.

Where to Start Each Resource Type

For day-to-day use updates, the official blog and help center are sufficient. For deeper context, follow a couple of independent voices and one or two newsletters. For the broader research and ethical questions, the academic and trade-book literature is growing fast — pick up new work as it appears in your specific field.

The most important resource, ultimately, is your own evolving practice. The NotebookLM you use in two years won't be the NotebookLM described in this book, and the workflows that work best for you will be the ones you've refined through use. Read, follow, listen — and then build, verify, and refine.

www.ingramcontent.com/pod-product-compliance
Lightning Source LLC
LaVergne TN
LVHW060026210926
848481LV00013B/3796
* 9 7 9 8 9 5 0 5 3 3 1 0 5 *